The Emergence of the Modern German Novel

This book treats both the literary history of the modern German novel and theoretical considerations about gender and eighteenth-century narrative strategies. It attempts to overcome a twofold division in scholarship by treating Christoph Martin Wieland's *Geschichte des Agathon* and Sophie von La Roche's *Geschichte des Fräuleins von Sternheim*, the two novels generally considered to be foundational in the development of the German Bildungsroman, in conjunction, rather than as examples of unrelated traditions, and by considering the reciprocal influence of fictional and theoretical writing dealing with the developing genre of the modern German novel. Baldwin also examines Wieland's *Don Sylvio* and Maria Anna Sagar's *Karolinens Tagebuch* and analyzes how gender as a relative construct functions in each of the four texts. In so doing she shows how the new German novel of the 1770s aligns reading and narrative practices with gendered attributes to establish narrative authority and cultural legitimacy for the new stories of identity they explore. The interpretations proceed from an analysis of the ways that reading and narration are represented in the novels, and in their poetological prefaces, to show that the texts take up, challenge, and contribute to contemporary literary and social theories of the novel.

Claire Baldwin is assistant professor of German at Colgate University in Hamilton, New York.

Studies in German Literature, Linguistics, and Culture

Edited by James Hardin
(South Carolina)

Jean Honoré Fragonard
A Young Girl Reading, c. 1776, oil on canvas
Gift of Mrs. Mellon Bruce in memory of her father, Andrew W. Mellon
© 2002 Board of Trustees, National Gallery of Art, Washington

THE EMERGENCE OF THE MODERN GERMAN NOVEL

*Christoph Martin Wieland,
Sophie von La Roche, and
Maria Anna Sagar*

CLAIRE BALDWIN

CAMDEN HOUSE

Copyright © 2002 Claire Baldwin

All Rights Reserved. Except as permitted under current legislation,
no part of this work may be photocopied, stored in a retrieval system,
published, performed in public, adapted, broadcast, transmitted,
recorded, or reproduced in any form or by any means,
without the prior permission of the copyright owner.

First published 2002
by Camden House

Camden House is an imprint of Boydell & Brewer Inc.
PO Box 41026, Rochester, NY 14604-4126 USA
and of Boydell & Brewer Limited
PO Box 9, Woodbridge, Suffolk IP12 3DF, UK

ISBN: 1–57113–167–1

Library of Congress Cataloging-in-Publication Data

Baldwin, Claire.
    The emergence of the modern German novel: Christoph Martin
Wieland, Sophie von La Roche, and Maria Anna Sagar / Claire Baldwin
    p. cm. — (Studies in German literature, linguistics, and culture)
Includes bibliographical references and index.
ISBN 1–57113–167–1 (alk. paper)
    1. German fiction — 18th century — History and criticism.
2. Bildungsroman. 3. Wieland, Christoph Martin, 1733–1813 — Criticism and interpretation. 4. La Roche, Sophie von, 1731–1807 — Criticism and interpretation. 5. Sagar, Maria Anna, 1727–1805 — Criticism
and interpretation. I. Title. II. Studies in German literature, linguistics,
and culture (Unnumbered)

PT759 .b25 2002
833'.609—dc21

                                            2001059855

A catalogue record for this title is available from the British Library.

This publication is printed on acid-free paper.
Printed in the United States of America.

Contents

Acknowledgments

I AM GRATEFUL TO MANY FRIENDS and colleagues for their support of this project. In particular I would like to thank Mary Bly, Peter Demetz, Carol Jenkins, Jill N. Levin, Helga Meise, Rebecca Messbarger, Lynne Tatlock, and Ferdinand von Münch for their generous advice and assistance. I thank James Hardin and James Walker for their patience and assistance in the publication process. I appreciate the careful attention that the anonymous readers for the press gave my manuscript and I thank them for their helpful comments. I also gratefully acknowledge the financial assistance I received from Washington University for publishing this volume.

Introduction

THIS IS A BOOK ABOUT the beginnings of the modern German novel around 1770. It investigates the narrative strategies developed in novels by Christoph Martin Wieland, Sophie von La Roche, and Maria Anna Sagar to defend the modern novel as a respectable literary form and to participate in contemporary debates over its influence as a genre. The following chapters examine the metafictional nature of texts by these three writers as a kind of practical poetics that positions them within eighteenth-century critical discussion on the genre and investigates relationships between the novel and various types of novel readers. These questions and the issue of gender and genre that was so central to the controversies over the novel in the eighteenth century are addressed by considering novels written by male and female authors together in the common contexts of eighteenth-century novel theory, eighteenth-century theories of gender, the cultural demand to justify the novel, and the emergence of the German novel described as modern. In the past, literary scholarship on the modern German novel has tended to examine novels written by men separately from novels written by women. This book seeks to bridge that divide by bringing together novels traditionally identified as foundational for those separate, gendered canons; it seeks thereby to offer a new look at the beginnings of the modern German novel.

Despite the popularity of the genre, eighteenth-century novelists felt compelled to defend their texts against charges of moral impropriety and against the stigma of low literary status. To assert a place of cultural, social, and literary legitimacy not hitherto accorded it, the novel aimed to reinvent itself: the good modern novel sought distance from what was considered novelistic. Indeed, the term "novelistic" had been used broadly to designate all that was anathema to dominant Enlightenment aesthetics and to contemporary cultural taste, as in the disparaging definition Johann Georg Sulzer gives for *romanhaft* in 1771 in his encyclopedic *Allgemeine Theorie der schönen Künste in einzeln, nach alphabetischer Ordnung der Kunstwörter auf einander folgenden Artikeln abge-*

handelt: "Man nennt eigentlich dasjenige so, was in dem Inhalt, Ton oder Ausdruck den Charakter hat, der in den ehemaligen Romanen herrschend war, wie das Abentheuerliche, Verstiegene in Handlungen, in Begebenheiten und in den Empfindungen. Das Natürliche ist ohngefähr gerade das Entgegengesetzte des Romanhaften."[1] Sulzer programmatically opposes "the natural" to "the novelistic," a clear example of his ambition to use his compendium to establish aesthetic standards and to codify aesthetic theory. He ascribes to each term a distinct literary style that he links to its particular historical position: the novelistic harks back to an age of tasteless immoderation, while the natural denotes a superior modern sensibility. The natural, which Sulzer aligns with "truth" and poetic progress, will ultimately triumph over the novelistic even in the modern novel itself: "Da sich in unsren Zeiten der Charakter der Romane selbst dem natürlichen Charakter der wahren Geschichte immer mehr nähert, und unsre Schriftsteller es sich immer mehr zur Regel machen, ihren Geschmack nach den Alten zu bilden . . ., so ist auch zu erwarten, daß es [das Romanhafte] sich allmählig unter uns gänzlich verlieren werde" (4:101).[2] To win poetic accolades, the eighteenth-century German novel must, then, renounce its legacy, realign its literary affiliations, and transform itself into a genre that promises truth. According to Sulzer, the antidote to the artificiality of the novelistic is to be found in classicism; contemporary authors are enjoined to emulate the ancients to lend authority to their narratives. Yet the positive possibilities implied in this assessment of the modern novel find no official corroboration in Sulzer's encyclopedia, since "the novel" as a genre is deemed unworthy of an individual entry and so denied formal literary status. In Sulzer's vision of literary history, the novel will rid itself of the characteristics he defines as novelistic in the process of its transformation into a viable modern form.

Sulzer's attempts at categorical clarity and his exclusion of the novel as a distinct entity expose tensions in the theoretical assessment of the novel that vexed critics, authors, and general readers. Nonetheless, many eighteenth-century theoreticians as well as subsequent literary historians have concurred with Sulzer that there was a qualitative generic shift around 1770 that marked the emergence of the modern German novel, in which the reformed genre successfully distanced itself from the negative associations of its history to establish itself as respectable: by 1774, exemplars of the form are identified in Friedrich von Blanckenburg's important treatise *Versuch über den Roman* and are celebrated as novel, rather than novelistic, and as innovative, not imitative. How did the novel assert itself in the face of literary and moral prejudice to attain cultural legitimacy at this time? How did the demands to define the new novel through negativity influence both fictional narratives and the understanding of what a novel could be? Seeking answers to these questions, this book examines the reciprocal relation between the theoretical discourse on the novel and the novelistic interpretation of such theory at this particular historical juncture.

By the 1770s, public opinion on the novel was expressed and shaped through many channels, including moral weeklies and other journals, pedagogical literature, reading circles and salons, medical treatises, iconography, and juridical tracts and documents, but not least within the novels themselves. Their prefaces generally drew on such topoi as a manuscript fiction or an authorial disclaimer to shape the reception of the texts they introduced. These prefaces commonly affected conformity with the reigning theoretical positions, including the demand for verisimilitude, and defended the novels against common aesthetic and ethical reproaches.[3] However, subtle and sustained reflections on the novel's changing status are also embedded in the body of novels themselves. These metanarratives emphasize the novel's self-conscious fictionality and justify its existence given the charges of the impropriety and danger of imaginative literature, and of the novel in particular. Furthermore, metanarratives not only underscore the novel's condition of fictionality, they also elaborate specifically on what type of fictions they embody and how they wish to be understood. Their narrative liaisons with existing literary traditions, genres, styles, and theoretical stances, and the pedagogy they offer their implied readers, position and define individual texts and the modern novel itself as an emerging genre. Investigating these metafictional narrative strategies that comment on and underpin the novel's generic innovation in the context of the vociferous debates of the period is an important step towards a fuller understanding of the novel's attempts to secure its modern literary status.

The emergence of the modern German novel in the last third of the eighteenth century was accompanied by rising literacy rates and an exponential increase in the number of novels published. There was a wide variety among the novels and there were many different narrative approaches to the predominant themes of love and adventure.[4] In response to this variety and proliferation of texts, scholarship has distinguished numerous sub-genres of the novel. Yet several authors and their novels stand out as innovative and historically noteworthy for their role in generating the new traditions of the German novel that later came to be differentiated by the infelicitous terms *Bildungsroman* and *Frauenroman* (women's novel).[5] Although these terms are inadequate as descriptive categories and certainly do not account for the great breadth of novel production at the time, they have been and remain important and consequential terms in literary criticism. Their widespread use both historically and in contemporary scholarship makes clear that modern German novel production, since its beginnings, has often been perceived and described as having two histories, one male and one female. Significantly, the first tradition or sub-genre of novels, written almost exclusively by men, has not always been recognized as gendered, whereas the second, those written by women, has been defined by gender and too often dismissed as a parallel, yet secondary development.

The reception of the novels by Christoph Martin Wieland and Sophie von La Roche can be taken as emblematic of this bifurcation in critical history. Wieland has been seen by eighteenth-century and twentieth-century critics alike as the originator of the first of these traditions and La Roche as the originator of the second. Wieland's earliest novels are commonly cited as the first examples of the modern German novel. *Agathon* especially is taken as a foundational text for the tradition of the Bildungsroman.[6] For his contemporaries, anxiously concerned with promulgating a bona fide "original German novel" equal to the fictions already well-established and flourishing in England and France, the young Wieland represented an author capable of achieving international stature by incorporating elements of other European novel styles in texts with their own unique signature. Blanckenburg lauds Wieland's *Geschichte des Agathon* (1766–67; The History of Agathon) as the morally instructive story of an individual's path to perfection and he makes this novel the cornerstone of his influential novel theory. Twentieth-century scholars have located the modern innovations and the significance of Wieland's novels in their sophisticated literary techniques, their pervasive irony, and their philosophical perspectivism. Sophie von La Roche was and is regarded as the first female German novelist on the basis of her successful first novel *Geschichte des Fräuleins von Sternheim* (The History of Lady Sternheim), published anonymously under Wieland's editorship in 1771. In a striking instance of dividing and gendering the emerging novel tradition, Wieland hailed La Roche's originality in his preface to the novel, but also emphatically designated her writing as feminine in style and content and best suited for a female audience. While he garnered severe criticism from some of La Roche's many admirers for his characterization of the text and its author, his presentation has had a lasting influence on the reception of the novel and thus on the understanding of the early development of the German novel as a whole. Although La Roche's significant adaptation of French and English narrative models has been recognized and the pivotal role of *Sternheim* in the development of German fiction is acknowledged within discussions of *Empfindsamkeit*, twentieth-century scholars, too, have considered La Roche primarily as an innovator in women's fiction and have treated her as the founder of a second tradition of the German novel defined by its exploration of female subjectivity and by the gender of the author.[7] Her status as a precursor to the increasing number of female novelists of the last third of the eighteenth century is also uncontested. Parallel to the story of the origins of the "modern German novel" (by male authors), then, runs the story of the origins of the German "women's novel."

The bifurcation of the German novel based on the gendered signature of the author into two traditions or sub-genres that simply happened to have emerged at the same time has determined how we read its history and continues to define much scholarly work. Although the term *Bildungsroman* has been widely, and loosely, adopted within the critical traditions of other national literatures, where it is often paired with such terms as "female," "ethnic," or "English," criticism on the German Bildungsroman has generally excluded texts by women from its purview.[8] Significant studies by feminist scholars in recent years have recovered and reconsidered eighteenth-century German novels by women and have challenged literary histories that have ignored female authors.[9] Yet there is very little critical work that considers together novels associated with one or the other of these gendered lineages and that shows a methodological interest in both the history of German aesthetic theory and gender.[10]

This book argues that it is fruitful to read modern German novels by men together with those by women in a common context, and that to do so illuminates important similarities generally overlooked when the dichotomy between these novels is upheld. Such an approach reveals that the modern German novel is concerned at its origin with the experiences of gendered subjectivity and the ways in which fictional narrative can shape it, and makes clear the influences of gender on the various narrative strategies developed to defend the novel in texts by men and women. Of course the divide constructed between novels written by women and novels written by men reflects real differences in the historical conditions of literary production faced by female and male authors, including their respective opportunities for education, their access to the literary market, and the prejudices encountered by women who ventured to publish. The relegation of women's literary expression to a separate, feminine sphere under the controlling aegis of male publishers and critics mitigated the threat, and thus the transgression, of women asserting a public voice, for example. In addition, the dichotomy reflects differences in the kinds of stories that were told about female and male protagonists in the novels at this time in German history, although the gender of the protagonist did not always correspond to the gender of the author. However, the separation of novels from this time into discrete categories by gender obscures their similarities. One fundamental commonality between the various forms of the modern novel is that they all create and assess the subjectivity of their protagonists in a new fashion and place the portrayal of individual identity at the center of their fictions. With an increasing interest in psychological interpretations, novels tell new stories about the emotional self and explore ideas about gender and identity. When narratives that focus on male protagonists are read as a separate phenomenon from narratives that focus on female protagonists, it is easy to lose sight of the fact that the polarized definitions of gender emerging as dominant in the late eighteenth century were defined reciprocally. Evaluations of literary style also employed gender distinctions that were relational: the masculine was understood as the not-feminine and vice versa. The assertion of these distinctions supported a developing definition of masculine literary style and masculine aesthetic judgment. Thus the new novel explores the discursive formation of gendered traits in stories of modern subjectivity and employs gendered categories in this exploration to define its own innovative poetics.

In the chapters that follow, I wish to reassess the gendered typology of the emerging modern German novel through interpretations of the strategies developed in the novel's defense by Christoph Martin Wieland in *Der Sieg der Natur über die Schwärmerey oder Die Abentheuer des Don Sylvio von Rosalva* (1764; The Victory of Nature over Enthusiasm or The Adventures of Don Sylvio of Rosalva) and *Geschichte des Agathon* (1766–67), by Sophie von La Roche in *Geschichte des Fräuleins von Sternheim* (1771), and by Maria Anna Sagar in *Karolinens Tagebuch ohne ausserordentliche Handlungen* (1774; Karoline's Journal with no Exceptional Events). While both Wieland and La Roche have been recognized as literary innovators whose early novels contributed importantly to the formation of a German national literature, and their personal relationship has always been of interest to literary historiography, their novels have not been discussed in conjunction. Instead they have been treated — separately — as the originators of the new gendered traditions of the novel, as sketched above. There has been a striking tendency in German Studies to construct elaborate typologies of the eighteenth-century novel that have served to create distinctions rather than to establish commonalities. The novels I bring together here are often examined in isolation, either as unique accomplishments or as exceptional examples of a particular novel sub-genre, or sub-sub-genre: Wieland, for example, has been read as the author of "pragmatic," "anthropological," or "pragmatic-philosophical" texts of development, La Roche as an innovator in the German "epistolary" or "sentimental" novel and the *Frauenroman,* and Sagar, who until recently had been nearly forgotten, as the author of the "rational Frauenroman." This desire to categorize and order the many guises of the emerging modern novel, while analytically useful, also reveals critical discomfort with the multiplicity of forms the emerging German novel could take. But such rigid typologies hinder efforts to consider broader commonalities among novels appearing nearly contemporaneously.

Another feature of German literary historiography further prejudices the perception of the German novel around 1770. The veneration of Goethe has caused the history of the eighteenth-century German novel to be commonly constructed as a trajectory (or even a teleology) culminating in his texts, which are then understood as the "real" beginning of the modern German novel. Both Wieland and La Roche, for example, are frequently considered, in differing and unrelated fashions, as literary precursors to Goethe: Wieland's *Agathon* as a step towards *Wilhelm Meisters Lehrjahre* and La Roche's *Sternheim* as an influence on *Werther* — if indeed the author is not dismissed from the literary context and primarily remembered for her role as "Mama La Roche," mother of Maxe, whom Goethe admired and who was said to be one inspiration for his first novel. Although such interpretations do illuminate important aspects of the development of the German novel, their predominance simultaneously overshadows other interesting literary relations.

In choosing to investigate novels by Wieland, La Roche, and Sagar alongside one another, I aim to reconfigure the context in which these texts, and thus the beginning of the modern German novel, are viewed. When these novels are approached in their own right, in relation to each other and to contemporary theoretical discussion, rather than being read through the lens of late-century models (particularly Goethe's *Wilhelm Meisters Lehrjahre*), a new sense of the challenges facing the genre and of its transformation comes into focus. Concurrent with the possibilities of metamorphosis open to the novel is the demand that its authors define and defend their narratives as modern, in relation to new social and aesthetic conceptions of what novels are and what they should be. The novels I examine in the following chapters employ differing narrative strategies to that end, but all are metanarratives, or "metafictions" in the sense theorized by Patricia Waugh: "fictional writing which self-consciously and systematically draws attention to its status as an artifact in order to pose questions about the relationship between fiction and reality."[11] Metafictional writers, Waugh argues, "all explore a *theory* of fiction through the *practice* of writing fiction" (2). Although her book focuses on the postmodern novel and its difference from the modernist aesthetic, Waugh sees the tendency to metafiction as generically inherent in the modern novel and points to Laurence Sterne's *Tristram Shandy* (1760) as "the prototype for the contemporary metafictional novel" (70). The eighteenth-century metafictions I examine in this study explore theories of fiction and of the novel through their presentations of reading and of narrative production. They thereby illuminate concerns about the German novel at a pivotal point in its history.

Metafictional reflexivity that foregrounds the activities of reading and of narrative production directly engages contemporary aesthetic and social concerns that converge in the discourse on reading practices. While proper reading was hailed as powerfully emancipatory, the self-appointed enlightened guardians of social order tended to shudder at the putative ill effects of unsanctioned reading materials and reading styles.[12] For these moralists, the discredited novel of old constituted a unique nexus of aesthetic and moral deficiencies. Through its fantastical adventures and romances, its histrionic characters, and its tasteless hyperbole of style, the novel supposedly appealed to its readers' baser desires, led them away from the firm ground of reality, and thus posed a danger to their moral well-being. Rapidly growing literacy and the burgeoning publication of novels in the expanding book market increased anxiety that reading would unleash readers' passions incommensurate with social propriety and impervious to social controls, and thereby would endanger the social order itself.[13] Most eighteenth-century theories of the novel were also preoccupied with the gender of the novel's readers and with the ways that gender was thought to correspond to the readers' desires. The novel, many pedagogues warned, threatened to promote dissoluteness in younger male readers and in impressionable female ones. In the numerous essays on the addiction to reading, *Lesesucht* or *Lesewut,* the most foolish, immoderate reader was usually imagined as a woman, while the follies of young men were embodied in the more noble, if still misguided, figure of the enthusiast, the *Schwärmer.* The novel was thus seen as a menace to the successful socialization of its readers. The internalization of false models of the self through reading would, it was feared, lead to widespread deviation from the gender roles required for social reproduction.

The fictions examined in the chapters that follow explore these and other theoretical scenarios of reading by incorporating reader figures into their narrative structures.[14] In the venerable tradition of Cervantes's *Don Quixote* (1605; 1615), this ploy enables metafictional reflection and self-definition and an investigation of the relationships among reading practices, narrative conventions, and the interpretation of experience. Characters' reading habits reveal them and advance the plots of the novels. In addition, the readers out-

side the text must engage reflexively with aesthetic questions in order to judge narrative virtues and failings. My first chapter thus introduces aspects of the eighteenth-century discourse about the
novel in Germany that figure centrally within the fictional texts
themselves. These include the theoretical controversies about the
genre and its relation to readers' desires, popular debates on reading and on interpretation, iconographic renditions of reader figures, and the changing cultural constructions of gender that helped
to shape conceptions of the novel. The remaining chapters present
my interpretations of Christoph Martin Wieland's *Don Sylvio von
Rosalva* (1764) and his *Geschichte des Agathon* (1766–67), Sophie
von La Roche's *Geschichte des Fräuleins von Sternheim* (1771), and
Maria Anna Sagar's *Karolinens Tagebuch ohne ausserordentliche
Handlungen* (1774). I proceed from an analysis of the ways that
readers and reading, narrators and narration are represented in the
body of the novels themselves, as well as in their prefaces on poetics. The project of the novel's self-legitimation and the delineation
of the poetics of the genre are accomplished by the plotting of
reading and narrative practices (in the tradition of *Don Quixote*).
As metafictions, the texts comment on reading styles and literary
fashion to educate their implied and desired readers in an art of
reading commensurate with the texts' claims to sophistication of
design. The reader's desires, which the narratives court, and the
reader's interpretive competence, on which they rely for their intellectually and aesthetically ambitious effects, are described within
the texts as predicated on age and gender. The inextricable link
between gender and genre theory is central to the frequent direct
and implicit narrative self-reflection that occurs in texts by men and
women alike.

The relationships that the novels set up between readers' desires (long associated with the genre as grounds for condemnation)
and their competence to judge literary value (a value not traditionally accorded to the novel) illuminate the dilemmas accompanying
the genre's attempts at self-justification in the face of charges of
impropriety. I argue that the novels boldly insist on their ability to
elicit their readers' varied and often transgressive desires as a sign of
their artistic quality. The novelistic discourse thus reconfigures the
relation between desires and narrative and shifts the burden of
moral and social responsibility from the self-conscious and self-
consciously fictional text to the reader, lifting it from the author,

and by extension, the text. By describing various types of readers and evaluating reader responses to passions within their fictions, the texts can surreptitiously condone the pleasures they offer the readers while overtly defining and countenancing a particular mode of reading with desire that is figured as masculine. This in turn validates the text's cultural legitimacy and literary standing and authorizes the novelistic narrative as art.

The novels' explorations of the art of reading and the arts of narration illuminate the difficulties and possibilities of impassioned, yet self-aware, reading as a mode of identity-formation. They reject the model of reading, anxiously propounded by the theoreticians most fiercely opposed to the novel, that assumes readers will blindly identify with and mimetically enact the plots and character types put forth in texts. Instead, the novel's new poetics allows for and indeed emphasizes the ability of readers to selectively adopt models of gendered subjectivity offered in fictional narrative. By appealing to the readers' fantasies and desires, the novels offer their tales as paradigmatic stories of subjectivity negotiated through reading and narrative. This negotiation is the basis of the adventure story offered by the new novel, an adventure of narrative for the reader and writer alike. Around 1770, as the German novel draws on and even flaunts traditions of adventure, romance, and fantastic fiction, it also develops new narrative techniques and self-consciously seeks approbation from the aesthetically competent contemporary reader as an innovative, artistic modern genre.

1: The Powers of Desire: The Debate on the Novel in Eighteenth-Century Germany

THE EIGHTEENTH-CENTURY NOVEL, as yet external to the classical poetic canon, posed an elusive threat to religious, social, and poetic controls. Eighteenth-century efforts to define the unruly form, to categorize and evaluate its features and functions, and to dictate rules for future novel production were also endeavors to understand and regulate its effects on its readers. The recurrent issues raised in the theoretical writings on the novel of how to guide reader reception through narrative techniques reveal the enormous influence attributed to this genre. Moral, social, and literary interests informed the debates on the fundamental terms of poetics such as truth, verisimilitude and the marvelous, character, originality, and narrative form. The terms considered crucial to narrative theory remained nearly constant throughout the eighteenth century, yet their definitions and relative emphasis changed dramatically with the general transformations in aesthetic orientation from the systematic poetics of the early Enlightenment to the cult of genius in the 1770s. The following sketch of the theoretical discussions on the novel attempts to present some of the polemic issues in the debates as they appear in Germany from the early eighteenth century to 1774, the year in which Friedrich von Blanckenburg published his influential theory *Versuch über den Roman*. Rather than providing a systematic overview, I wish to point to complexities and conflicts in the exchanges on the novel as a context for the interpretations of the fictional texts which follow.[1]

The theoretical efforts to comprehend and contain the novel's protean capacities led to considerations of the interactions between narratives and human desires. The ways in which these relationships were construed depended on diverse factors, such as religious beliefs, pedagogical zeal, or aesthetic ambition. Theoretical defenses of the novel as well as attacks on the genre proceeded, in the early part of the century, from the premise that the author determines the response of the reader through skilled manipulation of the reader's affects. Judgments of the aesthetic and moral qualities of novels, then, partly hinged on assessments of the legitimacy of the reader's emotions engaged by the novel. The novel found condemnation when it was thought to elicit and foster illicit passions; it found approbation when it was instead thought to acknowledge innate human desires and to respond to them in a culturally appropriate fashion. The term "desire" (*Begierde*) was both indeterminate and over-determined. It included fantasies of love and adventure and connoted sexual passion. In the context of novel theory, the amorphous term was applied to the reader's amorphous feelings that the suggestive capacities of the novel might direct or misdirect. Many writings on the novel betray the fear that the imagination, excited by fiction, could lead the reader from one type of desire to another, less sanctioned one. At issue in debates on the novel, then, are questions of which desires are met by fiction and whether they are socially acceptable, whether novels ought to accommodate the desires of their readers or to guide them, and by what means and to what end novels ought to court these desires. The poetic legitimation of the genre depended on creating a sanctioned form of reception for narrative fiction, since the imaginative pleasures it offers were not to conflict with the pragmatic socialization of the reader.

While the concern with reader reception continued throughout the century, the understandings of what reading entails and how a narrative influences the reader changed. By mid-century there was an increased interest in the subjectivity of the reader and in the roles that the reader's psychological traits play in the interpretation of a text. The location of moral responsibility for the effects of a novel on its readers began to shift from the author to the individual reader. The changing images of readers, theories of interpretation, and the concerns about how novels play on desires increasingly incorporated aspects of the modern, anthropological discourse of the eighteenth century, including its new elaborations of gender attributes. This chapter will show some of the ways these issues converged in assessments of the novel.

Theoretical Discourse on the Novel

Pierre-Daniel Huët's treatise on the novel, "Traité de l'Origine des Romans" of 1670, translated into German in 1682, marks a critical

point of departure for Enlightenment literary theories of the novel
(T 1:91–1:92). In contrast to his influential adversary Nicolas Boil-
eau, Bishop Huët defends the novel against moral condemnation
and literary stigma. Huët delineates the novel in relation to the ancient epic, thereby distancing fictional prose from the measure of
"true history" and bestowing upon it independent legitimacy and a
poetic orientation. The preliminary definition of the novel offered
in Huët's study highlights its thematic focus on love, the poetic
categorization of the novel as prose fiction, and the Horatian purpose "prodesse et delectare" of the narrative. Huët locates the origin of the novel in the universal human desire for fictions, thereby
staking the position that novels respond to, rather than initially in-
cite, the imagination and passions.

The fear that the novel engenders forbidden desires and the
corresponding damnation of the genre on religious and moral
grounds is vigorously articulated at the turn of the century by the
Protestant pastor Gotthard Heidegger.[2] His "Mythoscopia romantica oder Discours Von den so benanten Romans" (1698) represents the position of unequivocal criticism of fiction through its
polemics that novels are nothing but lies which deceive the reader,
inflame the passions and the imagination, make men dependent on
women, foster addictive reading, and cannot fulfill the didactic
purpose sometimes erroneously ascribed to fiction (R 52–56).[3]
Heidegger is pessimistic about the fate of the reader who reads
with desire. Novels, he maintains, "nehmen den Kopff gantz als in
Arrest, setzen den Menschen in ein Schwitzbad der *Passionen,* ver-
derben folgens auch die Gesundheit, machen *Melancholicos* und
Duckmauser" (R 54).[4]

Similar judgments on the novel and the seductive dangers it
poses to delicate or naive readers through its themes of love and its
capacity for creating illusion echo throughout the century: novels
are consistently viewed as instruments which can spark the flames
of "unchaste desires."[5] Such tirades, which often knowledgeably
engage literary theoretical debates on truth, probability, illusion,
and reader reception, were countered (for example by G. W. Leib-
niz)[6] with arguments that fiction can legitimately present a utopian
world without being mendacious. Other writers opposed to the
Heideggerian stance (one is C. Thomasius)[7] attempted to deter-
mine the narrative balance between didactic value and entertainment that would be both poetically proper and educationally

effective. These considerations presage the focus on the psychological constitution of novel characters and novel readers that becomes increasingly central to the theoretical reflections on the novel in the course of the century.

Another common defense of the novel constructs a historical distinction between the old and the new as a way to legitimize contemporary novels. In this view, obsolete, unprincipled novels stand in sharp contrast to the newer, more sophisticated, and acceptable works. Such division allows the theoretical rivals to censure each other on the basis of what writings they choose to define as novels. In his "Gespräch über Gotthard Heideggers Mythoscopia romantica" (1702), Nicolaus Gundling praises Huët and criticizes Heidegger on these grounds, speculating that the latter mistakenly equates older authors with contemporary novelists, but Gundling concedes that older novels often arouse improper passions rather than fostering acceptable love (T 1:325). The distinction between bad and good, old and new novels is drawn even more sharply in the "Raisonnement über den Roman" (1708), attributed to Erdmann Neumeister. Like Huët, Neumeister proceeds from reflections on human beings' innate desires for stories, which can even lead one to forego physical nourishment (T 1:392). Neumeister champions a graceful combination of education and entertainment which satisfies the desire for wonder; the imbalance between the two accounts for the faults of existing novels. These inadequate texts have a negative effect on both men and women, as they can lead readers astray by encouraging their "passions and vanities" (T 1:406). He criticizes the tendency of authors to accommodate the reader's desires and poor taste, and argues against idealized fictional figures. Yet he also condemns inelegant didactic efforts which are inconsistent with pleasing narrative. Neumeister sketches guidelines for the modern, respectable novel that would strategically steer reader response in an enjoyable fashion. Thus women, the presumed readers of the novel, would be led to recognize their "innate, indescribable weaknesses" and be guided from vanity to reason. The orientation toward gendered reader reception and a possible positive didactic function determines considerations about the novel's content as well as its style. Novels should, Neumeister argues, enable a rational person to recognize vices and learn good conduct. Novels appealing to a clever reader will include "nothing silly, nothing ineffective, and nothing vexing" (T 1:404).

Neumeister thus engages negative models to imagine the features of high-quality new novels which would fulfill a laudable social function, while pleasing the readers as literary works.

All positions in the debates on the novel outlined thus far share the opinion that the novel wields inordinate power and influence over its readers and consequently over society, a belief sometimes subjected to ridicule: "Gewiß es nimt mich Wunder / daß unser *Autor* nicht auch gesaget / Eva hätte kurtz zuvor / ehe sie vom verbottenem Baum geessen / einen *Roman* gelesen oder eine von der nichts würdigem Schlangen *präsentierte Histoire galante*" (Gundling, *T* 1:330).[8] Yet the Enlightenment postulate that novels can positively influence readers while entertaining them draws on the very convictions ironically criticized here. The novel's power derives from the pleasures it provides the reader and its hold over the reader's imagination, which in turn arouse passions or can appeal to reason. Relationships between text and reader are in the foreground of these theories. The interest in the reader is still, at the beginning of the eighteenth century in Germany, primarily directed to *what* the reader reads and to how the author and the author's text are to satisfy or manipulate the passions that prompt reading. The assumption is that readers are impressionable and that, while the readers' choice of reading matter reflects their morals and their judgments, the text itself channels their imaginations and desires. In the course of the century, the main concern shifts from what readers read to how they read. This crucial development in novel theory, one that is furthered, as I argue, by the narrative tactics of metafictional novels, gradually alters the aspects of moral responsibility associated with the genre.

The transformation around mid-century in the conception of reading and in the image of the novel reader, which influences the assessment of the novel genre itself, can be observed in the changing positions on the novel found in the moral weeklies of the 1740s.[9] Earlier, these journals had reiterated moralistic arguments against the novel and warned their female readers, who were considered most susceptible to the seductions of the genre, against the degenerate narratives. The ideal of the woman guided by reason was contrasted with the figure of the silly, immoderate female novel reader. Novel reading was thus associated with a negative expression of femininity. It lacked a utilitarian purpose and was perceived as a hindrance to pedagogical efforts to fashion a female subject who would best serve social interests. Following the enthusiastic reception in Germany of Samuel Richardson's novels, which propagated the middle-class values of sentimentalism, the novel was gradually accorded potential legitimacy if it offered edifying examples of virtuous behavior. Arguments for this view — initially in *Der Zeitvertreiber* (1745) and later, for example, in *Der Gesellige* (1750) — are built on the persuasion that the novel can have a socializing function for the subjects of the emergent civil society.[10] In this view, the responsibility for the effect of the novel still lies clearly with the novelists. If the novelist is morally unreliable, full of "fiery imagination" and anxious only to please the reader, the novel will abound with dangerous themes and expressions and become sugar-coated poison, rather than a sweetened moral lesson for sensitive souls (*R* 82). With time, pedagogues and moralists become increasingly interested in the individual reader as emotional subject and their theories of reading — although still predicated on rather rudimentary notions of readers' passions — do allow for greater differentiation between individual psychological and moral constitutions. The theorists focus more sharply on the particular qualities of mind valued and exhibited by the reader and they present the novel as a vehicle through which pedagogues can both cultivate and assess the minds of their charges. Good narrative, they conjecture, will develop its readers' moral sensibilities by revealing the workings of "the most secret springs of moral actions and the generation of the passions."[11] In turn, the passions that novels elicit become apparent in the visages of their readers. Youthful readers, especially, become open texts themselves when they read novels: "Die Begierde, welche den Leser hinreisst, erleichtert die Mühe, und er leget, ohne daß er das geringste davon weiß oder muthmasset, sein ganzes Herz an den Tag" (*R* 88).[12] These reflections on the dynamics of active reading begin to alter the image of the novel around the middle of the eighteenth century.

Judgments about the manipulation of the passions of readers are central not only for such moralistic assessments, but also for aesthetic considerations of novelistic narrative. The requirements of verisimilitude, of unity in character and action, and of a lively and natural narrative style all allow reason to contribute to better coddling and capturing the imagination. Johann Christoph Gottsched maintains that good narrative is founded on verisimilitude, itself founded on the imitation of nature.[13] For Gottsched, the crucial tension structuring fiction is that between historical truth and the moral ideal. His Swiss critics Johann Jakob Bodmer and Johann Jakob Breitinger relate verisimilitude to the category of the marvelous. Good narrative engages the reader's desire for amazement, but also challenges the reader to explain rationally the (apparently) marvelous in accordance with probability and the laws of nature. This approach combines a reliance on the Leibnizian concept of possible worlds that have inner consistency with a psychological interest in character portrayal. Bodmer's influential analysis and theoretical defense of Miguel de Cervantes's *Don Quixote* reveal this psychological turn, marking a new stage in this novel's German reception and spurring both theoretical and fictional considerations of narrative and reading.[14] Bodmer accepts as aesthetically valid the narrative strategy of expanding the novel's poetic possibilities by ostensibly criticizing its generic model. He argues that, since Don Quixote imitates romances, the narrative telling his story requires only the same degree of probability found in them; the marvelous (*das Wunderbare*) found in Cervantes's novel stems from his title figure's imagination and therefore remains within the bounds of what is probable. The characterization of Quixote as a symbolic and a moral figure, his unique combination of wisdom and foolishness, is psychologically motivated in the text and is comprehensible for the rational reader. This imbues the novel with poetic truth and legitimizes all potential flights of fantasy.

The license for greater poetic freedom that the novel gained through the impetus of the Swiss critics in the mid-century was augmented by its elevation from a position subordinate to the epic to a more independent poetic status and legitimacy. In 1751, Johann Adolf Schlegel suspended the distinction between poetry and prose drawn in the systematic poetics of Gottsched and promoted the novel and other "prosaic poetry" to the rank of "sister of poetic art."[15] Here, too, the concern with reader reception still dominates: these various poetic forms share the primary aims of pleasing the reader aesthetically through mimesis, entertainment, and edification. Schlegel distinguishes the modern novel from the epic, asserting that the novel enchants the reader with marvels of the world, rather than with the tales of the heavenly marvels found in the epic. Other literary theoreticians concurrently examined further genres for insights applicable to the novel and they added to the novel's legitimacy through these comparisons. Christian Fürchtegott Gellert underscores the epistolary virtues of immediacy in engaging the reader's imagination;[16] Karl Friedrich Troeltsch turns to dramatic theory for analytic tools, as Blanckenburg will later.[17] The importance of the action's "knot," the suspense leading to it and its denouement, for instance, are essential in capturing and guiding the reader's attention. Troeltsch argues that the successful poet must simultaneously arouse and hinder the reader's desires: "Je mehr also der Dichter Hindernisse im Wege legt, die die Ungewißheit des Lesers stärken und seine Begierde vermehren, desto besser und rührender weiß er den Leser einzunehmen" (*T* 2:165).[18] Troeltsch argues that the reader's desire, heightened by tantalizing uncertainties, is directed toward individual figures in the texts. The fictional protagonist ought, then, to be virtuous, and all figures in the narrative must be perfectly consistent. Although it may detract from verisimilitude, Troeltsch only allows small deviations from this inner stability of character.

The qualities of characters in novels and the manner of their narrative construction to best influence the reader become a central point of theoretical contention in the second half of the century. The position that only unchanging and unequivocal characters can inspire readers to emulate virtue and to spurn vice is countered with the assertion that such model figures are fully improbable and, as such, less capable of eliciting the identification or positive bias which guides readers to insights about their own human failings.[19] With the increasing interest in psychological introspection and analysis, the conceptions of verisimilitude in characterization shifted. The recourse to the literary precepts of probability and credibility found in the calls for consistency of character is likewise essential for authors who champion changeable figures with individual faults and strengths. The preoccupation with education also influenced demands on the novel to portray credibly a character's development from ignorance or foolishness to greater knowledge and wisdom. Among foreign models, Samuel Richardson's characters, once considered natural in opposition to the idealized figures of the older romances, were contrasted negatively with Henry Fielding's more probable ones.[20] Jean-Jacques Rousseau's fictional figures also elicited heated controversy over the construction of character. Moses Mendelssohn's criticism of Rousseau and the ensuing exchange between Mendelssohn and Johann Georg Hamann circle the issue of reader reception and the central role of characterization. Hamann attacks Mendelssohn's inability to accept the enthusiasm of Rousseau; Mendelssohn insists that the first art of the novelist must be to enchant the reader so as to make the enthusiastic flights of sentiment believable: "Wenn der ästhetische Zauberer mir seine Wunder zeigen will; so muß sein erstes Wunder seyn, meinen Glauben zu fangen. . . . Er muß entweder meine *Empfindungen* bezaubern, oder ich bin ungläubig" (*R* 119).[21] Despite Rousseau's theoretical tenets against ideal characters, Mendelssohn finds Rousseau's characters unconvincing. Julie, for example, despite her transgressions, becomes too virtuous to be believed; she is presented as an angel rather than as a virtuous woman (*R* 110).

Credible characterization, the critics agreed, must provide specific details depicting nationality and historical circumstance. The recurring lament that there were no good German original novels showing German milieus and values and elevating the nation's sorry novel production to the level of the foreign models was not only a reflection of national literary pride, but also a moment in the Enlightenment's concern for didactic and aesthetic influence over readers. The exhortations to produce German originals intensified polemics of the aesthetic and narrative theories at this historical juncture. The faith in the ability to construct good art by observing rationally formulated and transmissible guidelines conflicted with the conviction that artistic production and sensibility proceed from subjective experience and the natural expression of the imagination, stimulated by the senses. Johann Heinrich Merck's scathing reviews of Sulzer, for example, reveal the embattled state between the proponents of different literary positions, which Merck divides between Sulzer's pupils and the true artists and lovers of art. For Merck, the inner necessity of the artist to create holds primacy over the insights of the audience, the often incompetent public.[22] Merck mocks timorous efforts to follow theoretical and critical demands for German originality and criticizes narrative which imitates other narratives rather than nature.[23] Narrative quality, and particularly that of the modern epic, the novel, depends fundamentally on the senses. Thus the condition of narrative talent is not literary learnedness, but the ability to articulate immediate sensory impressions. Georg Christoph Lichtenberg ironically comments that the preoccupation with the dearth of German originals itself reveals aspects of the German epigonic character. The German is never more of an imitator, Lichtenberg writes, than when he aims to be original, just because authors of other countries exhibit originality.[24] Lichtenberg's impatience with the inability of German authors to free themselves from dulling literary conventions and to portray German character had, he thought, a simple solution: the authors ought to cultivate their powers of observation and perception, and offer characters from life in their national, social, linguistic particularity.[25] Lichtenberg's satiric criticism of the novel, particularly the sentimental novel, reflects his contemporaries' theoretical preoccupation with aesthetics, desire, and the novel: he believes novelists are motivated to write by erotic desire, yet must not reduce their perception, experience, and narrative expression to simple sexuality.

Lichtenberg's complaints, directed toward the facile self-indulgence of the novelists he attacks, diverge from the general tenor of novel theory in the 1770s, which focused not on the writer's but on the reader's desire, excited and manipulated by the calculating writer. Johann Georg Sulzer's theoretical foundation for his encyclopedia of aesthetic concepts offers a representative articulation of this relationship in the early 1770s. Art affects its audience through compelling sensual impressions which charm the imagination, as it aims to move the soul and elevate the spirit and the heart.[26] The arts' influence lies in their seductive power over their audience: "Sie sind die Syrenen, deren Gesang niemand zu widerstehen vermag" (20).[27] Yet such allure carries the dangerous power to corrupt as well as to enchant. The border between these effects must be closely controlled by the artist's moral purpose guided by reason: "Ohne diese Lenkung zum höheren Zweck, wären die Musen verführerische Buhlerinnen" (20).[28] The appeal of the arts figured here conventionally as feminine manifests itself through the strength of the erotic desire aroused in the audience, which is implicitly male. The assessment of the arts as muses, sirens, or coquettes depends primarily on the ends toward which this masculine desire is directed. For Sulzer, the perils lurking in the aesthetic capacity to excite the imagination through sensual images are manifold and alarming: amorous enthusiasm, political deviance, and religious fanaticism are all described as manifestations of sensuality abandoned by reason (31). Sulzer's theory dramatizes the Enlightenment belief in the prodigious power of art to influence individuals and social structures, for good or for evil. The import of literature for the body politic is explicit in Sulzer's text. He emphasizes the potential use of "good" literature as political propaganda and argues for the integration of such an enterprise into the machinery of the state. Concurrently he underscores his conviction that censorship of aesthetic production and distribution is imperative to ensure that this tremendous force not fall into treacherous hands. For Sulzer, the most significant issue in the evaluation of a literary text is ultimately its ability to promote behavior commensurate with his society's moral ideals. These aims are dependent on particular narrative qualities — in Sulzer's view the enhancement of nature through art and strict ethical discipline in content and style.

An orientation towards moral purpose, but with a different focus, also dominates Friedrich von Blanckenburg's *Versuch über den Roman* of 1774, the first extensive treatise on the novel to have a wide influence.[29] Blanckenburg's essay compiles many of the positions and issues found in the discourse on the novel of his time, and indeed his strengths lie more in synthesis than in originality.[30] The novel shaping his considerations is Wieland's *Geschichte des Agathon,* which Blanckenburg reads as the story of an individual's path to perfection. Blanckenburg significantly distinguishes between the "Bürger," the person as political being, and the "Mensch," the subjective identity of a person. The good novel will, in his view, present the inner history of a character as "Mensch" such that readers understand the causality of the character's development and can, in turn, apply the insights gleaned from the novel to their own maturity toward perfection. In this way, Blanckenburg's theory of the novel participates in defining the modern German novel as a new kind of narrative about the self, and as a narrative that contributes to shaping new understandings of subjectivity. Like Johann Jakob Engel, whose *Über Handlung, Gespräch und Erzählung* likewise appeared in 1774,[31] Blanckenburg applauds scenic narrative that conveys causal connections and the inner emotions of the protagonist with the heightened illusion of dramatic immediacy.

As has often been noted, although Blanckenburg takes Wieland's literary practice as the basis on which to establish theoretical guidelines for the novel, his reading of *Agathon* is idiosyncratic and selective.[32] His theory rests on the image of the author as a sovereign, omniscient creator of a fictional world that is fully harmonious, and in which perfectibility is indeed possible. He is, therefore, blind to those characteristics of Wieland's novel most striking for the reader today: his irony, the sophisticated figure of the narrator, the narrative ploys, the address to fictive readers, the playful emphasis on fictionality, the philosophical aporias. These features, however, are crucial elements of the text that shape its reception and help it stake a position in the contemporary debates on the social functions and the literary possibilities of the novel. The tensions between theoretical and fictional writings on the novel, between the efforts to grasp systematically the novel's workings and the practical means of exploiting and expanding narrative potential, are exemplified dramatically in the nexus of this influential pair — Blanckenburg's *Versuch* and Wieland's *Agathon* — each guided by different notions about the properties of fiction and the malleability of the reader.

The relationships between author, text, and reader shaped by desires are at the heart of eighteenth-century narrative theory. The conceptualization of these relationships change, but the efforts to provide a theory for the fluid and precarious force of passions in narrative production and reception are a consistent component of aesthetic considerations. Although theories of the novel were focused primarily on elements of narrative production, general theories of interpretation gave priority to narrative reception. The development and transformations of such theories, and their implications for concepts of reading, are important for the concurrent changes in the theoretical and fictional discourses on the novel.

In the early eighteenth century, language was conceived of as a secondary system of signs that represented prior mental ideas transmitted directly from author to reader. This view, which led to the effort to achieve an illusion of transparent language, gave way around 1770 to a growing suspicion of such interpretive clarity and to new notions of the historical and material nature of the text and of hermeneutical self-reflection.[33] The Enlightenment model of "semiotic interpretation" placed trust in the principles of reason and logic and in conventions of genre. In this model, the type of writing chosen by an author assured its proper reception, since both author and reader would comply with the appropriate, governing rules. A further guiding principle was that of "hermeneutic propriety," which states that "the reader must seek to maximize the truth of what is written, to render the text or discourse in a way which is consistent with reason."[34] This paradigm, which distinguishes between the ordering of ideas and the expression that represents them and allows for their accurate reconstruction by the receptive reader, underlies not only considerations of rational discourse, Robert Leventhal argues, but also the aesthetic theories of Alexander Gottlieb Baumgarten and Georg Friedrich Meier. "The supposedly emancipatory function of the aesthetic is already laden with rhetorical and hermeneutic requirements of proper reception and correct interpretation" (242). The theorization of a "hermeneutic-philological paradigm" of interpretation in the 1770s, for example by Herder, took issue with Enlightenment semiotics and conceptions of language, and developed understandings of the text "as a historically determined linguistic construct requiring a specific technology of disclosure" (247).

The transformations in theoretical articulations of interpretive practices imply parallel transformations in the conceptions of the reader. Enlightenment understandings of discursive interpretation proceeded from the idea of universal rules of reason and representation that were (theoretically) resonant in every human mind and soul. The hermeneutic model posited the need for privileged intellectual insight in order to decode textual obscurities. The discipline of philology as it developed in the late eighteenth century reflects the institutional distinction between professionalized, competent readers and the general readership. The altered images of "the reader's" activity and of various levels of competence among different readers shifted a major burden of responsibility for the impact of the literary work from the author to the reader's personal receptive capacities. Rather than automatically responding to and replicating the ideational and aesthetic concepts strategically expressed by the author, readers actively engage with the complexities of the text. They are characterized and assessed not only by what they read, but also by how they read. For readers of novels, the prescribed mode of literary reception underwent a transformation around mid-century from mimetic reading based on a reader's identification with characters, such as that championed by Gellert in theoretical and fictional works, to a more distanced position of cognitive enjoyment of the rational and sensual aesthetic experience deemed more adequate to the work of art in the last third of the century.[35] While ethical responsibility and aesthetic competence are thus newly defined and distributed between author and reader, the delicate balance realized in the reader between distance and desire remains decisive for the aesthetic impact of the text. Further insights into how the nexus of desire and reading figures in the cultural imagination of the eighteenth century, and how it is significant for the eighteenth-century novel, can be gleaned by considering the proliferation of iconographic and discursive images of readers.

Images of Readers and Their Desires

The eighteenth century, drawing on long cultural traditions, figures reading and desire together in several predominant fashions. The recurrent association of reading and sensual pleasures can be found in Western iconography at least since the early modern period.[36] Sixteenth-century images of books in proximity with food and wine reflect elite social standing or a dreamland of luxuries. The mutual magnification of the pleasures of reading and of the palate, including the newly imported exotic substances coffee and pipe tobacco, is more frequent in the seventeenth century. In the eighteenth century, reading and other pleasures are even more closely interwoven in the visual arts. New furniture designed for greater reading comfort appears.[37] Male readers are shown not only with a book, but also with pipe in hand or with a glass of wine or cup of coffee nearby. Additional images of sensual appeal — music, food, coffee — surround both male and female readers frequently. Fritz Nies concludes that such iconography portrays reading as the art of enjoying the pleasures of the imagination, further heightened by sophisticated sensual impulses.[38]

Sensuality and reading are markedly figured in scenes of erotic encounter or of erotic appeal, a topos familiar in literature — for instance in Dante's *Inferno* or Rousseau's *Nouvelle Héloïse* — as well as in the visual arts. The readers in such images are predominantly female; female reading and erotic desire are symbiotically linked in the Western cultural imagination.[39] In eighteenth-century images, the erotic, youthful female reader is depicted in a sensual environment, with emblematic statuettes, love letters, and fragrant flowers. Reading in bed is figured in the visual arts as a female occupation: the half-naked woman reader is surrounded by pillows and roses, perhaps with a lover in view. Her reading material is often designated in the image as a "dangerous novel" or as letters of love. In these images, the erotic exteriors of the women readers, who are lost in thoughts of love, mirror their inner preoccupations and reveal the cultural associations of reading, especially novel reading, with female desire. Furthermore, such images of female readers present seductive scenes to the viewer. Reading appears to heighten not only the desire, but also the desirability of the women portrayed. Scenes of erotic encounter, in which a man interrupts the reading woman, are frequent. Depicted in the private interiors of the bedroom, the female reader attracts the voyeur; her forbidden or inappropriate reading material and desirous receptive posture titillate the imagination of the (male) artist and viewer.

The significance that eighteenth-century society accorded to reading and the associations of reading with desires found further expression in the discourse on addictive reading, *Lesesucht*.[40] The victims of *Lesesucht* were thought to be young men, women, and those from the lower classes.[41] Consternation about the epidemic of passion-induced reading accompanied the growth of the book market in the second half of the century in Germany, and reached its height in the 1790s.[42] The case against inordinate reading particularly targeted novels, and rested on many old arguments newly presented: such reading is a waste of time and a sign of idleness; it encourages imaginative excess incommensurate with social realities and moral principles; it leads the reader to neglect duties; the reader is driven by unreflected passion which excludes understanding and contemplation. The aspect given that passion is, however, largely specific to gender. Excessive desire to read can lead to exaggerated learnedness in men, and the satire on the solitary scholar is common.[43] Young male students are most interested in social activities of drinking and carousing, but they too can be seduced by inappropriate reading material.[44] An immoderate, imaginative enthusiasm, *Schwärmerei*, is attributed particularly to the youthful reader. The fictional reckonings with such enthusiasms, as will be shown in the following chapters, depend greatly on the stereotypical, gender-specific images of reading and desire. Often, male enthusiasm is interpreted as the sign of a noble soul inspired by higher ideals, ones that prove incommensurate with social reality.[45] Female desires similarly subversive to the social order, however, appear too threatening to sanction.

The polemics against women's excessive reading were manifold. One set of arguments is directed against the activity of reading per se as an occupation which distracts bourgeois women from household and familial duties and wastes time and money. A second argument attacks the motivations for reading, asserting that the desire to read corresponds to other inappropriate desires. These may be desires for learnedness — ridiculed in attacks on the *femmes savantes* — or for ideal love or for sheer erotic passion; the particular desire becomes manifest through the choice of reading material. A further argument attacks how women read: women are designated as superficial readers who project their own personal emotions into the text and identify fully with literary figures. They are considered lacking in the exegetical and critical skills of men. Young men might share this feminine trait of simplistic reading, but they can mature to greater interpretative skills. When adolescent men read superficially, it is lamentable misreading in a feminine style, whereas when women read exegetically, they transgress the limitations of their gender roles and often become comic or berated figures.[46]

The idea that the reading styles of men and women are fundamentally different has a long cultural tradition.[47] "Good," exegetical, insightful reading is connoted as masculine, while "bad," frivolous, shallow reading is perceived as feminine. In the second half of the eighteenth century, this alignment informed the distinction being made between complex, philological reading and superficial, empathetic reading. Both reading practices are thought to be guided by desire, yet the masculine desire to read includes a controlled resistance and a connoisseur's awareness of the seduction efforts of the text, while the feminine desire to read is assumed to be unrestrained and instinctive. The male literary professionals embody the first type of reader. Mendelssohn, for example, asserts his critical right to resist — and thus to test — Rousseau's novelistic enchantment: "Als Kunstrichter habe ich ein Recht den starken Geist zu spielen, und in seine geheimnißvolle Künste ein Mistrauen zu setzen" (*R* 119).[48] Indiscriminate, feminine readers, in contrast, were thought by the male theorists to be immanently vulnerable to seduction, and of course, novels were considered the corollary of feminine desirous reading. Carl Friedrich Pockels reiterated a common position: "Die Sache ist ganz natürlich. Die Weiber finden in Romanen . . . fast immer etwas, das sie geflissentlich suchen. Dasjenige Frauenzimmer, welches sehr zur Liebe geneigt ist, sieht ihre eigenes Herz."[49]

Anthropology, Literature, Gender

The association of various reading practices with attributes of gender found support in the new anthropological disciplines that developed in the second half of the eighteenth century. These disciplines promoted fundamental shifts in the constructions and understandings of gender central to the establishment of the nascent middle-class society and its ideologies.[50] Whereas sexual differences had hitherto been understood as a matter of degree, women being imperfect versions of men, the new sciences proclaimed and correlated biological differences between the sexes and the division of gendered attributes as natural facts.[51] Physical differences and moral qualities were aligned, and the alignment was justified and established with reference to nature as reflective of an order and hierarchy prescribed by God (fortifying a long cultural tradition) and as a system accessible and interpretable through scientific method.[52] The new scientific wisdom supported and furthered the interests of other cultural institutions such as the structure of the family and bourgeois education.

The anthropological determination of sexual difference and biologically rooted gender qualities influenced literary production and reception profoundly. Not only did it support male primacy and the social prohibitions and controls of women's literacy, its paradigms also informed the epoch's aesthetics in general and poetics in particular. Johann Georg Jacobi's influential women's journal *Iris*, for example, which offered advice on appropriate readings for girls, employed the new scientific discourses propagating polarized gender roles to cultivate those attitudes and qualities of mind that were thought to make women desirable to men.

In the essay "Erziehung der Töchter" in *Iris*, a good mother's instinct, her "own heart," is guided to interpret the laws of nature in this fashion:

> Stärke und Schwäche. Bey der Schwäche Schönheit, Reitz und Lenksamkeit, dem Starken zu gefallen, ihn zu gewinnen, von ihm nicht unterdrückt zu werden. Muth und Furchtsamkeit; bey der Furchtsamkeit List, um der Gewalt zu entgehen. Gewalt, und Gehorsam; Strenge und Geduld; Schutz, und Treue; Tiefsinn, und Scherz Arbeit, und Hülfe, und Erquickung; Leiden, und Trost; Begierde, und Gegenbegierde mit Schaam, welche sich mäßigt, damit der Herrscher die unterworfene Schönheit verehre, und sich entwaffne zu ihren Füßen. Liebe zwischen beyden; und

ein neues Geschlecht, wofür sich ihre Sorge vereinigt: das ist *Mann* und *Weib*.[53]

Perhaps the most influential articulation of this normative conception of sexual and gendered difference built on the notion of the female as supplement to the male is found in Rousseau's novels, which were celebrated in Germany and had a profound effect on its literature.[54] Sophie, the ideal partner for Émile, is subordinate and supplementary to him, yet, like Woman in the quote above, she also wields impressive power over her mate through her charms, through which she both pleases and disarms him. Woman, in this vision, is ultimately responsible for maintaining the social order in which her desirability and her modesty are mutually dependent. Female modesty is necessary as a simultaneous control and provocation of desire: female desire, a powerful threat to the patriarchal order, must be restrained to ensure the domination of men over women, and male desire must be channeled toward virtue. The tool of such guidance is seduction, namely, the intensification of and the attendant influence over male desire.

The course prescribed for Woman as subordinate complement to Man is maintained through strict fetters on intellectual independence. Female minds are to be developed in accordance with male needs, but not beyond. Control over women's intellectual horizons is therefore a central male preoccupation, bolstered by scientific arguments. The determination of female intellectual capacity is made, for example, in an historical-anthropological guise in the article from *Iris* on the education of daughters cited above. In its version of the relations between the sexes, the historical evolution of the male, predicated on intellectual curiosity and an unquenchable desire for knowledge, is accompanied by female accommodation to his needs, whereby her function remains constant, immune to historical change:

> Der Geist des Mannes erwacht zu einem helleren Morgen, zu einer neuen Schöpfung. Er untersucht, entdeckt, untersucht wieder, vergleicht, erfindet. Kenntniß und Wißbegierde nehmen zu; sein Herz erweitert sich, er muß Gedanken ausreden, Gefühle mittheilen. . . . In dieser Gesellschaft, unter diesen Veränderungen, bleibt die Bestimmung des Weibes immer dieselbe. Sie muß dem Stärkern gefallen, die Gehülfinn ihres Gatten, und die Verpflegerinn ihrer Kinder seyn.[55] (1, 3 [1774]: 124–25)

The craving for knowledge and self-expression posited as essential for Man is not recognized for Woman. Instead, her intellectual development is causally bound to, and restricted by, male desires: "Auch an dem weiblichen Geiste will der männliche seine Lust haben; Daher entwickeln, schärfen, und erhöhen sich nach und nach die eigenthümlichen Fähigkeiten und Reitze desselben" (1, 3 [1774]: 125).[56] In the rubric "Zur Damenbibliothek" of *Iris*, J. G. Jacobi explicitly states the aim of aesthetic education for women of the upper bourgeoisie, namely, to make them more desirable, to "make the intellect more lovable through art" (*Iris* 4, 3 [1776]: 465). This purpose establishes rigid parameters, for the vision of excessive female interest in art is horrifying; it is said to threaten the very existence of the family and, by extension, the middle-class society through its effects, namely, the weakening of the nerves and the heart that leads to neglect of domestic duties, so that "the most prosperous families are gradually ruined and the sweetest joys of a wife, housewife and mother are squandered" (*Iris* 4, 3 [1776]: 465).[57]

Medical literature in the late eighteenth century provided a scientific basis for the male fear that women's intellectual engagements would detract from familial duties by linking women's cerebral activity causally with the neglect of their husbands, households, and children.[58] Medicine interpreted the precarious emotional and intellectual condition of women to be fully dependent on their sexual organs. The discipline of gynecology thus constructed a medical foundation for women's supposed intellectual incapacity, for the prohibition against anything more than superficial learning for women, and for the efforts to control female sexuality.[59] Similarly, sterility was explained as a result of excessive mental activity that led to underdeveloped sexual organs. Too much mental motion was thought to weaken the nerves and cause barrenness.

Infertility and illness, particularly weakened nerves, also appear in late eighteenth-century medical literature as symptoms of masturbation. The tracts on masturbation are marked by the same contradiction found in other discursive forums regarding female sexuality: between the denial of women's sexual desire, articulated as her natural modesty, and the fear of its force and its independence from men. Culturally inappropriate sexuality is thought to lead to the decay and abandonment of the sexual and social functions that are perceived as natural. While this is said to apply to both women and adolescent men, a man's symptoms are treated by his acquiring a wife and thereby productively integrating his desire into the social system. Female illnesses attributed to autoeroticism, however, appear as threats to the bourgeois order; they destroy women's beauty (so often equated with virtue), that is, the physical and moral desirability of women for men, and prevent maternity.[60] The heated imagination accompanying masturbation is thought to be a prime culprit in a woman's physical deterioration.

A common tenet of these scientific analyses is that the unfettered female imagination is dangerous. The imagination, spurred by excessive lust or by excessive intellectual or artistic engagement, is said to wreak havoc on the nervous system, making it a physical mirror of mental transgressions and rendering the sensitive woman incapable of fulfilling her female duties. One resilient idea about the novel, traced above, is that its appeal to the imagination is both intellectually and erotically seductive. The association of the novel with the erotic imagination lent the genre the reputation — and aura — of moral impropriety and trespass. The unseemliness of novels as reading material for young women correlated explicitly with their prescribed lack of sexual knowledge. An entry under the rubric "Frauenzimmerbibliothek" in *Iris* recommends withholding all books from one's daughters until marriage, at which point they may choose their own reading matter (1, 3 [1774]: 151–66). A later entry of "Zur Damenbibliothek" offers a summary of the difficulties in choosing reading material for girls and women. The few books worth perusing are too learned for women, "oder zu dunkel für die leichtsinnigen und flatterhaften; oder zu stark und gewaltsam, oder sonst irgend etwas zu für das zarte Herz und die Blumenphantasie der jungen Schönheit" (4, 2 [July 1775]: 102).[61] The suggested solution to this dilemma is to present excerpts of various texts that might benefit women readers. Despite its irony, the images used to figure this project reveal it as meticulous masculine control over the tantalizing knowledge forbidden to women:

> Wir halten deßwegen für wohlgethan, und hoffen den Dank des schönen Publikums zu gewinnen, wenn wir demselben aus diesen verbotnen, verschloßnen, oder mit Fußangeln gefährteten Gärten wenigstens einige der schönsten Blumen brechen und den besten Früchte pflücken, die jedermann, der weiß was gut ist, für heilsam anerkennen muß — wenn wir den Leserinnen aus den für

gefährlich gehaltnen, schwer zu verstehenden, u. s. w. neuher-
ausgekommenen Büchern einige der vortrefflichsten Stellen ab-
schreiben.[62] (4, 2 [July 1775]: 102)

The passage uses images that play on the topos of seduction as an
instrument of education: men offer selected fruits of knowledge to
women in a reversal of the gender roles in the Garden of Eden.
Simultaneously the passage underscores the imperiled position and
the potential repetition of trespass tempting these modern daughters of Eve, were they left to their own devices.

If women's reading was laden with restrictions and fears of impropriety, women's writing, if not strictly private, was even more
closely associated with ethical trespass.[63] This too has a long cultural tradition, shored up by the scientific tracts of the late eighteenth century that prove female intellectual inferiority. The
transgression of female authorship was long associated with sexual
transgression, and specifically with prostitution, as in Friedrich
Schiller's famous parody "Die berühmte Frau" (The Famous
Woman, 1788).[64] The desire or intent to publish was the first ta-
boo, as such an assertion of authority over an audience implied
distance from requisite feminine modesty and thus suggested sexual impropriety. Writing for an audience also drew the specific
criticism of a vain claim to the masculine domain of learnedness,
which included the establishment and judgment of aesthetic criteria, while the actual expression of such knowledge was considered
biologically impossible or, if acknowledged as present, aberrant.
Furthermore, virtuous women lacked not only literary experience,
they also lacked the experience of the world deemed necessary for
the successful novelist.

Socially acceptable writing by women drew on cultural constructs of the feminine as support, definition, and defense.[65]
Women might write for their own self-improvement or at the request and for the pleasure of their husbands, as long as their writing was solely intended for the personal sphere and assumed
knowledge only of that limited arena. Thus topoi of writing with a
female signature developed. An avowal of privacy and personal improvement was one common self-defense, as was the denial of responsibility for the publication of a work (usually attributed to a
husband or male friend). The writer often insisted on authorial incompetence and literary insignificance. She often underscored sincerity and spontaneity, that is to say authenticity, while denying

artistry. The authorial stance of the female writer is figured repeatedly through the esteemed social, feminine roles of educator and particularly of mother, as understood by the eighteenth-century German middle class. The image of mother serves multiple functions: it legitimizes the activity of writing as a natural female occupation and it confines the threat of female intellectual creativity to a figure of female biological creativity in the service of a patriarchal social order.

Certain genres proved more amenable to this authorial profile than others. Those with an aura of privacy and naturalness were considered the most legitimate vehicles for women's texts. The confessional autobiography in the religious tradition, written for a higher moral purpose and therefore immune to reproaches of narcissistic motivation, was one such form; the other classic feminine genre was the letter.[66] The personal epistle, defined in theories by Gellert and others in the second half of the eighteenth century as a form demanding a seemingly effortless, natural, and indeed feminine style, carried the promise of authenticity and the interest of confession also found in the autobiography and the journal. These genres bore the pretense of formlessness and mundane content, of everyday detail with no presumptions of artistic design.

The anthropological fixation of gender traits thus influenced aesthetics and poetics of the late eighteenth century by ascribing distinctive competence to men and women in matters of form, style, thematic content, and genre, and by conversely ascribing gender traits to these literary patterns: artistic, strategic structure is masculine, apparent fragmentation, loose detail, and formlessness are feminine; learned allusions and witty ambiguities as well as classical artistry are masculine, natural spontaneity, naiveté, and emotional authenticity are feminine; affairs of the world and the intellect are masculine, affairs of the home and the heart are feminine; theoretical speculation and poetic polish in dramatic and epic forms are masculine, epistles and private journals are feminine.[67] Wilhelm von Humboldt's anthropological writings codify such associations of gender and literary form, for example in his *Plan einer vergleichenden Anthropologie:* "Nur lehrt die Erfahrung soviel, dass Frauen sich nicht leicht an denjenigen Gattungen versuchen, deren Gelingen vorzugsweise auf ihrer künstlerischen, nur durch Genie möglichen Form beruht, wie die epische und dramatische Poesie und die plastische Kunst ist, sondern fast ausschliessend nur an denen, die gleichsam mehr Fläche darbieten, dem blossen Reiz und dem Reichthum des Stoffes mehr Raum verstatten, der Musik und Mahlerei, dem Roman."[68]

The eighteenth-century novel was, then, a genre that connoted gender, particularly femininity, in manifold ways, from the association of themes of love with the desires of female readers to market concerns at the end of the century when the readership of novels was predominantly female. As a genre struggling for definition and legitimacy in the literary canon of forms, the novel's indeterminate poetic profile placed it in proximity to what was considered the feminine propensity for formlessness. The efforts to elevate the novel to aesthetic and social respectability through theoretical defenses and definitions realigned the associations of the genre from the pole of the feminine to the esteemed narrative and interpretive practices identified as masculine. Blanckenburg distances the pragmatic novel "proper" from its associations with romance.[69] The new "anthropological novel"[70] delineated in Blanckenburg's theory requires a male protagonist, with whom male readers might identify, certainly written by a male author. The inner development towards perfection and maturity of a female protagonist in the 1770s necessarily would imply a focus on her relationship with the man whom she supplements to achieve her female destiny and to perfect her female character.

Lessing's famous accolade of Wieland's *Agathon* as the first German novel for the thinking mind points to shifts in the way the relationships among author, novel, and reader were construed, toward greater independence and active participation in the literary enterprise on the part of the understanding reader. The shared interests and experiences of author and reader meet in the text; the reader must have literary skills related to those of the author in order to read adequately. The hierarchical relationship between author and reader remains in place, yet the two are potential intellectual equals in such theories.[71] This assumes a male author and a male reader, for women are denied the interpretive competence necessary to participate in such an exchange. Yet while the growing professional literary caste determining the theoretical establishment of the novel was male, women found increasing opportunities to write and publish in the last decades of the century. The practical development of the novel in eighteenth-century Germany was dependent on and oriented toward a female readership.[72] Novelists sought the approbation of both a male and a female readership; their novels promised pleasure to readers whose desires to read and whose desires elicited by novels were delineated as either masculine or feminine. The new novel around 1770 played on these attributions in the narrative strategies it employed in its own defense. Wieland, La Roche, and Sagar rely on notions of gendered reading and authorship and explore the gendered description of desires linked to narrative reception and production to describe the generic innovations offered by their own texts and to establish the novel's cultural legitimacy.

The reconfiguration of these issues in the German novel around 1770 corresponds to developments in German politics and society of the time. The intemperate desires of the young male enthusiast were of concern to social commentators because of the fear that, if they were generated through reading, their force would be spent outside the social order rather than contributing to its establishment. Yet, as Isabel Hull has shown, the expression of mature masculine sexual desire channeled through marriage and other institutions was perceived as crucial to the health of the individual and of the collective, even as the very foundation of the emerging civil society.[73] Simultaneously, expressions of autonomous female desire were increasingly decried and women's active sexual desire and expression of any independent wishes in general became metaphors for each other. The imaginative excesses the novel was thought to elicit were posited as the cause for just such immoderation of desire and gender confusion, yet imagination and its expressions (such as the creation of ideals) were also fundamentally valued as a cornerstone of the newly emerging social order: ". . . imagination, far from being against morality, actually founded the new morality, for it made possible the republican virtue at the base of the new, abstract, principled form of society and government" (275). The basis for citizenship in that new society was found in the newly defined model of male sexual maturity; the valued citizen was defined as a man both virile and capable of the rational self-control that provided the philosophical basis for freedom. "The ability to regulate one's appetites was the hallmark of the rational man and, later, the sine qua non for admission to civil society" (162–63).

The delineation of desirous reading in metafictions of the novel contributes to and is a function of these aspects of the emergent modern civil society.[74] Jeffrey Masten insists on the importance of recognizing "that texts are produced within a particular sex/ gender context and that gender and sexuality are themselves in part produced in and by texts."[75] This means attending to the historical particularities of sex/gender, as well as to the importance of gender to historical investigation, as many theorists have emphasized.[76] The novel, so often judged to be a crucial object of the public interest in regulating individual behavior in accordance with the social sex/gender system, explores the discursive formation of gendered traits at this historical moment. Its fictions self-consciously address the power and mechanisms of narrative convention as an important mode of shaping and ascribing significance to individual and collective experience. The following chapters will discuss how the self-reflective novel of the 1760s and 1770s aligns gendered attributes with forms of poetic production and reception to create the story of two new beginnings of the German novel divided along the lines of the gendered signature of the author.

2: The Pleasures of Fiction: Christoph Martin Wieland's *Der Sieg der Natur über die Schwärmerey oder Die Abentheuer des Don Sylvio von Rosalva*

"WIE MAN LIEST": the laconic essay title of 1781 captures *in nuce* a pervasive concern of Christoph Martin Wieland's extensive literary production.[1] How is literature read by the general public? he often asks. Are there any readers a poor author can rely on to read intelligently and with appreciation for literary talent? How can one evaluate narrative judiciously in both poetic and social terms? Throughout his opus Wieland tenaciously engages these questions of literary imagination, ingenuity, and influence. His first novel, *Der Sieg der Natur über die Schwärmerey oder die Abentheuer des Don Sylvio von Rosalva* (1764), dramatically manifests his concerns with reading, readers, and narrative.

Wieland wrote *Don Sylvio* swiftly in 1763, in part as diversion from the more arduous work on *Geschichte des Agathon,* in part in order to produce the income he badly needed. Despite the tendency of scholars to view *Don Sylvio* in isolation from the rest of Wieland's novelistic production, this first novel can be read productively as counterpoint to *Agathon,* the weightier second novel. Wieland worked on both novels simultaneously and the two texts have much in common, not least their sensitive and idealistic protagonists and their self-reflective exploration of the arts of narrative. Together, they represent Wieland's early and influential experimentation in the mutable genre of the novel. In a letter of August 5, 1763, to his publisher and friend Salomon Gessner, he points to his serious purpose in *Don Sylvio,* notwithstanding the playful trappings of his "little novel," and writes: "Es ist eine Art von satyr. Roman der unter dem Schein der Frivolität philosophisch genug ist, und wie ich mir einbilde, keiner Art von Lesern die austere ausgenommen, Langeweile machen soll."[2] In the same letter, Wieland states his intention to entertain a two-fold audience encompassing both clever and foolish readers, as well as to amuse himself, and he declares this compatible with a more serious aim: "Dieses Amüsement interessirte mich unvermerkt so stark, daß ich eine Arbeit daraus machte und daß ich beschloß aus meinem Fond, der an sich närrisch genug ist, etwas so gescheidtes zu machen, als mir nur möglich wäre" (169).[3] Wieland's efforts to expand the serious literary possibilities for the novel form through the fanciful tale of *Don Sylvio* proceed through his overt and satiric treatment of the themes of reading and literary reception.

In the tradition of *Don Quixote,* the novel is set in Spain and its plot is produced and propelled by the enthusiastic misreadings of its protagonist, Don Sylvio. While Quixote favored chivalric romance, Don Sylvio is a voracious reader of fairy tales. The conventions of this genre are the filter through which he interprets his own experience. He therefore confuses his reality with a fairy-tale world and embarks on a search for his fairy princess. But although Sylvio's misunderstandings are the occasion for much of the novel's comedy and are subject to satiric exposure, his perceptions of his experience are largely validated by the novel in the end: he is, in fact, a fairy-tale figure who, after withstanding a series of adventures, indeed finds his fairy princess.

Thus the novel is no simple satire against fairy tales; it is itself a fairy tale that incorporates conventions of other genres.[4] Like Quixote, Sylvio misreads his world but, in the process, creates a new, poetic reality that illuminates aspects of the self-reflexive literary construct which features him as protagonist. And while Sylvio is the most prominent reader in the novel, the other major figures are also characterized by their distinctive reading habits and literary judgments. Like Sylvio, many of these characters create "second realities."[5] The narratives that the characters relate about themselves and about their experiences are structured by the generic conventions of the literature each one favors. These personal narratives raise questions of how literary models influence notions of subjectivity and reveal that the activities of textual reception and textual production are profoundly intertwined. Conflicts that further the plot of *Don Sylvio* often stem from the differences between various characters' interpretations of events, and these differences of interpretation can be explained through the characters' divergent literary preferences or reading practices.

Wieland's thematic focus on the reading practices of his novel's characters is a fundamental metafictional strategy, by means of which he incorporates a broad spectrum of attitudes about reading and readers, from debates on *Schwärmerei* and *Lesewuth* to points of contention in the emergent theory of the novel. The presentation of fictional readers allows for fluid movement in the narrative between the plot and poetic self-reflection and it cultivates self-consciousness in its own readers about their personal modes of literary reception. The thematic centrality of reading thus illuminates the novel's position within eighteenth-century poetic theory and gives greater depth to an investigation of the implied readers of the novel. Yet these aspects of *Don Sylvio* have often been treated in isolation from each other. There are studies of the fictional readers[6] and other studies of the implied readers, notably the trenchant analysis of W. Daniel Wilson.[7] Some critics have examined the novel's self-conscious proclamation of fictionality[8] and its strategies of emancipating itself from strictures of literary theory that mark it as modern.[9] *Don Sylvio* has indeed been designated by one critic as the first modern German novel, based on its personal narrator who mediates such signs of a modern sensibility.[10] Friedhelm Marx cogently relates the presentation of fictional readers to the theoretical discourse on poetics and psychology in mid-eighteenth-century Germany and he discusses Wieland's integration of various generic conventions into his novel.[11] But the metafiction in *Don Sylvio* extends even further. Wieland presents his novel as highly stylized fiction and self-conscious artistic construct through fiction that disregards the boundaries between theory and literary practice. He engages the topical discussions of the personal and social influences of literature in order to address questions of the narrative appeal of *Don Sylvio* itself. In that process, Wieland offers comments on the novel's style and its generic qualities and constructs a distinct literary lineage for his novel, even while presenting it as distinctly modern.

The following analysis of the links between the thematic focus on reading and the novel's theoretical treatments of reading and narrative brings to the fore the centrality of gender for the particular metafictional assertions of *Don Sylvio*. One important way in which the narrator constructs relationships with the novel's readers and defines his theoretical allegiances is by associating himself with certain characters and dissociating himself from others based on their literary taste. The metafiction through which Wieland defines the literary profile of his novel as both modern and legitimate hinges on questions of the readers' desires. That is, the narratives

of the self that the main characters of *Don Sylvio* tell reveal their
desires and the relation of their desires to their reading habits, both
of which are assessed by other characters as well as by the narrator
in terms of gender, literary fashion, and relevance to the contemporary context. What kinds of desire do the readers bring to a text?
Which desires are satisfied or legitimized by various kinds of narrative? What kinds of desirous readers does a narrative woo in turn as
legitimation of its literary value? Or, how can one justify the pleasures of fiction, especially the pleasures of the novel, so long disdained in the literary canon, but valued by its readers? *Don Sylvio*
seeks the approval of readers with cultural authority. But by making both its plot and its playful theoretical reflections turn on the
powers of desirous reading and on the precarious relationships
between author, text, and reader, the novel also aims to define the
type of desirous reader it would successfully court as validation for
its narrative arts.

The Demands of Reading: a Satirical Preface

The preface to *Don Sylvio* exuberantly displays the novel's fictional
constructs and its design to entertain. The frivolity characterizing
the overture to the lighthearted opus that follows is by no means
antithetical to its sophisticated introduction of the thematic and
theoretical concerns with the art of reading and the powers of narrative. On the contrary, such playfulness makes possible the provoca-
tive manipulation of narrative convention and the destabilization of
poetic categories which define the entire novel. The preface prepares Wieland's readers for the tale of Don Sylvio by satirizing desirous and uncontrolled reading. In the preface, the fictional editor
of the novel narrates a story about his experience of reading the
manuscript and then justifies his decision to publish it. However,
this character proves an unreliable guide in literary matters and
himself becomes an object of Wieland's satire on inadequate reading practices. The preface functions like a verbal frontispiece: familiar emblems of satire are transcribed into a narrative prelude
alerting the novel's readers to the need for self-scrutiny, critical
judgment, and attentive interpretation. The satiric preface presents
itself both as a mirror for the external readers and as a reflection of
(and on) the novel that follows; the manuscript read by the fictional figures of the preface is the same text the external readers
will read. These specular qualities are extended through the pref-

ace's thematic focus on reading patterns and narrative production, leaving the readers of *Don Sylvio* with descriptions of various interpretive practices — of both fiction and subjective experience — that they can compare to their own habits of reading and their explanations of the world.

The novel's metafictional commentary already begins with its full title — *Der Sieg der Natur über die Schwärmerey oder Die Abentheuer des Don Sylvio von Rosalva: Eine Geschichte worinn alles wunderbare natürlich zugeht* — and continues in the title to the preface: "Nachbericht des Herausgebers, welcher aus Versehen des Abschreibers zu einem Vorberichte gemacht worden."[12] This introduction to the fictional editor's preface explains the discrepancy between his intent and the actual presentation of the written text, but also draws attention to it. Hence the title provokes questions about the editor's authority and competence and warns the readers to be vigilant and discerning, although it appears at first glance to clarify the text. Similarly, the title implicates other aspects of the novel. For example, irreverence toward literary conventions is made evident through their exaggerated use — the title underscores the novel's fictionality through its hyperbolic insistence on employing topoi of authenticity. By representing the preface as both foreword and afterword, the title effectively frames and encloses the entire novel. Simultaneously, this gesture of closure and its attendant authority are questioned by remarking the manuscript's status as a material object susceptible to capricious transformation, a point reiterated and reinforced at the end of *Don Sylvio*. In a manner reminiscent of Laurence Sterne's *The Life and Opinions of Tristram Shandy* (1759–67), the conditional status of the text, particularly of its beginning, is accented and a linear narrative progression is suspended through the suggestion of a circle or spiral of reading and writing, linking beginning and end.[13] Finally, the title to the preface implicitly directs the reader to reread the editor's comments after completing the novel and to assess them critically from this remove.

The preface itself takes up its title's attention to the process of narrative production and also considers a variety of reader responses to the manuscript. The first of its three sections dispenses with the conventional manuscript fiction. The editor relates the translator's story of the manuscript's "curious fates," confesses that it would be too laborious to doubt the veracity of "such a compli-

cated and well-composed story" and leaves it to the reader's good
will to accept these conventions of textual credibility (9). In the
second section, the complacent editor describes his own exuberant
response to the manuscript. He enjoys its comic scenes and characters immensely and suggests to the readers that this unreflective
delight is the appropriate reception of the text. The third section
takes up potential theological objections to the manuscript and relates the editor's search for a moral authority through which to legitimize his own reading. He surmises that his receptive stance has
been sanctioned by the enlightened priest, a faulty conclusion too
quickly echoed in Wieland criticism.[14] A more attentive reading of
the preface instead reveals the editor's position to be the object of
benevolent satire.

The editor's reading practice, revealed through his first-person
narrative, is motivated by his wish for effortless diversion. While
this desire is presented largely as harmless (in contrast to the omi-
nous warnings found in much novel theory about the unreflective
pleasure to be gained from reading), the editor is not an ideal
reader but rather an unsophisticated one. Instead of offering an
analytic or authoritative literary judgment, he tells a story of events
in his household. He laughs so hard at Don Sylvio's story that he
alarms his wife: "sie besorgte in der Tat, ich möchte närrisch geworden sein, ein Besorgnis, womit sie, ich gestehe es, meinem Ver-
stande eben keine Ehre antat" (9).[15] Her fear succinctly prefigures
the underlying plot of the novel: the hero Don Sylvio, whose rea-
soning and understanding are otherwise stellar, has become a fool
through reading. The editor, who wishes to counter his wife's concern and to exonerate his reason from blame, then reads aloud
from the manuscript so that others will corroborate the validity of
his response. His wife is an upright woman who, unlike most female figures in the novel, has not "ruined her eyes through much
reading" (9). Her response to the novel is offered by her husband
as one based on common sense: she stands in here for the un-
learned but reasonable reading public, in the editor's view, for she
has "enough reason to know when one must laugh and when one
must cry" (10). She too becomes hysterical with laughter, leading
their dour scribe to believe "we had escaped from the loony bin"
(10). But the scribe, too, eventually yields, breaking into "a braying laughter" (10). And still another person appears to add "the
fourth voice in this sardonic concert" (10). One by one the entire

household joins to form a "braying symphony" (10) which infects even the passers-by on the street. The editor concludes: "Kurz, es lag nur an mir alle meine Nachbarn mit ins Spiel zu bringen, und wer weiß, ob das Gelächter sich nicht von Gasse zu Gasse fortge- wälzt und endlich die ganze Stadt samt den Vorstädten in Er- schütterung gesetzt hätte, wenn ich nicht so klug gewesen wäre, mein Manuscript wegzulegen" (10–11).[16] Such laughter — crazed, sardonic, braying, and dangerously intoxicating — seems to threaten the very stability of society. Although the editor's tale is comically exaggerated and satirically directed against similar dire predictions about the result of reading novels, this cacophonous laughter is far from a positive model of reader reception.[17] Instead, it reveals a reading practice as artless as those reading habits which are deline- ated in the very manuscript that elicits these readers' mirth.

The description of the manuscript's impact on the editor's household prefigures the satiric treatment of reading that follows in the main body of the novel. But furthermore, it emphasizes the novel's satiric character by citing the emblems of satire and ani- mating them, as it were, through narrative. That is, instead of em- ploying an allegorical frontispiece as a preface, Wieland draws on conventions of visual representation to cast the preface itself as an emblem. Satire was still associated with satyrs, due to the false ety- mology common in the eighteenth century. It was further linked with the satyric drama of antiquity featuring a chorus of Dionysian satyrs represented with horses ears and tails, half-human creatures considered to be lustful revelers who knew no limits in their intoxi- cated enthusiasm. The laughter of the editor's household alludes to these notions of satire. It is extreme and uncontrolled. It is repeat- edly described as animalistic, specifically akin to horses or donkeys, and thus suspended between the image of satyrs with horses' ears and the image of the donkey as emblem for foolishness. Moreover, it evokes Horace's introduction to *Ars Poetica,* which figures bad, that is, inconsistent, literature through imagery of part-human, part-animal traits. Satire, however, is understood (without con- demnation) precisely as such a mixed genre that aims to distort its object to better reveal the foolishness it mocks. It is therefore a genre freed from prevailing theoretical dictums, a privilege that ac- commodates Wieland's narrative practice in *Don Sylvio*. Distortion is underscored by the adjective "sardonisch," meaning both scorn- ful and "cramped, leading to muscle contortions."[18] Wieland thus introduces his satiric intent and the topic of reading practices by figuring the first readers in his novel, the editor and his household, as a satyric chorus.

Yet the novel's satire, so emphatically presented in the preface, clearly extends beyond the ridicule of particular reading habits. Its reach includes the contemporary theoretical discourse on reading practices and on the novel's social influence, as apparent, for example, in Wieland's mockery of fears for the social fabric, or in his derision of employing literature in the service of rigid moralization. Already in the preface, Wieland's multi-dimensional narrative playfully complicates the novel's thematic, poetic, and social concerns.

Considerations of enthusiasm, another focus of the social and literary attention given to the reader, are brought to bear in the third section of the preface. The figure of the Jansenist is shown to be an unreasonable reader afflicted with religious fanaticism, which is also considered *Schwärmerei*.[19] In his effort to burn the manuscript, he attempts to carry out the sentence leveled against fiction by the theologians in *Don Quixote*.[20] The editor, looking instead for religious sanction of his position, calls on another cleric to legitimate the novel's publication theologically. This priest's response pleases the editor, since the latter interprets it complacently as a license to laugh at the work "to his heart's delight" (13). The editor's misreading of the priest's letter again demonstrates the deficiencies of his reading skills, for the priest reads the work as satire, cautiously venturing to judge the author's intention as one of enlightenment and education in an entertaining form. He values the usefulness of satire against enthusiasm and superstition as long as it remains within "its appropriate measure and limitation" (12), a sentiment the novel seems designed to support. Yet the editor neither reads with concern for satirically mediated lessons nor is he thoughtful or moderate in his response.

In a final gesture, the editor admits his actual lack of concern about the reader's response to the manuscript. He suggests that his focus on the comic elements of the novel is primarily an advertising ploy for the publisher, who hopes the book will prove itself economically profitable. Part of the task of the eighteenth-century preface was indeed to sell the product on the expanding book market[21] and references to satire marked a text as a desirable commodity.[22] The editor's last remarks, then, allude briefly to materialistic concerns of the book market while further undermining the validity of his literary judgment.

The Female Quixote:
Donna Mencia as Adversary of the Narrative

Issues of narrative reception and evaluation, anticipated in the preface of *Don Sylvio*, assert themselves immediately and forcefully in the novel proper. Critics have read the novel's opening passages as paradigmatic examples of its striking stylistic features and have studied Wieland's art of characterization with respect to the figure of Donna Mencia, who is introduced in the first chapter of the novel ("Character einer Art von Tanten").[23] The significance of eighteenth-century discourses on reading and gender for the portrayal of Donna Mencia, however, has received insufficient critical attention. Like the other characters, Donna Mencia is characterized by what and how she reads; her depiction and the presentation of how she interpolates her literary experiences into her lived reality are essential aspects of the metafiction in *Don Sylvio*. But also, analysis of the satire of Mencia illuminates her significance as the prime antagonist in, and of, the narrative of *Don Sylvio*. Her negative qualities help to define the positive qualities of other figures as well as the positive literary qualities for which the narrative itself seeks recognition.

The misogynist sketch of Mencia, true to her role as the evil stepmother in Sylvio's fairy tale, depicts her as, simultaneously, the embodiment of negative feminine traits and a figure transgressing gender norms. Her deviant desires are directed defensively against the expression of desires posited as properly feminine and motivate her zealous crusade against "beauty and love" (17). She and her sisterhood, which forms a celibate, hermetic state in the feminine beau monde analogous to that of a monastic order in the masculine political world, earn for themselves the name of anti-graces "indem sie mit dem ganzen Reich der Liebe in einer eben so offenbaren und unversöhnlichen Fehde stunden, als die Maltheser-Ritter mit den Musulmannen" (18).[24] The comic effects of hyperbole and anachronism in the comparison to the Maltese knights are heightened by Mencia's deviance from positive female roles. The classic "bad woman," her transgressions against normative ideals of femininity are, paradoxically, underscored and explained by those negative traits that are cast as typically feminine ones: jealousy, spite, vanity, bitter prudery, and ugliness. She is a shrew who rails against pretty women as devious female monsters ("Harpye," "Hyäne," "Syrene," "Amphisbäne") — ostensibly to defend "the poor men" (18). The satire against the false gender identification is developed further in the ironic suggestion that Mencia attempts to emulate a masculine, imperial stance through "a mode of thought that she had perhaps copied from the great Caesar" (19).

The comparison of Donna Mencia to the Maltese Knights anticipates the damning evidence against her, namely her reading habits; for the novel's reader, her reading habits substantiate the validity of the narrator's negative judgment. She reads chivalric novels passionately and is consistently ridiculed for the manner in which she incorporates them into her life and discourse. In the final scenes of *Don Sylvio,* for example, she becomes amenable to the plan of double marriages because she finds Don Sylvio's role in freeing his sister Hyacinthe worthy of any famous literary knight and — ultimately — because Don Gabriel flatters her through compliments delivered in the discursive style fashionable in the previous century. Despite the obvious anachronism, she responds positively to the bombastic sixteenth-century formulas gleaned from reading *Amadis,*[25] and thereby performs the inverted mimesis of literary models often imputed to female readers in eighteenth-century debates on the novel.

Mencia's literary predilections are shown both to shape and to reflect her poor judgment and her inappropriate social behavior. Her reading habits and literary taste are associated in the narrative with forms of female desire that are socially condemned. Like Quixote, Mencia mistakes chivalric novels for viable models of behavior, but as a woman, she cannot enact her fantasies directly in the masculine role of an adventurous hero. The sarcastic designation of her as a knight emphasizes that her crusades against other women in the name of higher morality are misguided. The pleasure she takes in enacting the feminine role of honored damsel, in her stilted exchange with Don Gabriel, is equally ridiculed by the narrator to underscore the vanity and foolishness that give rise to her fancy for such flattery. Mencia also views chivalric novels as a source of worthwhile knowledge. She is mocked for this error in judgment as well as for her self-delusion that she is learned. Even were the novels considered fonts of wisdom, her ambition to be knowledgeable represents a further transgression of sanctioned femininity and a confirmation of female vanity. The narrator thus reveals and derides Mencia's self-image and her desires, shows them to be intertwined with her reading practices, and interprets both her reading habits and her desires as signs of deviance from those feminine roles that are socially acceptable.

Mencia's improper passions in literature and in life make her the figure most open to harsh satire and render her the only purely negative Quixote-figure in the novel, a foil to the male protagonist and his follies. Mencia's misreading corresponds to negative eighteenth-century notions about female reading; her gender may explain her errors but it does not excuse them. Her nephew Don Sylvio, however, is largely exonerated in the novel for his initial desire to imitate the very heroes Mencia most admires. His tendency to read tales of adventure as models for behavior is interpreted in the narrative as a sign of his youthful propensity to indulge an enthusiastic, even intoxicating imagination that is highly valued and ultimately rewarded.

The conflict between Mencia and Sylvio is fundamentally literary. It is based on differences in the respective genres they employ as paradigmatic structures for reading the world, and on differences in the kinds of desires that motivate their reading. Their discord is prefigured in the disputes between Mencia and Don Pedro, the absent father figure from whom Sylvio has apparently inherited his literary taste as well as his books. Don Sylvio and Don Pedro share an enthusiasm for fairy tales. Don Pedro's attitude as reader is remarkably similar to that of the editor in the preface, for he seeks diversion and nothing more: "je schnakischer die Einfälle sind, die der närrische Kerl, der Autor, auf die Bahn bringt, desto mehr lach' ich, und das ist alles, was ich dabei suche" (24).[26] While this is not the sole reading practice supported by the novel — for it does reward Sylvio's idealistic enthusiasm, even as it also demands intellectual, critical engagement from its readers — the pleasure of reading that such laughter reflects and the ability to become absorbed in the literary world are encouraged by the narrative. Mencia, in contrast, has no appreciation for humor and deplores the witty and lighthearted fairy tale, a sure sign of her inadequate literary discernment. She is presented as a poor critic unable even to distinguish basic generic differences: "Denn in so großem Ansehen die Ritterbücher bei ihr stunden, welche sie mit den Chroniken, Historien und Reisebeschreibungen in einerlei Classe setzte, so verächtlich waren ihr alle diese kleine Spiele des Witzes, die bloß zur Unterhaltung der Kinder oder zum Zeitvertreib der Erwachsenen geschrieben werden, und durch nichts als die angenehme Art der Erzählung sich Leuten von Geschmack empfehlen können" (24).[27] Here Mencia is shown to be not only the antagonist of her nephew, but also of the genre and narrative project of the enchanting and witty novel *Don Sylvio* itself. Wieland's ruthless treatment of her serves in his narrative strategy as a defense of his own literary enterprise, for no reader will want to acknowledge kinship with such a ridiculous character, least of all share her inferior literary judgment.

While the narrator develops the satire against Donna Mencia under the guise of an objective presentation, the negative portrayal allows him to indicate the superiority of his own literary practice. Through this scheme of contrast and competition, the tale *Don Sylvio* is marked and valued as masculine. The narrator continues his feud with Mencia by offering his readers irrefutable proof of his claim that her outward stance of a moral and chaste lifestyle is mendacious. Her "true" character is revealed through further insight into her literary taste and her secret reading habits: "Der Abscheu, den sie vor den Erzählungen eines Bocaz und selbst vor den unschuldigsten Scherzen eines Lope de Vega bezeugte, hinderte nicht, daß die Gespräche, die irgend ein moderner Sotades der berühmten Aloysia Sigea aufgeschoben, das Buch waren, welches allezeit unter ihrem Hauptküssen lag; eine Gewohnheit, die sie vielleicht mit dem Exempel des heiligen Chrysostomus zu rechtfertigen glaubte, welcher den eben so sotadischen Comödien des Aristophanes die nämliche Ehre widerfahren ließ" (59).[28] The scene of secret reading in bed and the danger it poses to a woman's virtue was a familiar cipher in contemporary discourse on reading and gender for the perils posed by novels to genteel society. The image also recurs in the pictorial art of the time and it remains a constant anchor in the *Lesesucht* debates focused on the moral status of the novel.[29] The eighteenth-century assumptions that female virtue need be guarded more closely than male virtue and that women, whose social role it was to uphold morality, may be duplicitous in their outward moral stance, are thus brought to bear in the satire against Donna Mencia. She who claims to protect masculine virtue from feminine seduction turns secretly to titillating reading matter, while her ugliness and "men's lack of compassion" (58) toward her deny her the experience of sexual seduction. The narrator is quick to separate himself, however ironically, from this masculine view. He is compelled to make such unflattering revelations, he avers, by nothing less than poetic principle, which obligates him to fulfill "the duties of historical faithfulness in this matter" in order to convince the suspicious reader of the "truth of our story" (59).

In the context of the revelations about Mencia's secret reading matter, the protestations of narrative propriety and honesty further distance both the narrator's persona and the text of the novel from any association with Mencia. The narrator professes his personal virtue through an exaggerated explanation of his lack of discretion. His text, by extension, claims to conform to precepts of literary theory such as historical truth. Moreover, as Donna Mencia's literary antagonist, both the narrator and his narrative stand in contrast to the literature she embraces and are akin to the literature she opposes. In this regard, the narrator's remark that the work under Mencia's pillow is ascribed to a female author is noteworthy, for the opposition between the respective literary tastes of Mencia and the narrator is thereby shored up by describing the narratives themselves, as well as their readers, through terms of gender. The imputation that the author of the dialogues Mencia reads is, however, actually a man emphasizes the aberration of female authorship, even while specifying inferior, disreputably sexual and scatological literature as feminine and effeminate. The narrator thereby recalls a longstanding association drawn between effeminacy and the cinaedic — sexual and scatological — poetry of Sotades, invoked here as the literary ancestor of the texts Mencia prefers to read. For himself, in contrast, the narrator creates an honorable literary heritage. He relates himself by analogy to Boccaccio and Lope de Vega, whose wit is unappreciated by Mencia. *Scherz* (playfulness) is likewise emphasized throughout *Don Sylvio* in the generic descriptions of the fairy tales disdained by Mencia. To strengthen the narrator's alliance with his chosen literary models, *Scherz* is flaunted even as the narrator disparages Mencia. For example, the chapter heading, "Ein Exempel, daß Sprödigkeit den Zorn der Venus reizt" (II, 1, 58)[30] achieves both goals: it playfully situates itself as exemplum near didactic literature, an object of scorn throughout the narrative, but reverses the expectations about the moral to be told, for it argues against excessive chastity as prudery in order to criticize Mencia. The presentation of Donna

Mencia as at once a bad woman, an aberrant reader, and the primary antagonist of the literary style adopted in *Don Sylvio* is thus one central device of the novel's theoretical self-reflection and an important tactic in its aim to shape an ideal reader who delights in wit and playfulness and who also desires literary sophistication.

The characterization of Donna Felicia as the most positive female figure in *Don Sylvio* further underscores Mencia's position as the novel's symbolic antagonist, while extending the novel's metafictional commentary on its own narrative profile. Again, this commentary relies on assessments of various reading practices and narrative styles associated with the different characters. As shown above, gender traits are correlated in the novel with the predilection of characters for particular literary genres. The nexus of gender and genre is not only used to define differences between women and men. It is also used to define differences between women — or between men — of different reading habits. Such a contrast is clearly drawn between the unequal rivals for Don Sylvio's affections, Mergelina, who is Mencia's cohort and pawn, and Felicia. Mencia conspires to wed Sylvio to Mergelina, but it is Felicia who is the true object of his desire and who gives meaning to his fairy-tale adventure. These characters not only represent competing plots within *Don Sylvio;* they also represent divergent literary modes. Mergelina, like Mencia, favors chivalric novels and the narrator clearly disapproves of "women of her genre" (75). In contrast, Felicia's elaborate realization of "arcadia" is based on her reception of pastoral novels. She is thus affiliated both as a reader and as a creator with the realm of "beauty and love" that is posited in the novel as properly feminine but is opposed by Mencia and Mergelina.[31]

In the character of Felicia, the apparent dichotomy between art and life — a dichotomy that is a cornerstone for the plot of the quixotic reader's confusions — is suspended. Sylvio's enthusiastic but immature passions are aroused by the artistic image on the medallion that appears to be a portrait of Felicia, but instead portrays her grandmother. After the clarification of this confusion, the substitution of the real for the imagined love resolves the plot of the novel. Felicia's ability to guide Sylvio's desire away from fiction and toward mature social integration through marriage thus assures the victory of life over illusion, or the "victory of nature over enthusiasm" that is promised in the novel's title. In the metanarrative of *Don Sylvio,* however, Sylvio's enthusiastic imagination and his natural sentiment are commensurate. Indeed, his desires for fiction and for Felicia are equivalent and are both fulfilled in and through fiction, since Felicia is the overtly fictional, literary descendent of figures in the picaresque novel *Histoire de Gil Blas de Santillane* (The History of Gil Blas of Santillane, 1715–35) by Alain-René Lesage, from which many of the characters and place names in *Don Sylvio* derive.[32]

The resolution of the novel's metafictional conflict thus depends on a different kind of substitution, namely a diachronic substitution of modern art for art that is passé. Sylvio's fantasy is nourished by narratives of adventure and enchantment that presage the tale in which he and Felicia figure as protagonists. The portrait on the medallion seems, and indeed is, the promise of his own fairy-tale adventure. But the art that attracts the youthful Sylvio proves to be dated. Although Felicia appears remarkably similar to her grandmother when she dons her guise to pose for a parallel portrait, she is a younger figure self-consciously enacting a role. She is a modern descendant playfully usurping the costume of her ancestor, just as the narrative in which she is a protagonist takes on the trappings of older genres. Felicia is thus simultaneously the embodiment of Sylvio's fairy princess and the embodied corrective to his imaginative excesses that are fueled by outmoded fiction. Both as the apotheosis of Sylvio's princess fantasy and as the imagined descendant of well-known fictional characters, Felicia is a representative of fiction, but of a self-assured, modern fiction.

Thus, with the help of Felicia's enlightening guidance, Sylvio soon acknowledges that she, and not the image on the medallion, is indeed the more appropriate recipient of his affections, the better incarnation of his desires sparked by reading. Yet Sylvio's seduction through art did lead him, felicitously, to his beloved. As inheritor of the medallion and the art it represents, Felicia legitimizes Sylvio's passion for imaginative fiction, even as she educates him to a more suitable means of drawing on literature to enhance life. The self-conscious modern narrative that Felicia can be seen to represent triumphs over the anachronistic novels which Mencia champions and replaces the simplistic fairy-tale conventions hitherto guiding Sylvio. Felicia becomes a figure for the kind of fiction that can attract and hold the desire of the mature masculine reader, for the kind of fiction that Sylvio may legitimately embrace, for the kind of alluring modern fiction that Wieland offers his readers.

Wieland thus creates a stylistic profile for *Don Sylvio* through his characterization of the figure of Donna Mencia in her role as antagonist within the plot and in her role as antagonist to the narrative itself. In doing so, he explicitly points to specific texts and authors to construct a literary lineage for his own narrative and to illuminate and emphasize its defining qualities and values. He claims narrative authority for his novel by casting wit, playfulness, enlightened insight and sophisticated pleasure in fiction's many charms as attributes of a modern masculine style. Such narrative derives further legitimacy by not appealing to incompetent readers (those guided by desires presented in the text as inappropriate) and by attracting mature and intelligent readers. The character of Felicia, overtly the masculine author's fictional creation, figures the appeal of such fiction for the mature masculine reader. And in this role, she becomes a model of positively valued femininity to emulate for the female reader who ought to be, like Felicia, a mature and wise reader able to integrate her appreciation for literature into her own life story in a socially appropriate fashion.

Symbolic Siblings

Both the stylistic self-reflection of the novel and its interest in literary inheritance and lineage are further developed through the characterization and plot entanglements of the protagonist Don Sylvio. His poetic appropriation of the fairy-tale paradigm to construct his own story of identity and the ways that it informs the theoretical profile of the larger narrative are best understood in relation to the practices of narrative reception and production of two other characters, namely Hyacinthe and Pedrillo. In turn, the literary functions of the embedded narratives of Hyacinthe and Pedrillo become clearer when read in connection with Don Sylvio's mode of reading. These three figures are related in the text not only by their youth, their enthusiastic reception of literature, and their proclivity to interpret their experience through the generic conventions of the stories they love. They are also linked explicitly as symbolic siblings. However, these sibling figures do not share one literary inheritance: their differences in this regard are explained in the novel by their social separation. Hyacinthe was kidnapped at a young age and thus not raised with Sylvio, while Pedrillo's social inferiority to Sylvio determines the narrative material that nurtures his imagination. Together, Hyacinthe and Pedrillo serve as foils who position the protagonist in a social and a literary hierarchy. And in the metafictional discourse of the novel, the narrative style of *Don Sylvio* is further defined through contrast and association with these storytellers. Together, then, the narratives of these symbolic sibling figures elaborate the novel's thematic and theoretical focus on the power of literary paradigms and on the social status and influence of literature.

Hyacinthe's Tales of Virtue

Critics have generally found Hyacinthe's story disruptive and have struggled to integrate it into a broader reading of *Don Sylvio*.[33] From the first reception of the novel, they have remarked the dullness of the narrative and found it incommensurate with the novel's modern style. In the words of one early reviewer, Hyacinthe "erzählt ihre Komödiantengeschichte in einem so elenden Tone, daß gewiß auf der Insel Felsenburg die Lebensläufe besser erzählt werden."[34] Wieland chose to shorten Hyacinthe's story considerably in later versions of the text, yet its tedium was clearly part of the original narrative design. Hyacinthe's narrative reflects the discourse of femininity exemplified and firmly established by Richardson's *Pamela, or Virtue Rewarded,* and as such is juxtaposed in the novel with the genre and style of *Don Sylvio,* a comparison in which Wieland's novel is favored. The entire episode can be read as a parody of Richardson, but this parody does not rest on the moral condemnation of the figure Hyacinthe, as has been argued, nor is it unrelated to the novel's "inner bond," namely "a reckoning with Schwärmerei."[35] Such a critique is, rather, firmly embedded in the novel's obsession with enthusiastic reading, for Hyacinthe is very much her quixotic brother's sister. Her story presents her as a reader whose understanding of the world is determined by the literature she reads and whose narrative directly articulates this relationship. Novels provide her with the interpretive model through which to read her experience. Her narrative, therefore, paradigmatically reproduces that discourse which Nancy Miller has termed the "heroine's text."[36]

The way in which social constructions of gender inform both the style of Hyacinthe's narrative and her conception of her femininity becomes clear immediately in the introduction to her story:

> Wenn es richtig ist, wie ich zu glauben geneigt bin, fing die
> schöne Hyacinthe ihre Erzählung an, daß ein Frauenzimmer de-
> sto schätzbarer ist, je weniger sie von sich zu reden macht, so bin
> ich unglücklich genug, daß ich in einem Alter, worin die meisten
> kaum angefangen haben unter den Flügeln einer zärtlichen
> Mutter schüchtern hervor zu schleichen, eine Erzählung meiner
> Begebenheiten zu machen habe; und ich würde in der Tat un-
> tröstbar deswegen sein, wenn ich die Schuld davon mir selbst
> beizumessen hätte.[37] (229)

Hyacinthe begins with a confession and a defense. Although respectable women ought not to be the subject of narrative, Hyacinthe does have a story to tell. She explains this circumstance
through the condition of motherlessness — her defense is the lack
of a positive female guide and protector. Already the topoi of the
heroine's text are in play. Hyacinthe believes herself an orphan,
since she is separated from her family at a young age. She must
prove her virtue, which serves as an indicator of her true social class
(nobility of heart and lineage), under extreme circumstances in
which the only alternatives seen for her are "to seduce others" or
to "let herself be seduced" (230). She repeatedly passes tests of
virtue: she maintains her purity despite the dances of the gypsies,
the advances of a single suitor, the sexual threats of a roomful of
men, the predatory intentions of the man who has bought her, and
even despite her experiences in the morally questionable institution
of the theater. Needless to say, the heroine is indeed a heroine. She
resists various forms of temptation, such as vanity and sexual
arousal, as well as physical assault. Her responses to these threats
reproduce those responses prescribed by the sentimental heroine's
text: she cries, throws herself at her aggressor's feet, threatens sui-
cide, becomes breathless and weak, and in the last instance man-
ages to flee. In the theater she places herself under the watchful eye
of a surrogate mother figure, thereby demonstrating and protecting her virtue.

As both narrator and protagonist of her tale, Hyacinthe faces
poetic dilemmas occasioned by the conflict between the demand to
fashion her own story well and the demand to embody the feminine ideal of virtue. The following confession, for example, reveals
her difficulties in this regard: "Ich stellte mir vor, wie ich mich gegen den Marquis bezeugen wollte, meine Einbildung malte mir eine Menge von Abenteuern vor, die ich in alten Romanen gelesen

hatte, und meine kleine Eitelkeit fand sich durch den Gedanken geschmeichelt, daß ich vermutlich selbst die Heldin eines Romans werden könnte" (241).[38] Hyacinthe tells her listeners that the literature she read fortified her during her trials and offered her the hope that her own virtue would someday likewise be rewarded. But here Hyacinthe admits that she dreamed herself to be a literary heroine, a thought thoroughly incommensurate with the social attitudes and self-understanding with which she introduced her feminine tale. While her brother Sylvio's perception of himself as the protagonist of a fairy tale is portrayed as foolish, but not immoral, Hyacinthe's parallel conceit is one she must reject as a moral fault revealing her vanity. Although she may not adopt the pose of a heroine who has "many adventures" as described in "old novels," she does embrace the image of feminine virtue modeled in the texts she reads and applies it as a measure of her own experience. Hyacinthe finds herself in a paradoxical bind inherent to the genre of the modern sentimental novel and its discourse, which she adopts. To be properly feminine requires modesty and, indeed, the lack of the experiences that make a story worth telling, but to narrate her story so as to prove her virtue, she must present herself convincingly as a heroine. The virtue of the sentimental heroine must demonstrate and enact itself physically to be believed, but this enactment instantly becomes suspect as theatrical duplicity.[39] Indeed, the necessity and inherent problem of the theatrics of virtue is one which her narrative addresses. Eugenio, for instance, emphasizes Hyacinthe's lack of talent as an actress, a failing which, as a sign of her true virtue, endears her to him. Similarly, Hyacinthe's pedestrian narrative style exonerates her from any suspicion of deceiving her audience with seductive artistry. An eighteenth-century Scheherazade who defends her virtue as her life, she knows fairy tales and ballads by heart and narrates them to put lustful suitors to sleep, a skill which reflects well on her virtue but quite poorly on her skills as an engaging storyteller.

The novel *Don Sylvio* grants Hyacinthe the status of literary heroine which she herself, as proper heroine, must disavow. Her virtue *is* a sign of her noble birth that corresponds to her noble heart; she *is* reunited with her long lost family; she *is* rewarded through marriage to the man she loves. Such confirmation of Hyacinthe as a heroine who enacts the prototypical plot of the sentimental novel underscores her status as a fictional figure and points to the narrative hierarchy of *Don Sylvio*, for the narrator ultimately controls her story within his design of the larger tale. The narrator of the novel reasserts his voice and his authority after presenting sections of Hyacinthe's story told by herself and by Eugenio. He interrupts their tale and distances himself from the tedious narrative styles ascribed to these figures: "So interessant vermutlich die Liebesgeschichte des Don Eugenio und der schönen Hyacinthe ihnen selbst und vielleicht auch ihren unmittelbaren Zuhörern gewesen sein mag, so wenig können wir unsern Lesern übel nehmen, wenn sie das Ende davon zu sehen wünschen. Es ist in der Tat für ehrliche Leute, die bei kaltem Blut sind, kein langweiligeres Geschöpf in der Welt als ein Liebhaber, der die Geschichte seines Herzens erzählt" (262).[40] Hyacinthe's story of virtue rewarded by true love, guided by narrative conventions that are associated with the feminine, is repeatedly described as, and is indeed shown to be, poetically uninteresting. It bores readers rather than involving them in an imaginative world and its emphasis on ideal feminine virtue proves a narrative liability. Hyacinthe may be a perfect Richardsonian heroine but she is a poor literary judge. Such characterization of Hyacinthe highlights the superior poetic sensibilities of her brother, while the literary inferiority of her chosen generic model allows the tale of *Don Sylvio* to shine in contrast as a witty and enchanting masculine narrative.

The metafictional definition of Wieland's narrative continues with respect to Hyacinthe's story as the characters discuss their divergent literary expectations and comment on the art of narration. The listener Don Sylvio is unable to understand his sister's tale, shaped by unfamiliar generic conventions — he is primarily bemused by the absence of fairies in her story. Hyacinthe's response illustrates her greater awareness that narratives are constructed. Rather than being transparently representational, they interpret events according to particular discursive rules, she explains: "Wollten sie dann, sagte Hyacinthe, daß ich ein Feen-Märchen aus meiner Geschichte gemacht haben sollte, warum ließen sie mir nichts davon merken? Wenn ich geglaubt hätte, sie ihnen dadurch angenehm zu machen, so wäre es mir ein leichtes gewesen, die alte Zigeunerin in eine Carabosse, die gute Dame zu Calatrava in eine Lüminöse, und Don Fernand von Zamora, wo nicht zu einem schelmischen Zwerg, doch wenigstens zu einem Sylphen oder Salamander zu machen" (263–64).[41] Hyacinthe would have been willing to translate her story into the terminology and signifying structures Don Sylvio anticipated. The boring elements of her story that Felicia chides are a commentary, therefore, on Hyacinthe's choice of convention, in turn a reflection on her literary taste and on the way in which social gender constructions correlate with particular literary genres. Felicia, like the narrator, distances herself from Hyacinthe's style. She simultaneously teases and humors Sylvio with her assertions that Hyacinthe's story would have been better, certainly more entertaining, had she turned it into a fairy tale. A poetic description following fairy-tale convention, Felicia maintains, would lead her and others to believe "that the poet had executed his office and presented nature as he should" (264). And indeed, Hyacinthe's story, as shaped by the novel's narrator, can be read as a fairy tale with many parallels to her brother's adventures, as W. Daniel Wilson has shown.[42] Once again the narrative slyly incorporates a subversive reassessment of the theoretical mandate to imitate nature that ironically reflects and legitimizes Wieland's own practice in the fanciful novel *Don Sylvio*.

Don Sylvio's Tales of Enchantment

Don Sylvio and Hyacinthe share similar responses to the literature they read. Each of them imaginatively identifies with the protagonists of these tales to such an extent that they adopt the fictional narratives as models on which to base their own stories. The intensity of their common reading practice seems to be innate, yet the development of their literary taste is determined by their immediate environment. Don Sylvio's susceptibility to enchantment by the fairies is anticipated in his response to the chivalric novels through which Donna Mencia educates him. The knightly protagonists, "whose great deeds and heroic virtues delighted him to the point of enchantment" (21), inspire him with the zeal to imitate them. But as Sylvio gets older, he turns away from the novels that are the domain of his surrogate mother to mimic the literary taste of his father, inherited in the form of Don Pedro's books of fairy-tale adventures. Don Sylvio's initial reading attitude toward fairy tales repeats that of both his father and the editor from the preface to the novel. In short, he gives himself over to the pleasure of pure entertainment. Gradually, however, the fairy tales ensconce themselves so firmly in his mind that he begins to reconstruct his surroundings through their terminology: "er las nichts anders, er staunte und dichtete nichts anders, er ging den ganzen Tag mit nichts anderm um, und träumte die ganze Nacht von nichts anderm" (27).[43]

Don Sylvio is not passive in his literary reception. He actively engages in transposing signifying terms from the literary realm to his more immediate reality. One form of his poetic creativity is his tendency to bestow new names upon the objects and beings in his universe. His reality is transformed through this naming, and soon gains independence from his initial authoritative act. And just as the two spheres of poetry and reality merge for Don Sylvio through renaming, so their boundaries are blurred and dismantled in the novel. Initially the narrator distances himself explicitly from Sylvio's poeticizing vein by explaining the phenomenon of literary influence psychologically or by attributing fairy-tale nomenclature specifically to Don Sylvio's personal narrative. The narrator does not maintain such a stance, however. Shielded by the disclaimer of irony, the narrator introduces fairies as agents in Don Sylvio's story, a practice repeated, for instance, in the chapter headings throughout the novel and through strategic shifts in narrative modality between subjunctive and indicative.[44] The early metaphoric description of Sylvio's enchantment through literature becomes increasingly literal in the text, both as indictment and as confirmation of Sylvio's understanding of his experience. While Hyacinthe possesses a degree of awareness about the function her reading plays in shaping her narrative, Don Sylvio must yet learn to recognize the characteristics of his reception of literature, but he proves steadfast — and in the scheme of the novel, quite justified — in his own notion of the relation between the world of fairies and his own.

If the narratives of Hyacinthe and Sylvio illuminate their reading habits, the responses of critical listeners to their stories reveal the social framework against which these definitions of subjective experience must be measured, while such exchanges between narrator and audience within the novel's plot allow metafictional commentary on the narrative of the novel and on the interaction between text and reader. While Hyacinthe has a circle of listeners, Don Sylvio's primary audience is Pedrillo, whose role as listener and critic of Sylvio's tales proves to be as crucial to an understanding of the novel as are Don Sylvio's foibles as a reader and a storyteller. The role each character adopts in these exchanges and the interaction of the two characters underscore theoretical dimensions of the novel's metafiction, frequently found in proximity to Pedrillo.

The two longer stories which Don Sylvio tells to Pedrillo reveal the extent to which fairy tales come to dominate Sylvio's perception of reality, while Pedrillo's response as audience of these tales points to issues of aesthetic judgment and narrative skill. Don Sylvio's account of his adventures during the night he failed to return home to Rosalva is his first longer narrative (I, 10). Not surprisingly, it is the tale of a beautiful princess, good and bad fairies, reward, enchantments, and evil spells. As narrator, he adopts a tone of absolute authority. He forbids Pedrillo to interrupt him and is angered by Pedrillo's commentary. Pedrillo agrees to let him continue undisturbed, but he feels compelled to object to a detail of Sylvio's story which he finds incredible, namely, the condition placed on the disenchantment of a malicious green dwarf. Pedrillo, well versed in fairy-tale convention, does not object to the dwarf or to the elements of enchantment, but rather to the implausibility of a particular character. Even within the sovereign logic of the fairy-tale world, Pedrillo feels that Don Sylvio has transgressed the limits of poetic license. Don Sylvio's insistence on enacting the continuation of the story by seeking a blue butterfly in the woods further disconcerts his listener. Despite Sylvio's outrage at Pedrillo's lack of faith, Pedrillo dares suggest that his friend and master might have been dreaming, a psychological explanation that grants Sylvio's sincerity, even while questioning the veracity of the story.

Pedrillo's tone soon changes when Don Sylvio offers him a locket with the image of his princess as concrete evidence corroborating his tale. Pedrillo's exclamations unwittingly resound with central criteria of poetic judgment: truth, truthfulness, and the marvelous: "Nun muß ichs freilich wohl glauben, daß alles die Wahrheit ist, was ihr mir erzählt habt; wahrhaftig, wenn ich sie nicht mit meinen eignen Augen sähe, so hätt ichs nicht geglaubt. Das ist wunderbar! Aber von wem könntet ihr es auch sonst haben als von einer Fee?" (51).[45] Pedrillo's response is fully consistent with the absolute confidence he has in his vision as epistemological foundation. The ability he had shown to separate his aesthetic appreciation from his judgment about its relation to his experience disintegrates when he is confronted with pictorial rather than narrative art. On seeing the "miraculous" locket, he believes that Don Sylvio's story indeed corresponds directly to his actual experience.

Pedrillo's confusion here as to modes and methods of artistic presentation soon becomes emphatically apparent, for it is not limited to his belief in the locket as a guarantor for the truth of the marvelous. While he does understand that the painting is not real, he finds the image so authentic that he conceives of it as a fully mimetic representation of the person depicted, and therefore imagines the princess to be as tiny as her portrait. Now it is Don Sylvio who can explain the conditions and functions of artistic devices: "Sie ist hier nur so klein gemalt, weil es die Kleinheit des Raums nicht anders zuließ, aber das verhindert nicht, daß sie nicht zum wenigsten so groß sei als die Diana . . . und gesetzt auch, daß sie etwas kleiner wäre, so wäre sie nur dadurch den Gratien desto ähnlicher, welcher von den Poeten und Malern kleiner vorgestellt werden als andre Göttinnen, um die Anmut und Lieblichkeit dadurch auszudrücken" (52).[46] Linking the literary and the pictorial spheres, Sylvio indicates the fallacy in Pedrillo's understanding of representation, pointing to the material limitations the painter faced as well as to the artistic effect intended. This discussion between Don Sylvio and the less educated Pedrillo, in which the comedy rests on hyperbolic extension of the underlying concept of mimesis, reflects on the similar confusion from which the hero suffers regarding literature. It simultaneously criticizes a rigid exegesis of such theoretical terms as *Nachahmung* (imitation), *Wahrscheinlichkeit* (probability), and *das Wunderbare* (the marvelous), terms under constant surveillance and playful modulation in the novel. The fictive reader is thus cautioned against a misapplication of the aesthetic criteria current in the literary theory of the mideighteenth century that could lead one, like Pedrillo or Don Sylvio, to bypass the essence of art.

The discussion between the two adventurers after the second longer story of fantastic adventures with the green dwarf related by Don Sylvio to Pedrillo (III, 3) explicitly refers back to points of contention in Pedrillo's reception of the first story, specifically the probability and inner consistency of the narrative. Pedrillo, who has been rudely awakened by Don Sylvio's attempts to throttle him, is skeptical of Sylvio's initial explanation of the incident; once again, he suspects Sylvio of dreaming. Sylvio, however, will admit no concessions, stating imperially: "I am telling you that I was awake, and that ought to be enough for you" (99). Thus Pedrillo again adopts the role of listener. He accepts Sylvio's arrogated authority as narrator, suspends his disbelief, and settles in to enjoy the story. Pedrillo's doubts about the truth of the narrative do not detract from its value for him as entertainment. His disappointment at the lack of a happy ending to such a tale suggests that he is evaluating the story according to fairy-tale convention. "Das ist eine verzweifelte Historie, sagte Pedrillo, meiner Six, sie fing so schön an! es ist Jammerschade, daß sie nicht besser aufhörte. Aber — wenn einem einfältigen Kerl eine Frage erlaubt ist, glaubt ihr also, gnädiger Herr, daß euch das alles würklich begegnet ist?" (102).[47] While he cannot convince Sylvio of the story's implausibility or persuade him about his alternative version of their shared experience, he does catch him in the logic of his own narrative framework and insists on the need for inner consistency. Since Pedrillo had finally accepted the improbable conditions for the release of the green dwarf in the last narrative, Don Sylvio must now admit that such a release is unlikely to have taken place so quickly. It is, however, the locket rather than theoretical arguments that again serves as their ultimate criterion of judgment, this time disproving the truth of Sylvio's story through its presence, as Pedrillo observes (102). As the audience and critic of Don Sylvio's narratives, Pedrillo employs the categories of truth, credibility, plausibility, and possibility — of the marvelous and reality. He judges Sylvio's tales with reference to literary convention. And he appreciates Don Sylvio's rhetorical skill and narrative constructions, in spite of his skepticism about their viability as representations of reality. Despite his ignorance of theoretical aesthetic concerns, Pedrillo thus challenges the stories Don Sylvio tells and functions in the self-reflexive text of the novel to draw reader attention to aesthetic criteria, to questions of interpretation and evaluation.

Little Pedro's Old Wives' Tales

Pedrillo has been described as "the comic voice of truth" who shows that Sylvio's world is indeed one of fairy-tale extravagance and that his adventures are indeed a fairy tale.[48] In this respect he serves the metafictional strategy of the narrative, but his role as "wise fool" who reveals poetic truths extends further. As the audience for Sylvio's tales, his naive responses show the controlling narrator's playful elaboration on aesthetic concerns and the larger issues of the novel. And as narrator, Pedrillo shows himself to be a crucial foil not only to the protagonist, but also to the narrator. As with Sancho Panza, an obvious literary ancestor, the humor associated with Pedrillo is often elicited through contrast to his master, yet much of the comedy centering on literary reception and production is founded on the kinship of the two figures with respect to their traits as imaginative readers and storytellers. In the novel's preface and within its main text, but also in Wieland's letter to Salomon Gessner of November 7, 1763, Wieland expressed the intention to address the related phenomena of enthusiasm and superstition in *Don Sylvio*.[49] Although Pedrillo is not generally examined as a "reader," Wieland's statements suggest a profound similarity between him and the hero. The similarity is reinforced by their symbolic sibling relationship. As with Sylvio's sister, Hyacinthe, the bonds drawn between the characters in this fashion point to their respective literary frameworks for reading the world. The differences in their literary references are presented as a difference in inheritance and also serve, through contrast, to define the narrative *Don Sylvio*.

Although Pedrillo is not a blood brother of Sylvio's, he states that he has grown up with his master and was suckled at the same breast: "he is my milk-brother" (133). This formulation emphasizes a bond from infancy created through a shared maternal figure. The symbolic sibling relationship is also made explicit in Pedrillo's name, which provides the paternal link, since he was named after Sylvio's father Don Pedro: "he was my godfather . . . and therefore I was christened Pedro" (133). The renaming in the diminutive, "Pedrillo," initially reflected his youth, but is also a linguistic inscription of the hierarchical difference in social status between the two. Pedrillo suggests that he might lose the diminutive ending of his name if he were to receive a noble title as a result of Sylvio's fantastic adventures — otherwise he will remain "Pedrillo" (133).

Pedrillo's literary inheritance is described in detail, just as it is for Sylvio and Hyacinthe, and his relative position in the social hierarchy, like theirs, also influences his literary taste. While Pedrillo is knowledgeable in the world of fairy tales and can hence participate in the Don Sylvio's discourse, his own literary background, unique in the novel, informs his perceptions and beliefs. It encompasses the oral tradition of stories passed on to him by his grandmother, including folk tales, ghost stories, and proverbs (the last also being another kind of literary inheritance from Sancho). Significantly, the difference in social hierarchy is reinforced as a difference in literary hierarchy described in terms of gender. The narrative tradition that shapes Pedrillo's interpretive framework is explicitly and repeatedly defined as feminine by Don Sylvio, by the narrator of the novel, and by Pedrillo himself. Don Sylvio criticizes Pedrillo's superstition as "Hirngespenste, welche die alte Hure, deine Großmutter, von ihrer Älter-Mutter geerbt" (90).[50] The narrator describes Pedrillo's storytelling as "einer sehr umständlichen Erzählung aller Histörchen von dieser Art, die seit undenklichen Zeiten den Tanten und Großmüttern in seiner Freundschaft, vermöge einer ununterbrochenen Tradition von Großmutter zu Großmutter, begegnet sein sollten" (162).[51] Pedrillo confirms this feminine tradition as the source of his literary knowledge in more positive terms with respect to an actual book:

> ihr wißt ja die Historie, Herr? sie steht in einem alten Buch, das ich aus der Erbschaft meiner Großmutter für dreizehn Maravedis annehmen mußte, ob es gleich keinen Deckel und kein Titel-Blatt mehr hatte; es waren die Menge gemalter Figuren darin, woran ich mich erlustigte, wie ich noch ein kleiner Junge war, und dann las mir meine Großmutter die Historien, die daneben stunden, es ist mir, als ob ich sie noch vor mir sitzen sehe, die gute alte Frau, Gott tröste sie![52] (42)

The literary tradition passed on to Pedrillo is thus defined socially by the hierarchy of both gender and class, as the description of the exact value and the poor condition of the book in question attest. The conflicts between Don Sylvio and Pedrillo in the readings of their common experience correspond to this difference of literary inheritance.

The similarities in the ways narrative influences the perceptive structure of Don Sylvio and Pedrillo are raised early in the novel in the chapter entitled "Psychologische Betrachtungen" (Psychological Observations, I, 3). Here the narrator muses that Nature herself can be the first source of the imaginative excesses that find expression in and that are furthered by narratives, be they the old wives' tales and ghost stories favored by the superstitious lower class or the kind of poetic chimeras that Sylvio embraces. The figure Pedrillo exemplifies this parallel with respect to his master, as is best illustrated in III, 1. Pedrillo's fear turns the trees in the dark into giants, a process informed by the narratives he knows: "Es fielen ihm auf einmal alle Gespenster-Historien ein, die er von seiner Kindheit an gehört hatte, er glaubte alle Augenblicke etwas verdächtiges zu sehen, und zitterte bei dem mindesten Geräusch, das er merkte, so laut oder noch lauter als ein Klopfstockischer Teufel" (85).[53] This description draws attention to the difference in literary register between the ghost stories which frame Pedrillo's perception and the polished verses of Klopstock's successful *Messias* which fall within the narrator's purview and thereby pertain to the literary profile of the novel *Don Sylvio*. Its protagonist Don Sylvio is able, in this instance, to correctly identify the source of Pedrillo's confusion and he articulates this insight through his complaint that Pedrillo wants to make a Don Quixote out of him, yet he comically fails to draw the obvious parallel between himself and Pedrillo. When Pedrillo mistakes Don Sylvio's "salamander" for a fiery man, Sylvio blames his misperception on his "ruined imagination" (92), comparing his confusion to a previous one between oak trees and giants. Pedrillo doggedly responds: "Ich dächte, eine Höflichkeit wäre gleichwohl der andern wert, und wenn ich euern Salamander gelten lasse, so könntet ihr meine Riesen wohl auch in ihrem Werte beruhen lassen. Wer weiss ohnedem, ob sie nicht näher mit einander verwandt sind als man sich einbildet" (92).[54] Indeed, the relation between the two is repeatedly emphasized in the narrative. Each figure's practice of the reception and reapplication of literature is fundamentally similar, although developing out of different literary material. Pedrillo's confusion of particular literary references which elicits Don Sylvio's condescending remarks functions as comedy precisely because Pedrillo forays into foreign literary terrain. Aspiring to classical literary learning, he transgresses the borders of the lower-class, feminine realm of popular tradition and superstition. In allusion to similar situations of transgression in *Don Quixote* in which Sancho, who can neither read nor write, "speaks like a professor"[55] or confuses words by inverting syllables or transposing letters,[56] the scene underscores the difference in literary register and status circumscribed by the class and gender appropriate to each figure.

As a narrator, Pedrillo is juxtaposed both with Don Sylvio and with the narrator of Don Sylvio's adventures. Accordingly, his narratives accrue great importance in the contexts of the novel's concerns with poetic theory. Two of Pedrillo's stories in particular merit investigation for the theoretical issues that inform their presentation in the novel. The first is Pedrillo's account to Don Sylvio of his meeting with Felicia and Laura (III, 9). The experience has so challenged the structures of interpretation available to him that in his confusion, we are told, he even begins to doubt his very identity. Pedrillo defers to Don Sylvio's judgment as to his own existence. Yet the confusion he feels profoundly influences his narrative and indeed, the narrator humorously claims, even the narrative of the novel: "Die Verwirrung, die diese Erscheinung in seinem Kopf und in seinem Herzen zurück ließ, war so groß, daß uns die bloße Bemühung eine Beschreibung davon zu machen, beinahe in eine eben so große Verwirrung setzt" (148).[57] As with the figure of Hyacinthe and her tale, the narrator's introduction to Pedrillo's story underscores the hierarchy of authority in the text, reminding the reader of Pedrillo's status as a literary servant who takes shape through the narrator's description. The stratification of narrative authority is repeated in the chapter heading of Pedrillo's narrative by offering the chapter as an example within the narrator's text: "Ein Beispiel, daß ein Augenzeuge nicht allemal so zuverlässig ist, als man zu glauben pflegt" (IV, 2, 150).[58] The title can be read as an ironic subversion of Sylvio's affirmation that Pedrillo actually exists. Furthermore it dismisses Pedrillo's primary epistemological category of vision that leads him to accept fairy-tale terminology as adequate to his experience.

The situation in which Pedrillo tells his story is an inversion of the circumstances attending Don Sylvio's second story. Pedrillo wakes the sleeping Sylvio, just as he had been awakened. And, whereas then Don Sylvio had doubted Pedrillo's identity, now it is Pedrillo who begs Don Sylvio for confirmation of his identity: "tell me first of all if I am really Pedrillo or not?" (150–51). In the first instance, Don Sylvio had to placate Pedrillo by insisting that he listen to the story. Here, Don Sylvio is impatient for Pedrillo's promised explanation. Each proceeds to tell a fairy tale of sorts.

Don Sylvio has no patience with Pedrillo's prologue to his narrative proper. He exclaims: "Tell me clearly and from the beginning" (152). It soon becomes apparent, however, that the rule of sequentiality is not the key to the ultimate narrative structure. Pedrillo's natural inclination is to begin from the center, the "appearance" or "apparition" of Laura which so dominates his impressions. (The narrator indirectly compares Pedrillo's narrative rendition of his experience with Petrarch's poetic praise of his Laura, again pointing to differences in literary spheres between the character and the narrator.) Yet Pedrillo proceeds detail by detail in a valiant attempt to obey Sylvio's demand to tell the events in order. His efforts fully exasperate Sylvio, who compares Pedrillo's style to that of the literature associated with him: "mußt du deswegen alle diese nichts bedeutenden Umstände mit dazu nehmen, wodurch deine Erzählung so schleppend und einschläfernd wird, als ein altes Kunkel-Stuben-Märchen?" (152–53).[59] Don Sylvio is now in the position Pedrillo previously occupied, interrupting the story with his criticisms and questions, wishing to override the belabored descriptions and the moralizing tendency (always an object of satire in the novel). Like Pedrillo after Sylvio's story, Sylvio now demands proof of Pedrillo's judgment that the figures he saw truly came from the fairy realm. Pedrillo, as usual, refers to the credibility of his vision. He asserts that he has seen what he has seen, and that he will of course favor the proof of his own eyes over that of Sylvio's conclusions. Pedrillo's insists naively on the primacy of his visual impressions rather than on the truth or plausibility of his narrative. Unlike Don Sylvio, Pedrillo is utterly unconcerned with a transparent relationship between what he saw and what names he gives these visions. He maintains that, as descriptions, the terminology from the fairy-tale world is the most appropriate to his experience. To Sylvio's objections, he simply speaks of the "fairy, whoever she may be" (159) or asserts: "If that was no fairy, you can throw all your fairy tales into the fire" (155). Pedrillo's attitude is most clear in the following statement addressed to Sylvio: "Gnädiger Herr . . . ich hätte doch gedacht, daß ich ein besseres Zutrauen von euch verdient hätte, als daß ihr glauben sollt, ich wolle euch was weis machen. Wenn die Salamander, die ich bei den Maultieren stehen sah, keine Salamander waren, so ist das ihre Sache und nicht die meinige; was geht das mich an; oder warum soll ich subligiert sein zu wissen, ob sie dieses oder jenes sind?" (158).[60] He insists on his sincerity and on the truthfulness of his story, which is independent of any correspondence between his narrative description and actual beings to which he refers. While Pedrillo uses literature to interpret his experience structurally, he is willing to change discourses as long as they offer a reading commensurate with his vision.[61] Don Sylvio, on the other hand, demands a more simplistic and illusory relationship of identification between referent and manner of signification, and he overcomes the displacements and gaps in his experience only by ascribing them to fairy enchantments.

The chapter dedicated to Pedrillo's second important narrative, "Exempel eines merkwürdigen Verhörs" (Example of a Curious Interrogation, IV, 6), opens with a passage in which the narrator requests that the reader interpret the description of fleas in Don Sylvio's bed as a sign of the narrative's truthfulness and loyalty to the mimetic principle: "Der günstige Leser wird so höflich sein, und die Anführung dieses Umstands als einen abermaligen Beweis der Genauigkeit ansehen, womit wir die Pflichten der historischen Treue zu beobachten beflissen sind, da es uns, wenn wir nur für die Ehre unsers Witzes hätten sorgen wollen, ein leichtes gewesen wäre, unsern Helden durch irgend eine edlere oder wunderbare Veranlassung aufzuwecken" (173).[62] While appearing to emphasize his reliability, the narrator simultaneously asserts his authority and control over the text, reminding the reader of how easy it would be to deviate from the historical truth for the sake of poetic polish. Furthermore, his gesture of stressing the banal detail illuminates the lack of such detail elsewhere in the text and thus calls attention to the incredible nature of the rest of the narrative. The narrator further subverts his claim to truthfulness when he prescribes a reader's attitude of courtesy in accepting the suggested interpretation of the narrative style. As the reader will remember, "courtesy" was the term chosen by Pedrillo to designate his and Don Sylvio's acceptance of each other's representations of the events in the woods. In this passage, while avowing credibility, the narrator repeatedly suggests that he may be unreliable. Hence, he asks the polite readers to accept his assertion and the pretext of authenticity as an adequate gesture toward allaying fears of the text's fictionality. The biting fleas, then, stand at the head of the chapter as the sign for the courteous arrangement between narrator and reader.

The chapter establishes a parallel between Pedrillo and the narrator. The narrator reveals and indeed explicates properties of his text and of his relationship to the implied reader through such apposition. Pedrillo attempts to deceive Don Sylvio about a nighttime rendezvous through the story he tells. The only way to do so, he feels, is through "brazenness and denial" (175). Pedrillo, like Sancho before him, manipulates his master's literary discourse to free himself from blame. In the ensuing story, through which he successfully convinces Don Sylvio of both his truthfulness and his loyalty, Pedrillo, like the narrator, repeatedly stresses the detail of fleas in his bed to underscore the plausibility of his tale. They are the device of his fiction designed to delude Sylvio by implying that his entire story rests on a direct correspondence to Don Sylvio's own experience. Pedrillo integrates descriptions of the fleas into his deceptive story to stress his innocence, and even incorporates them into his oaths of sincerity: "Das ist die reine Wahrheit, und wenn ihrs anders findet, so mögt ihr mich umbringen, oder den Flöhen vorwerfen, die in diesem Hause so hungrig sind, wie die Wölfe in den Pyrenäen" (178).[63] Pedrillo's narrative thus emphatically discredits the flea as the emblem of truth. But the larger novelistic narrative continues to play with it. After Don Sylvio accepts this story, Pedrillo chatters with relief:

> Sapperment! ich dachte doch gleich, wie ich die Flöhe so Legionenweis auf mich eindringen sah, daß es nichts gutes bedeuten werde. Ich versichre Eu. Gnaden, ich bin am ganzen Leibe nur eine Wunde, und ich wollte auf ein Buch schwören, daß es keine natürliche Flöhe, sonder lauter bezauberte Igel und Stachelschweine waren, mit denen uns dieses boshafte Zaubervolk zu Tode zu hetzen hoffte. In diesem Tone plauderte Pedrillo so lange fort, als er mit Bepackung seines Zwerchsacks zu tun hatte; denn er besorgte immer, sein Herr möchte, wenn er ihm Zeit zum Nachdenken ließe, hinter die Wahrheit kommen.[64] (180)

The fleas, in Pedrillo's words, may well be as magical and wondrous as the rest of Pedrillo's and Don Sylvio's adventures. Pedrillo strengthens this suspicion by swearing on a book — a notable oath in this context, for what lesser guarantee of truth and what better guarantee of the unnatural, fictional properties of these legions of fleas! The final paragraph reiterates the point for those readers who have not yet made the connection between Pedrillo's narrative and the poetic issues the narrator raises. Whereas Pedrillo fears that his master may yet, with some reflection, perceive the truth that his fiction conceals, the narrator is anxious to lead the reader to considerations of the self-conscious fictionality of his text. The structure of the chapter prompts the reader to appreciate the role of detail as a fictional device while simultaneously agreeing to accept it as an indication that the narrator has skillfully fulfilled his obligation to offer a pretext of authenticity.

Pedrillo's function within the discussions of narrative and reading illuminates an aspect of the figure's neglected centrality in the novel. Pedrillo is prominently featured in the preface, in the introductory chapter to the second part of the novel, and in the first chapter of the final book. Here the narrator asserts: "Allein Pedrillo hat, wie man längst bemerkt haben sollte, eine weit wichtigere Rolle zu spielen; und wenn auch bei seiner Einführung in diese Geschichte unsere Absicht zum Teil mit auf die Belustigung des Lesers gegangen ist, so ist doch gewiß, daß dieses (um uns gelehrt auszudrücken) nur ein finis secundarius war" (348–49).[65] Pedrillo is more than merely a comic character. This claim is embedded in commentary ascribed to the Spanish author on poetic rules of drama and narrative. It is ironically addressed to the reader, even as it condemns the literary practice of such address and other forms of catering to the audience. The text here circles back to the preface, in which Pedrillo as comic figure was celebrated by the editor. The passage explicitly negates the simplistic assumptions put forth by the editor about Pedrillo's role and the purpose of the novel as a whole. The humor accompanying Pedrillo functions, like the novel itself, in multiple ways and serves not only to entertain, but also to illuminate topical aesthetic issues: Pedrillo's practical poetics point to larger concerns of Wieland's novel and are central in its metafictional strategy. Yet, lest one begin to muse too intently on authorial or narrative intent, a turn to "Biribinker" is also in order.

Narrative Reliability: "Biribinker"

Views on the precise function of the interpolated fairy tale "Biribinker" range from the reading that it fulfills the rhetorical position of "confirmatio"[66] to the statement that, as a "parody of a parody," the story has little to do with the poetics of the original genre "fairy tale."[67] Most critics read the fanciful, erotic episode as a literary parody of the genre which enchants Don Sylvio and also point to similarities between the narrative and the novel *Don Sylvio*.[68] Don Gabriel's story of Prince Biribinker is purportedly designed to discredit fairy tales in Don Sylvio's eyes. Gabriel devises a tale so outrageous in its claims to veracity and in its style that even Sylvio will recognize it as sheer fantasy. He employs the gamut of fairy-tale conventions, straining them to the utmost and attempting to draw his listeners' attention to improbability and narrative unreliability, for example in his opening sentence, which tells of a conspiracy among historians to mislead future generations through false accounts. But Sylvio is deaf to such indications and applies his own logic in interpreting the tale. He is by no means dissuaded from his evaluation of fairy tales by Gabriel's narrative extravagance, for he holds an unshakable belief in the reliability of the author akin to his insistence on his own absolute authority as narrator. Gabriel must therefore enlighten him about the fallacies of such a premise, and shocks Sylvio by admitting that he invented the tale. Yet simultaneously Gabriel must recognize his failure to educate his audience through satire. Gabriel enumerates further arguments against Sylvio's premise of authorial credibility and narrative reliability:

> Woher könnten wir wissen, ob ein Autor, der vor drei tausend Jahren gelebt hat, und dessen Geschichte und Character uns gänzlich unbekannt ist, nur im Sinn gehabt habe uns die Wahrheit zu sagen. Und gesetzt, er hatte sie, konnte er nicht leichtgläubig sein? Konnte er nicht aus unlautern Quellen geschöpft haben? Konnte er nicht durch vorgefaßte Meinungen oder falsche Nachrichten selbst hintergegangen worden sein? Oder gesetzt, das alles fände nicht bei ihm statt; kann nicht in einer Zeitfolge von zwei oder drei tausend Jahren seine Geschichte unter den Händen der Abschreiber verändert, verfälscht und mit unterschobenen Zusätzen vermehrt worden sein?[69] (344)

Gabriel's questions remind the readers of the fate of the novel's preface, which allegedly suffered revision at the hands of such a careless copyist. In the course of these elaborations, Wieland inserts another glaring indication of the relevance of such comments to the reception of his text. Gabriel's anachronistic reference to Hume is remarked by the editor in a footnote that breaks into the narrative, highlighting for the reader that Gabriel is but a character in a novel whose narrative credibility ought to be questioned. Gabriel is unable to achieve his intent of enlightenment directly through his story, yet this failure confirms his position on the unpredictable contingencies affecting narrative and its reception. Ultimately, Gabriel's assessment of fairy-tale fiction as a game designed to amuse the imagination applies equally to Wieland's novel. Gabriel's delight in such tales is unlike that of the fictional editor in the preface, however, for it is shown to be founded on appreciative recognition of literary quality. Gabriel would seem to most closely approximate any ideal reader for the novel *Don Sylvio*, which entertains and engages the imagination with sophisticated literary diversion as well as with simple comic scenes.

By considering how readers read and how generic paradigms and literary inheritances affect interpretations of experience, *Don*

Sylvio reflects on the possible roles narrative can play for individuals and society. For there is a serious side to the exaggeration and playfulness in the satiric treatment of the figures. Their characterization through distinctive reading practices that structure the novel's plot helps Wieland position *Don Sylvio* on the literary stage. The novel is aligned *against* particular readers and the narrative conventions and styles they favor — those primarily associated negatively with femininity — and *with* the qualities of wit, playfulness, self-conscious fictionality, and theoretical sophistication associated with the masculine. The narrative casts itself as an engaging modern text with ancestors as distinguished as Cervantes and Boccaccio, one that appeals to the desires for literary quality of the most competent masculine readers, like Don Gabriel, even as it also delights in lighthearted entertainment. Don Gabriel's parodic erotic tale designed to educate Sylvio and the other listeners underscores the blindness of Sylvio's as yet immature desires. Yet the narrative collusion with Sylvio's enthusiasm and the promise at the novel's end that his fairy-tale wishes will find fulfillment in a socially and literarily acceptable fashion suggest that such quixotic passion itself is essential in the process of learning to read like a man.

Don Sylvio's strategy of approaching concerns of novel theory and pedagogy from many perspectives through its fiction foregrounds the complexities involved in ascertaining literary and social qualities of narrative, and propagates practical aesthetic freedoms. Wieland's epistemological stance of perspectivism, based on the conviction that truth is splintered rather than unified and that insight may be gained only through social dialogue and consideration of multiple points of view, informs theoretical as well as thematic dimensions of the text. Continual self-reflection, inversion and transposition of crucial terms, extensive irony, and the attendant displacement of authority upset literary theoretical categories such as *Wahrheit, Wahrscheinlichkeit,* and *Nachahmung.* The destabilization that undermines the text's own authority strengthens the novel's resistance to simple functional appropriation and supports its arguments against such use of literature as it asserts autonomy from social strictures. Yet the novel still claims a position of influence for literature in eighteenth-century society by engaging conflicts between the signifying structures of various discourses, their relational nature to one another, and their social and individual efficacy in interpreting empirical reality.

3: Seductive Strategies and the Promise of Knowledge: Wieland's *Geschichte des Agathon*

C HRISTOPH MARTIN WIELAND'S NOVEL *Geschichte des Agathon* became known, in literary history, as the most important precursor (if not the first example) of the German genre par excellence, the Bildungsroman. Its status as pivotal text was established by Friedrich von Blanckenburg's reading of the novel as the core of his influential novel theory, *Versuch über den Roman* (1774).[1] Such prominence obscures the fact that when *Agathon* first appeared in 1766–67, Wieland, like other authors, had to contend with debates on the viability of the novel as genre.

In *Agathon,* as in *Don Sylvio,* Wieland addresses the contemporary discourse on the novel through metafictional commentary on the kind of narrative fiction he offers. As in his first published novel, Wieland develops this metafiction not only through his narrator's digressions, but also through elements of his novel's plot. Like *Don Sylvio, Agathon* focuses on aesthetic reception and aesthetic creation. And specifically, *Agathon,* too, takes up the central question of how best to narrate stories of identity. In the earlier novel, these issues were addressed overtly through the novel's characters, whose tales about their own experiences were modeled directly on the generic conventions of the stories they favored. In *Agathon,* the questions of aesthetic reception and creation are approached less schematically. Instead, the novel assesses various autobiographical and biographical stories by means of abstract rules of good narrative. In ways that reflect on his own practice in *Agathon,* Wieland explores how to portray the relationship between historical truth and moral precepts and how to balance entertainment and edification in the design of a story. Underlying these and other narrative quandaries are the recurrent questions of how to capture the readers' desires and how, simultaneously, to educate the novel's readers to appreciate the qualities of the new type of novel that *Agathon* represents.

Wieland held high expectations for the first work he claimed he was writing for the world: "Ich sehe den *Agathon* als ein Buch an das kaum anders als einen grossen Succeß in der Welt haben kan; es ist für alle Arten von Leuten, und das Solide ist darinn mit dem ergötzenden und interessanten durchgehends vergesellschaftet."[2] His endeavor to captivate his readers was not entirely successful, as is evident in *Agathon's* controversial reception by contemporary reviewers.[3] Many critics did recognize *Agathon* as, indeed, a new type of novel. The praise for the novel emphasizes its originality and distances it from other contemporary novels through terms like "wit," "strength," "classicism," and "intellect" that were associated with masculinity. Albrecht von Haller writes, "überhaupt ist Agathon der witzigste Roman, den die Deutschen aufweisen können."[4] Gotthold Ephraim Lessing offers this famous parenthetical judgment: "Es ist der erste und einzige Roman für den denkenden Kopf, vom klassischen Geschmacke. Roman? Wir wollen ihm diesen Titel nur geben, vielleicht, daß es einige Leser mehr dadurch bekömmt."[5] Johann Georg Meusel praises the narrative as "noble, masculine, strong."[6] Yet some critics, even some who lauded aspects of *Agathon*, also charged the novel and its author with the kind of ethical improprieties that are often associated with the genre as a whole.[7] Heinrich Wilhelm von Gerstenberg, who praises Wieland for his "nearly attic eloquence," chides him for his skepticism and eroticism;[8] Christian Friedrich Daniel Schubart misses "a heart purified by the spirit of religion";[9] the reviewer for the *Allgemeine deutsche Bibliothek* complains that there is an unethical emphasis on amorous affairs;[10] in private, Lessing allegedly likewise attacked the immorality of *Agathon*.[11]

The acclaim given *Agathon* as intellectually ambitious and therefore new and the critique of it as dangerously erotic both rely on a negative image of the novel form and on moral and aesthetic standards of judging novels that Wieland was attempting to overcome. Wieland complained that no reader had comprehended the novel: "Insonderheit wird der arme Agathon so abscheulich gelobt, und so dumm getadelt, daß man nicht weiß, ob man lachen, weinen oder nach dem spanischen Rohre greifen soll. . . . Das Lustigste ist, daß keiner, auch nicht ein einziger, die Absicht und den Zusammenhang des Ganzen ausfindig gemacht hat."[12] And he asserted in a letter to Johann Georg Zimmermann: "Die Art wie Agathon aufgenommen worden ist, hat mich radicaliter von dem

Einfall geheilt, mir Verdienste um die Köpfe und Herzen meiner Zeitgenossen machen zu wollen."[13] The critics found the narrative propriety of the philosophical novel marred by Wieland's thematic interest in love and his enticing depictions of sensual scenes, its wisdom diminished by a disregard for virtue. The amorous aspects of the novel were thus cast as aesthetic weaknesses that detracted from the novel's appeal for the "masculine" thinking mind, a concession to readers attracted to the novel form by a "feminine" desire for affairs of the heart that directly engaged the senses. But one of the foundational themes of the novel is that an appeal to the intellect depends on and proceeds through sensory impressions, and that the relationship between "wisdom" and "virtue" is complex. Wieland's novel champions both intellectual and sensual pleasures and persistently investigates the ways in which good art depends on their synthesis.

The Horatian citation Wieland offers his readers as the motto to *Agathon* — "Quid Virtus, et quid Sapientia possit/ Utile proposuit nobis exemplar" — at first suggests a conventional understanding of his novel's purpose as morally instructive example. The life story of the hero Agathon, "the good," appears to be the vehicle through which to illustrate virtue and wisdom. Yet the traditional expectations raised by the motto are challenged in an adept fashion typical for Wieland: the authoritative gesture of the motto is transformed into an investigation of earnest questions accompanying the reader throughout the narrative. What, indeed, constitutes "wisdom" or "virtue?" What are their respective capabilities and limits? Such queries are raised with respect to Agathon's developmental journey, as he seeks wisdom and a virtuous lifestyle. The questions likewise refer to the way that Agathon's story itself is told. The narrator asks the readers to consider what makes a biographical narrative virtuous or wise and what makes it credible and compelling. The narrator leads the readers to ponder how an individual's story can best illuminate virtue and wisdom, and how it stands in relation to the exemplary function of literature lauded by Horace.[14]

Wieland addresses the theoretical concerns of aesthetic education and the status of art by making the tension between the two key terms of his motto a constant dilemma in Agathon's biography. The apparent incompatibility of virtue and wisdom occasions many of Agathon's trials. Furthermore, the novel stresses how hard it can be to differentiate between being guided toward wisdom and being led astray. In doing so, *Agathon* takes recourse to one of the most volatile terms in the debates on the novel as a cornerstone of its narrative scheme. It embraces seduction — the worst censure against the novel from the side of the moralists — as a figure through which to explore questions of narrative propriety. In order to expand the narrative possibilities of the novel, Wieland adopts the reproach of seductiveness as the description of his own efforts to arouse readers' desires and to captivate the audience, yet he does not accept the charge of immorality. Seduction functions in the novel to draw attention to matters of narrative style and strategy, to the relationships between reader and text, and to those between aesthetics and ethics. The nature of desire is at issue in the novel beginning with its opening scenes, which contrast images of the uncontrolled and threatening female passion of the Bacchic worshipers with images of the chaste, idealistic love of Psyche and Agathon. And plots of seduction structure much of Agathon's story, as he faces repeated challenges to his virtue and seeks to direct his own passions wisely. Seductive enchantment is often considered in relation to artistic enchantment in *Agathon;* thus Wieland underscores ways in which the narrative charms its audience and probes the acceptable limits of this quintessential poetic power.

Wieland uses Homeric texts to represent the power of poetic enchantment in *Agathon,* and their authority provides him with one legitimation for styling his novel itself as seductive. The motto from Horace's epistles that introduces *Agathon* is a comment on the *Odyssey* and the parallels between the heroes of the ancient epic and Wieland's modern philosophical novel, drawn throughout the text, suggest a noble literary ancestry for *Agathon.* But Homeric texts also appear in the plot of the novel prominently in scenes of seduction, and the power of these narratives to captivate an audience is apostrophized repeatedly as magical. In addition to Greek epics, Wieland calls on another text to emphasize literature's potent sway over its readers, for Agathon, like Don Sylvio, is likened to Don Quixote. This parallel is first drawn in Book I and recurs near the end of the novel in the metafictional chapter identified as the apology of the Greek author, "Apologie des griechischen Autors" (XI, 1), in reference to both Agathon's appealing enthusiasm and the novel's task of reconciling virtue and wisdom. Wieland's direct reference to Cervantes's novel as a point of comparison for his story of Agathon makes one of the guiding themes of his metafiction more conspicuous, namely, the role of the arts and specifically of literature in shaping stories of identity. By placing his protagonist Agathon in relation to both Quixote and Ulysses and by evoking both the modern and the ancient narratives in the context of literature's capacity to enchant its audience, Wieland points to the generic innovation of *Agathon*. His seductive narrative of a male protagonist's development claims status as the legitimate heir to the exalted epic, but also self-consciously and unapologetically incorporates aspects of the more lowly novel tradition into its modern form.

Seductive Arts: Agathon's Aesthetic Education

Plots of seduction in *Agathon* are a vehicle for the novel's metafictional reflection on its own aesthetic qualities. Agathon is marked for seduction in various fashions by Theogiton, by Pythia, by Hippias, and by Danae, while Agathon's own aims to lead the sybaritic ruler Dionysius to a path of virtue prove similar to seductive efforts directed at him. Each ploy involves efforts to use the influence of art to manipulate the object of seduction and thus integrates into the novel's plot issues fundamental to the novel's metafictional commentary: aesthetic enchantment, the intent of the artist and the artistic performer, and the role of the audience in assessing and responding to aesthetic quality.

Hippias and the materialist philosophy he advocates present the first serious threat to Agathon's idealistic virtue, a threat of both physical and intellectual seduction. In an early theoretical text, Wieland describes the Sophists as "masters in the art of seduction."[15] In *Agathon,* he endows his fictional figure Hippias, the master Sophist, with this trait: "Er hatte alles, was die Art von Weisheit, die er ausübte, verführisch machen konnte."[16] Hippias believes that the similarities he perceives between himself and Agathon will allow him to make of his new slave a disciple who will further propagate his sophistic wisdom and fame. And indeed, the two characters share many traits. Like Hippias, Agathon is extraordinarily handsome and makes a strong, positive first impression on others. Like Hippias, Agathon is intellectually distinguished. He is a connoisseur of the arts and a lover of beauty and he too has powerful rhetorical skills. Each of the two men presumes to accurately assess the other based on his ability to "read" visages and souls.[17]

Despite these affinities, Hippias errs in his assumptions that he can win over Agathon, for they disagree on what motivates human behavior and on what provides pleasure and happiness. The conflict between the two is initially drawn as a battle between the calculating, manipulative Sophist, who lives hedonistically at the cost of others and whose wisdom amounts to a system for achieving this goal, and the guileless Platonist given to introversion and reveries. Yet the apparently distinct moral contours of this contest between Hippias, the consummate seducer, and Agathon, the youthful champion of ideal virtue, soon become obscured. While Agathon, like Don Sylvio, perceives the world naively, Hippias is an intelligent and attractive immoralist — indeed, so attractive that Wieland was compelled to defend and refine his attitude toward his character in later editions of the novel. The celebrated wisdom of Hippias rests on psychological insight and a logic constructed on the principles of nature, reason, empiricism, and critical thought. Hippias's arguments echo many of the standard eighteenth-century theories of knowledge, while Agathon's enthusiasm and melancholy are typically deviant, a sign of an overactive or underemployed imagination: "romanhaft" is the epithet Hippias chooses for Agathon's behavior. Hippias believes that Agathon deceives himself as to the truly sensual source of his philosophical pleasures, which Agathon believes derive purely from his intellect and a disembodied moral sensibility. Hippias thus pursues an Enlightenment program of curing Agathon from his enthusiastic follies by demonstrating the logical errors in his ideological system.[18] The program of Hippias's seduction is to educate Agathon from idealistic excess to greater understanding of the laws of Nature.[19] In this fashion, the contest between the two characters becomes one between wisdom and virtue; the terms of the novel's Horatian motto are played off against each other disruptively rather than appearing in harmony.

Wieland complicates the assessment of the two characters Hippias and Agathon and the conception of the terms virtue and wisdom and hinders an easy judgment about the characters. While the Sophist's wisdom remains subject to moral criticism, the philosophical system he expounds at great length is superior to Agathon's in its realistic assessment of the world. And while Agathon's Platonic enthusiasm sustains his exemplary virtue and reveals his noble character, the narrator also presents it as a sign of immaturity and opens it to skeptical critique through the arguments of Hippias and the narrator's own gentle irony. As in *Don Sylvio,* Wieland sets up an apparent contest in his narrative between nature and enthusiasm, but instead mediates between the two poles, a convergence that his "philosophical novels" represent. As in *Don Sylvio,* the teachings of nature prove a problematic and insufficient weapon against enthusiasm, for nature provides the enthusiast with inspiration and justification. Agathon's imaginative visions, like those of Don Sylvio, also reveal aspects of the poetic fiction that tells his tale. If in *Don Sylvio* Wieland refused to condemn his protagonist's enthusiastic imagination, here he refuses to celebrate it without qualification. The novelistic enthusiasm and the ideal virtue of the hero reinforce each other and reflect the novel's fictionality, for only in a novel could such unwavering virtue be upheld. This in turn calls attention to the narrative's conceit of offering a solid, probable biography rather than a fanciful novelistic tale, while the ambivalence shown toward the protagonist's ideals simultaneously allows for narrative distance from the common conceptions of "the novelistic." The protagonist's youthful ideal of virtue is tempered through experience and he matures in his knowledge of himself and the ways of the world. The parallel metafictional commentary of the novel emphasizes that the narrative portrayal of Agathon's incredible virtue gains poetic validity not through the celebration of an ideal morality, but rather as realistic biography that reveals insights about human nature through astute psychological interpretation of its characters.

The unsuccessful efforts of Hippias to seduce Agathon to share his sensualist understanding of the world proceed through the allures of the young women in his household, through the art that adorns his home, and through his own persuasive rhetoric. Agathon's responses to these seductive measures reveal how the philosophical differences between him and Hippias lead to opposing positions on what constitutes or vitiates aesthetic power. For Hippias, aesthetic pleasure derives from the direct excitement of the senses and the task of art is to arouse and manipulate human passions. The artist or performer wields power over the passions of a malleable audience through psychological insight, founded on careful study of human nature. The more sensually overwhelming the art work, the better it achieves its aim and the better the artist can direct audience response to his or her own ends. For Agathon, the foundation of aesthetic pleasure is spiritual harmony. He claims that love of beauty is concurrently a love of truth and a recognition of ideals, and that art should speak to the innermost soul. Art wields a sensual power over its audience which, however, derives from a spiritual response rather than merely sensual excitement. The moral judgment of an artwork centers not only on its aesthetic effect but also on the artist's intent, on whether the artist abuses the power which good art necessarily holds over its audience. For Agathon, not all seductive art is good art, but good art is always seductive and this seduction is justified by its principled beauty, while for Hippias, seductive art is always good.

Agathon delineates these differences in taste and aesthetic judgment as a conflict between art that is under the guidance of the muses and art defined by the wanton tones of the sirens. The first two paths to convert the idealist to sensualism — the attentions of the seductive Cyane and the impressions mediated through art — offend Agathon's moral sensibility and disturb his equanimity, for Hippias's art and the arts of Cyane indeed evince exquisite talent and achieve the desired effect of arousing Agathon's passions. However, Agathon anticipates Hippias's efforts at intellectual seduction with pleasure. As a talented speaker himself, Agathon can appreciate the skill involved in effective rhetoric. He thus approaches the demonstration of Hippias's renowned eloquence as artistic spectacle and is anxious to witness the performance, "weil er sich von der Beredsamkeit desselben diejenige Art von Ergötzung versprach, die uns ein geschickter Gaukler macht, der uns einen Augenblick sehen läßt, was wir nicht sehen, ohne es bei einem klugen Menschen so weit zu bringen, daß man in eben demselben Augenblick nur daran zweifeln sollte, daß man betrogen wird" (69).[20] The comparison of the rhetorician to the illusion artist describes the relationship between illusion and deception — the artist must tease both the senses and the intellect with the illusion of something not actually there. The pleasure in this appearance derives precisely from the knowledge of its illusory nature. Agathon reveals his increasing maturity and his growing understanding of art through these expectations. In Delphi he was easily fooled by the seductive plot of Theogiton, who donned the guise of Apollo, precisely because of his initial inability to distinguish between deception and illusion. Hippias's eloquence, Agathon imagines, is a tool of fabrication and fiction, which challenges the intellect, yet cannot deceive it outright. While sophistic rhetoric does aim to seduce and deceive the audience for political or personal gain, Agathon's notion of brilliant eloquence prizes linguistic dexterity and the capacity to create illusion. The effect of the Sophists' ideal rhetoric is to overwhelm the impressionable listeners to passivity.[21] That of Agathon's ideal is aesthetic pleasure, which actively engages the audience intellectually, spiritually, and sensually.

Agathon is confident that he will remain impervious to Hippias's eloquent assault on his idealistic virtue. Since his receptive stance allows him to withstand the seduction Hippias represents, he can indulge in the pleasures of Hippias's art, rather than avoiding them as he attempts to avoid the other seductive snares set out for him. This ability demonstrates progress in Agathon's aesthetic education in comparison to Delphi, but he is still unwilling to give the sensual pleasures of art the recognition they deserve. As Don Gabriel similarly discovered with his efforts to enlighten Don Sylvio, the appeal to reason, for all his eloquence, is ineffective in curing the enthusiast. Hippias therefore turns to the lovely Danae for help in bringing the stubborn youth to his senses. Through her artistic performances, Agathon learns that it is more difficult than he imagined to distinguish between the arts of the sirens and those of the muses. And through the portrayal of the love between Danae and Agathon, Wieland again represents a mediation between the poles of sensualism and idealism.

Agathon stages issues of aesthetic production and reception central to the self-reflection of its narrative through scenes of Danae's successful seduction of the protagonist.[22] Danae's plan to capture Agathon's heart and senses proceeds in a methodical and calculated fashion. The penultimate step in this strategy is the musical performance of the battle between the sirens and the muses that she stages at her country house. Here seduction and pure artistic appeal are set up through these familiar feminine archetypes as opposing qualities, yet Danae's designs rely on the close relation between the two. As Danae courts Agathon's desire through her performance, she casts him in the role of judge and calls upon him to render an aesthetic verdict on two counts. He is to be the audience for the work considered a musical masterpiece by connoisseurs. His good taste ought to concur and to confirm the artistic merit of the piece and the artistic talents of its performers. Agathon thus functions as distanced critic of the entire performance, but he also has a second, participatory role to play within it, for he is to be the adjudicator between the two parties that are, in the conceit of the piece, competing. In the scheme of the novel, Agathon's two-fold judgment entails negotiating the aesthetic and ethical dilemmas debated in the eighteenth-century controversies on the genre of the novel and posited in *Agathon* as fundamental to the protagonist's conflict with Hippias. However, the division between the artistic appeal to sensual and sexual desires indulged by the Sophist and the artistic appeal to a more abstract aesthetic imagination championed by Agathon is profoundly challenged through Danae's performance. While the distinction between the two aesthetic ideologies proves less than clear, the subjective desirous attitude of the interpreter takes on great significance when assessing aesthetic achievement.

The contest between the two styles and philosophies of art represented by the figures of the muses and the sirens recalls the conflict between the ideological systems of Agathon and Hippias described in these same terms. Thus the choice required of Agathon for either the sirens or the muses is a further test of his own personal virtue: he ought (as upright hero) once again to reject the seduction instigated by Hippias. In addition, Agathon's verdict in the competition is implicitly a matter of aesthetic principle, a statement on the proper criteria for evaluating beauty and art, and a demonstration of how aesthetic judgments are formed. A predilection for one style or the other, however, is integrally linked with the ethical dimension of the choice Agathon faces. The performance enacts and literalizes the contest between Hippias and Agathon, incorporating and thus appropriating the aesthetic positions of each.

The role imposed upon Agathon as judge between two discrete and dissimilar styles proves to be falsely defined. Even a choice for the muse Danae as the winner of the competition is still paramount to succumbing to Hippias's system and would mean the triumph of the Sophist's philosophy represented by the sirens, since the entire performance of the battle is Danae's elaborate seductive ploy and the culmination of the conspiracy between her and Hippias to seduce, and convert, the young Platonist. Danae's strategy of seduction and the importance of her performance in this design are clearly outlined. She aims to inflame Agathon's imagination and his senses and to weaken his resistances while heightening his desire for her. Her skill in arousing and thwarting desire simultaneously is itself a highly developed art: "Die große Kunst war, unter der Masque der Freundschaft seine Begierden zu eben der Zeit zu reizen, da sie selbige durch eine unaffektierte Zurückhaltung abzuschrecken schien" (153).[23] The ultimate maneuver in her strategy of seduction repeats this duplicity. Under the mask of the muse she pursues the siren's aim of arousing Agathon's desires, enrapturing his senses, and winning his heart. As in the pantomime of Daphne and Apollo, the first such enactment designed to charm Agathon, Danae proves herself here to be both consummate artist and irresistible seductress. There, too, Agathon becomes ensnared by Danae's exquisite enactment of his ideal of virtue and, as shown in Kurt Wölfel's perspicacious interpretation of this pantomime in *Agathon*, Agathon's roles as critic and participant become profoundly entangled.[24]

Danae's talent on the lute and in song manifests itself through the magical powers of her music, the "Zauberkräfte der Kunst" (157), which efface even the visual impression of her initial pose:

> Man muß ohne Zweifel gestehen, daß das Gemälde, welches sich in diesem Augenblick unserm Helden darstellte, nicht sehr geschickt war, weder sein Herz noch seine Sinnen in Ruhe zu lassen; allein die Absicht der Danae war nur, ihn durch die Augen zu den Vergnügungen eines andern Sinnes vorzubereiten, und ihr Stolz verlangte keinen geringern Triumph, als ein so reizendes Gemälde durch die Zaubergewalt ihrer Stimme und ihrer Saiten in seiner Seele auszulöschen. (156)[25]

The "magical power of music" announced in the title of the chapter (V, 7) already reminds the reader of the magical power of literature, which the priestess Pythia drew on to enhance *her* chances of seducing Agathon. Pythia's attempt to adorn herself with the magically seductive power of Homer's poetry is likened to the way Juno sought the magical belt of Venus to seduce and ensnare Zeus. Danae appears dressed for her performance as muse in a pure white gown with a golden belt, and is compared favorably with Juno. This again recalls the Homeric passage Pythia asked Agathon to read in her efforts to seduce him; it describes the shimmering veil "that glimmered pale like the sunlight" and Aphrodite's magical belt adorning Juno, "the elaborate, pattern-pierced / zone, and on it are figured all beguilements, and loveliness / is figured upon it, and the passion of sex is there, and the whispered / endearment that steals the heart away even from the thoughtful."[26] Danae's performance thus suspends the sharp distinction between the muses and the sirens. Her art of seduction and her artistic talent mutually reinforce each other. Similarly, the performance of the sirens is artistically exquisite. The enacted battle of the sirens and muses reveals how thin the dividing line truly is between disreputable and acceptable art, between deceitful artistry and artistic illusion.

Agathon's physical position as judge of the performance under Danae's direction gives him the distance necessary for aesthetic appreciation. He is separated from the singers by water, which both stages the mythical danger of the sirens' song and offers a measure of protection from the danger of their art. It also establishes an additional barrier between Agathon and the seductive muse Danae. On hearing the "nearly irresistible seduction" in the song of the siren performers, Agathon still has enough presence of mind to reflect on Ulysses's wisdom in binding himself to the mast: "'Wenn die Sirenen, bei denen der kluge Ulysses vorbeifahren mußte, so gesungen haben,' (dachte Agathon) 'so hatte er wohl Ursache, sich an Händen und Füßen an den Mastbaum binden zu lassen'" (157).[27] He himself can barely avoid succumbing to the lure of Danae's tones, as her performance as muse tempts him to flee his safe position. Danae registers "wie sehr er außer sich selbst war, und wie viel Mühe er hatte, um sich zu halten, aus seinem Sitz sich in das Wasser herabzustürzen, zu ihr hinüber zu schwimmen, und seine in Entzückung und Liebe zerschmolzene Seele zu ihren Füßen auszuhauchen" (158).[28] This response is far from the exalted one Agathon normally associates with the muses. It does correspond to the expectations Danae harbored before the performance and to her plan to test the entire force of her charms on him, which demands: "eine zärtliche Weichlichkeit mußte sich vorher seiner ganzen Seele bemeistern, und seine in Vergnügen schwimmende Sinnen mußten von einer süßen Unruhe und wollüstigen Sehnsucht eingenommen werden" (153).[29] This is reminiscent of the artistic style favored in Hippias's household, "Syrenen-Gesänge . . . welche die Seele in ein bezaubertes Vergessen ihrer selbst versenkten, und, nachdem sie alle ihre edlere Kräfte entwaffnet hatte, die erregte und willige Sinnlichkeit der ganzen Gewalt der von allen Seiten eindringenden Wollust auslieferten" (55).[30] Danae as muse is even more compelling than the sirens; her musical art is greater. Yet her song, which attests to the superior art of the muses, poses the sirens' threat of a watery death. While Agathon's status as competent critic of the aesthetic performance is indeed threatened, it may seem extreme to compare his position to that of Ulysses. The performance is ostensibly a harmless artistic entertainment rather than an existential ethical dilemma. Nonetheless, in the novel's plot, Agathon is at yet unable to control his own desires while still indulging them and cannot maintain the epic hero's distance from danger. The seductive artistic performance does lead to the modern hero's actual seduction and to the loss of his independent, masculine self in his true love for Danae.[31]

Danae's final performance fully transforms Agathon: "Sein ganzes Wesen war Ohr, und seine ganze Seele zerfloß in die Empfindungen, die in ihrem Gesange herrscheten" (158).[32] This seems to confirm the triumph of Hippias's aesthetic sensibilities over Agathon's, for it precisely captures the expectations he placed on Agathon as reader — as Homerist — in his household, and is the measure of artistic quality for him: "Ein Jonisches Ohr will nicht nur ergötzt, es will bezaubert sein . . . kurz, die Art, wie gelesen wird, soll das Ohr an die Stelle aller übrigen Sinne setzen" (51–52).[33] Agathon's dilemma as judge and the substance of the battle staged by Danae, then, recast the quandaries explored in and for the novel *Agathon* itself, for it questions the nature of aesthetic and ethical judgment and explores the psychological standpoint and engagement of the audience, the reader. The consideration of Danae's intended influence on Agathon also occasions self-reflective gestures of the novel more directly, namely by weighing Danae's skills as a storyteller and explicitly evaluating the qualities and the quality of her narrative.

Danae's Autobiographical Tale: A Model Poetic Narrative

The narrator's extended deliberations on how best to interpret and judge Danae's autobiographical tale again direct reader attention to the complexities of assessing the aesthetic value that Agathon faced as participant-critic of Danae's *Gesamtkunstwerk*. Generic definitions and common criteria for measuring narrative worth come under scrutiny in the commentaries on Danae's story. The narrator puts theoretical distinctions to the test of critical reflection, analyzing the concrete practice of constructing narrative to specific ends and pondering the symbiotic relationship between author and audience, still openly explored through figures of seduction, that both defines and is defined through a text. Subjective

interests and desires influencing narrative production and reception
are taken as significant aspects in the exchange between storyteller
and listener, and these interests become part of the basis of judgment over Danae's tale for the narrator of *Agathon*. These specular
reflections underscore for *Agathon's* readers the interested, participatory role of the audience in establishing an interpretation of a
narrative and insist that rendering a considered, self-aware aesthetic
judgment is a serious and demanding task.

The self-interested story of Danae's life that she constructs for
Agathon is prized in many respects as a model poetic narrative,
and the qualities of Danae's autobiography that the narrator of
Agathon commends are closely bound to her talents as seductress,
as well as to her fine artistic sensibilities. The narrator denotes
Danae's narrative principles as "the laws of beauty and decency,"
which shape her tale, he surmises, to the disadvantage of "the duties of precise historical faithfulness" (307). Danae's priority of
aesthetics over factual truth corresponds to the effect she intends to
produce in Agathon, for whom her narrative is specifically conceived. Her desire to please him and to appear in the best possible
light so that his love for her is intensified leads her to embellish
certain aspects of her tale while slighting others. The design of her
narrative is thus also an extension of her seductive designs on
Agathon, as its aim is to further secure his affections and desire.
The means of realizing this goal, the technique of her narrative, is,
furthermore, described in terms strikingly similar to those used to
specify her art of seduction. Her narrative art consists primarily in
achieving a tantalizing and favorable balance between revelation
and concealment through the skillful and tactical control of language: "es gibt eine gewisse Kunst, dasjenige was einen widrigen
Eindruck machen könnte, aus den Augen zu entfernen; es kömmt
soviel auf die Wendung an; ein einziger kleiner Umstand gibt einer
Begebenheit eine so verschiedene Gestalt von demjenigen, was sie
ohne diesen kleinen Umstand gewesen wäre" (308).[34] Danae alters
the shape of events with attention to minutiae and carefully
chooses which details of her life to divulge. Where artistic skill cannot beautify an aspect of her tale, she hides it strategically with
simple silence: "Allein was diejenigen Stellen betraf, an denen sie
alle Kunst, die man auf ihre Verschönerung wenden möchte, für
verloren hielt . . . über diese hatte sie klüglich beschlossen, sie mit
gänzlichem Stillschweigen zu bedecken" (308–9).[35] Danae weighs

the variables of her story matter and the taste of her intended listener when shaping her narrative. The character of her audience influences the narrative design as both limitation and challenge; her artistic and amorous success in captivating her audience is contingent upon her ability to manipulate her listener's responses through well-considered linguistic disclosure and secrecy.

Despite the proximity of Danae's autobiographical tale to the realm of seduction in technique and intent, the narrator makes Danae no reproach. On the contrary, he even takes a stand in her defense, insisting that she neither deceives Agathon with fiction nor distorts her tale inappropriately through omission, for she tells him everything: "Sie sagte ihm alles" (308). Indeed, this narrative technique, with attention to aesthetic detail and the beautiful effect of the whole prized by good artists above all else, attests to Danae's artistic skill. Aesthetically pleasing narrative is contingent upon an encompassing design and upon a selective recounting of the story's material.

Danae's autobiographical narrative as told to Agathon is considered under the rubric of history, *Geschichte*. Her style and her decision to follow the aesthetic dictums of beauty and propriety is initially contrasted with the principle of historical faithfulness that the public generally demands from its authors. Yet instead of faulting Danae for the priorities she sets, the narrator questions the appropriateness of such clamor for rigid adherence to fact. Rather than striving for a definitive judgment about the truth of the story, the narrator focuses on the characters' psychological constitution and raises questions about their narratives from this perspective. The narrator draws on insights gleaned from the analysis of Danae's autobiography to venture suggestions on how to read other works, even those of authoritative authors like Xenophon and Montaigne. Her narrative is taken as an example to illuminate the general possibilities and perils of historical narrative. Absolute factual truth as the primary criteria of judgment, it is suggested, is quite misplaced. Autobiographies in particular must be read with consideration of the truths of human nature, for example the power of human vanity — such are the exigencies of even historical narration.

Modern historical narrative, in the theory of the time, was contrasted with the notion of the chronicle, in which every detail was listed with encyclopedic extravagance. The primary opposition was understood to lie between styles of presentation rather than between fact and fiction. The good narrator ought to order the crucial moments and events of the story at hand so as to reveal an inner and necessary causality, and ought further to adhere to rules of probability and to distinguish the narrative by a clarity and harmony achieved in large part through sparseness. (Pedrillo's ignorance of this rule was the fault which so exasperated Don Sylvio, as Pedrillo's attempt to include all details of his experience only led to incoherence in his tale.) Only fundamental elements of the story, with selective elaboration and embellishments to enhance the vigor of the writing, should appear. Explicit explanations or excessive details bore and insult the readers. The task of the good narrator is to engage and satisfy both the imagination and the intellect of the creative and critical audience.

History was further contrasted with the fantastic falsehood of novels. Yet the terms *Roman* and *Geschichte* as generic classifications were unclear and fluctuating. Lieselotte Kurth traces these shifts in historical and literary criticism, and exposes how historians explicitly redefined their task over and against poetic histories.[36] The novel as immoral romance was derided, but the novel as fictional history of human emotions, including love, had the advantage of offering models of moral behavior. *Geschichte* communicated truths, whether factual or fictional, by corresponding to and reflecting what were taken to be universal natural laws. As stated programmatically in the foreword to *Geschichte des Agathon:*

> Die Wahrheit . . . bestehet darin, daß alles mit dem Lauf der Welt übereinstimme, daß die Charakter nicht willkürlich, und bloß nach der Phantasie, oder den Absichten des Verfassers gebildet, sondern aus dem unerschöpflichen Vorrat der Natur selbst hergenommen; . . . und also alles so gedichtet sei, daß kein hinlänglicher Grund angegeben werden könne, warum es nicht eben so wie es erzählt wird, hätte geschehen können, oder noch einmal wirklich geschehen werde. Diese Wahrheit allein kann Werke von dieser Art nützlich machen. (11–12)[37]

To adhere to this truth, then, the author must portray credible human characters rather than exemplary moral heroes — must follow the example of Fielding rather than Richardson, authors taken to represent two poles in literary orientation.[38] No moral scheme, but only the varieties and peculiarities of human nature can truly capture the imagination and concern of readers and ultimately contribute to their moral betterment.

This interest in psychological complexity motivates biographical histories. The value and appeal of autobiographies lies likewise in readers' consideration of human nature. Thus Danae's narrative fulfills the demands placed on good history writing. She presents an aesthetically ordered, harmonious whole in an interesting, engaging fashion. Her ability to enchant the intended audience is a measure of her skill, and is in turn the primary criterion for judging her story. As long as the standards for reading are clear, the narrator concedes freedom of composition within this realm. Danae is exonerated from moral blame, for her tale follows the rules of beauty and propriety.[39] Yet by describing her exemplary narrative ploys in terms similar to those of seductive strategies, the narrator pointedly revisits the issue of the nexus between ethics and aesthetics. Indeed, the consideration of Danae's narrative also reveals the extent to which aesthetic beauty and propriety is ethically suspect. Loveliness fosters Danae's seductive schemes, disarms the audience, and deviates from absolute factual truth. It can be quite deceptive. Specifically, aesthetic propriety can serve to mask ethical impropriety. Danae conceals the impropriety of her past as part of her strategy of propriety in narration. The refinement in her story leaves her audience room for misunderstanding and for a multiplicity of interpretations.

Hippias can, therefore, influence Agathon's reading of Danae's autobiography by revealing additional facts. The inclusion of this supplementary information does not, however, make Hippias's version of the story more true than Danae's account. The narrator again defends both Danae's virtue and the value of her narrative: "Danae erzählte ihre Geschichte mit der unschuldigen Absicht zu gefallen. Sie sah natürlicher Weise ihre Aufführung, ihre Schwachheiten, ihre Fehltritte selbst in einem mildern, und (lasset uns die Wahrheit sagen) in einem wahrern Licht als die Welt" (315).[40] Hippias's rendition of Danae's life is, like Danae's, a construct designed to affect Agathon in a specific manner, in this case to arouse his passions to Danae's disadvantage. Hippias skillfully spurs Agathon's jealousy and reignites his dormant love of an ideal virtue, figured in Psyche, in order to destroy his trust in Danae and to end their relationship. Under the sway of the adept Sophist, Agathon reinterprets Danae's story to confirm his new fears: "Er verglich ihre eigene Erzählung mit des Hippias seiner, und glaubte nun, da das Mißtrauen sich seines Geistes einmal bemächtiget hatte, hundert Spuren in der ersten wahrzunehmen, welche die Wahrheit des letztern bekräftigten" (319).[41] Agathon's divergent readings of the same story reveal the importance of the reader's particular approach to a narrative in constructing an interpretation, yet they also point to the storyteller's responsibility in this process. Allowing that too much discretion can invite readers to misconstrue the story, the narrator of *Agathon* reflects on the balance between narrative decorum and narrative clarity with respect to his own practice. He then uses this theoretical front to cover for his narrative practice, for he justifies transgression of social etiquette — namely explicit love scenes — as a means of counteracting the potential ambiguity of decorous presentation. Narrative virtue, the narrator muses, lies in correctly assessing the appropriate degree of candor required, in weighing the demands of artistry and ethics.

> Es ist ohne Zweifel wohl getan, wenn ein Schriftsteller, der sich einen wichtigern Zweck als die bloße Ergötzung seiner Leser vorgesetzt hat, bei gewissen Anlässen, anstatt des zaumlosen Mutwillens vieler von den neuern Franzosen, lieber die bescheidne Zurückhaltung des jungfräulichen Virgils nachahmet, welcher . . . sich begnügt uns zu sagen: "Daß Dido und der Held in Eine Höhle kamen." Allein wenn diese Zurückhaltung so weit ginge, daß die Dunkelheit, welche man über einen schlüpfrigen Gegenstand ausbreitete, zu Mißverstand und Irrtum Anlaß geben könnte: So würde sie, deucht uns, in eine falsche Scham ausarten; und in solchen Fällen scheint uns ratsamer zu sein, den Vorhang ein wenig wegzuziehen, als aus übertriebener Bedenklichkeit Gefahr zu laufen, vielleicht die Unschuld selbst ungegründeten Vermutungen auszusetzen.[42] (165)

Narrative impropriety is justified as a means of revealing the virtue of the characters, for a modest silence is open to misreading. The narrator provocatively adopts the pose of apologizing for presenting the love scenes, which are precisely those the reader (and especially, Wieland teasingly claims, the female reader) most desires. Here the text, as if grudgingly, tells of novelistic romance while posing as more serious educational history.

Yet the narrator also employs the opposite strategy as part of his program to enchant readers, for, as he well knows, marked silence directly invites interpretation. By choosing at times to conceal pointedly, rather than to disclose, Wieland's narrator aims to seduce the readers under the mask of propriety. The text plays with the readers' anticipation and curiosity to arouse the imagination under the pretext of corralling it, and teases the readers with silence after piquing their interest. After introducing the central love scenes with protestations of the need for historical precision, the text affects understanding for reader disinterest and leaves these scenes, in the end, to the readers' fantasy: "Und hier, ohne den Leser unnötiger Weise damit aufzuhalten, was sie ferner sagte, und was er antwortete, überlassen wir den Pinsel einem Correggio, und schleichen uns davon" (168).[43] Correggio's sixteenth-century painting of Danae depicts precisely the suspension between revelation and concealment and its concurrent suspense for the imagination that Wieland's narrative employs. As Danae reclines on a bed, she and Cupid, who faces her, each hold a corner of the sheet partially covering her naked body, while two cherubim sharpen their arrows in a corner. The moment between covering and uncovering Danae is captured in the erotic image in which Cupid catches and guides the golden rain, the guise Jupiter adopts to mate with Danae. Wieland's reference to Correggio's painting evokes this visual image and thereby enhances and emphasizes his own tantalizing narrative tactics in *Agathon,* rather than diffusing them, as the narrator innocently suggests.

The narrator's theoretical digressions on poetics lead him to challenge the novel's readers to question the sincerity of Agathon's own autobiographical story as told to Danae. The dilemma of how to evaluate its virtues and those of the hero is thereby raised once more. If the reader approaches Agathon's story with suspicion, as Agathon did Danae's, his tale appears in another light. The voice of such a skeptical reader is raised and it provides the impetus for a reconsideration of Agathon's narrative: "Und woher wissen wir auch, daß Agathon selbst, mit aller seiner Offenherzigkeit, keinen Umstand zurück gehalten habe, von dem er vielleicht, wie ein guter Maler oder Dichter, vorausgesehen, daß er der schönen Würkung des Ganzen hinderlich sein könnte. Wer ist uns Bürge dafür, daß die verführische Priesterin nicht mehr über ihn erhalten habe, als er eingestanden?" (307).[44] Seduction is again the focus of this renewed investigation. The narrator recalls the situations in which Agathon found himself the intended target of seduction in Delphi and underscores the temptations that placed him in jeopardy. The authority of the priestess, not to mention her beauty, was bound to threaten any young man's virtue, the narrator reasons. Moreover, Pythia ingeniously heightened her chances of successful seduction by weaving the magical power of literature over the soul — a force with indisputable impact on the enthusiast Agathon — into her schemes to fully overcome his resistance. Given such consideration, the narrator reflects, Agathon's story as he told it becomes increasingly incredible. If Agathon were truly able to withstand the combined charms of the priestess and Homer's seductive poetry expressly depicting seduction scenes, then literature must not possess its acclaimed power of enchantment. But the enchanting qualities of Agathon's own narrative invalidate this hypothesis: the skeptical fictive reader judges Agathon's story itself to be so seductive in the mere retelling of the plots against his virtue that it belies his reported stoicism. The figurative potency of Agathon's narrative would communicate the effects of Pythia's allures more truly than his allegations.

The power which Agathon's narrative exerts over this vocal fictive reader thus attests to his artistic skill as a storyteller while marring his moral reputation. The narrator of *Agathon* is ostensibly concerned with weighing the truth content of Agathon's story, yet in reconsidering the scenes of Agathon's seductions, he piques the novel reader's voyeuristic interest and curiosity. Although he approaches the investigation of the narrative with the criterion of truth, he returns quickly to the examination of narrative enchantment and indirectly praises exactly the quality in Agathon's autobiography that initially arouses the suspicions of the moralist.

Seduction is portrayed throughout the novel, then, as clever, artistic, and artful manipulation, effected by establishing and controlling the tension between revealing and concealing the object of desire. Good narrative, the text implies, functions similarly: it excites and maintains reader interest by manipulating the relationship between revelation and concealment, and induces readers to continue reading in order to satisfy their desires for the pleasures of fiction. Like the art of seduction, narration fascinates by what is shown to be hidden. The narrative plays on the boundaries between silence and expression, and points to language as a medium of dissemblance as well as of disclosure. By explicitly leaving particularly intimate or erotic scenes to the imagination of the reader, provoking through prankish omission, the narrator can absolve himself of any blame. This ruse points to reading as deciphering, reassigning much of the responsibility for the moral quality of the work from the text to the reader's interpretive style. Yet Wieland also reconsiders the traditional notions of virtue. The virtue of the narrative lies precisely in its ability to seduce the reader. By exploring issues of aesthetic and ethical judgment, he subverts rigid categories of moral understanding and encourages the readers to approach the novel's complex questions of truth, wisdom, and virtue with greater sophistication.

Telling Tales of Virtue

Danae's and Agathon's autobiographical narratives provide one opportunity in *Agathon* for metafictional reflection on what makes the story of an individual life both artistically and ethically refined. Yet the intentions and uses of autobiography are not the same as those of biography. The narrator prizes Danae's artistic skill and examines Agathon's presentation of his life, but he also shares with his readers the particular difficulties he faces as author of Agathon's personal history, and these difficulties arise from Wieland's efforts to transform the novel genre. In *Don Sylvio*, Wieland did not eschew the fairy-tale structure in which true love and the promise of marriage provide a conclusion to the story. But the traditional romance ending is inadequate for the kind of story that Wieland wishes to tell in *Agathon*. Agathon's love for Danae removes him from the larger world and emasculates him, like Hercules in the thrall of Omphale, the narrator suggests. While this profile of the protagonist may please the female readers, who delight at being able to conquer their heroes similarly through love, the narrator teases, it does not provide an appropriate resolution to Agathon's story. The narrator stages his own masculine strength, which is equated here with the use of healthy reason to oppose love and female wiles, by removing his male protagonist from this effeminate position even at the risk of incurring the wrath of his female readers. Just as Ulysses left the island of Calypso, so Agathon must leave Danae to continue on his journey. As the narrator positions Agathon on a ship to Syracuse, he digresses from the plot to navigate between his own Scylla and Charybdis, for he must defend his narrative actions against the various interests of his readers. The narrator anticipates the anger of his female readers at Agathon's abandonment of Danae, and he also anticipates the irritation of his male readers with Agathon's lengthy observations about his experiences. But the narrator's greatest feud is with the moralists, who, he imagines, take issue with many aspects of Agathon's tale. Al-

though he won't shape the story of his protagonist as pure romance, he does defend Agathon's love for Danae. And although he
decelerates the pace of Agathon's adventures through philosophical
reflection and chides his male readers for their impatience with
such contemplation, these observations will not conform to the
rigid expectations of the moralists. The narrator insists, however,
that the aim of his story is to consider Agathon "as a moral person" (356) and to offer a portrait of his soul. The protesting moralists, the narrator asserts, are simply unable to read properly or to
perceive the value of his work. *Agathon* integrates and transforms
aspects of the novel conventionally associated with the desires of
male and of female readers. The narrator suggests that those readers who wish only for romance or adventure ought to read with
greater patience and sophistication and to consider the moral wisdom pursued through the novel. Yet he also wishes to please these
readers and to gratify their desires as he writes an innovative moral
history of his protagonist.

At the heart of the debate the narrator stages in *Agathon* with
the moralists is his conviction that virtue is not something that can
be taught easily. The demand that literature provide examples of
virtuous heroes and heroines is based on the idea that the readers
will emulate such figures, but the narrator reproaches such tales
and their proponents with their distance from the reality of human
nature and human needs. "'Löblich, vortrefflich, göttlich!' — rufen
die schwärmerischen Bewunderer der heroischen Tugend — wir
wollten gerne mitrufen, wenn man uns nur erst zeigen wollte, was
diese hochgetriebene Tugend dem menschlichen Geschlecht jemals
geholfen habe" (369).[45] The narrator expounds his views on such
heroic virtue in his introduction to Agathon's adventures in Syracuse. Here he reflects on the character of Dion as portrayed by
Plutarch. Plutarch's account of Dion's celebrated virtue strikes the
narrator of *Agathon* as highly incredible. The implausibility of the
narrative is not held personally against the author, the "virtuous
and good-hearted Plutarch" (365). Rather, by stressing this quality
of Plutarch's history, the narrator offers commentary on the relationships between this story and its readers and on possible modes
of reader reception. If readers placed unlimited faith in historians'
accounts, Dion's character (as presented by Plutarch) would necessarily appear awesome and indeed divine. The narrator tenders a
corrective to such a credulous and naive reading, for the sake of his

own concerns with historical truth, narrative style, and the persistent questions of what constitutes real virtue, yet he concedes that Plutarch's tale holds great appeal: "Ein solcher Charakter fällt allerdings gut in die Augen . . . und erweckt den Wunsch, daß er mehr als eine schöne Schimäre sein möchte. Aber wir gestehen, daß wir, aus erheblichen Gründen, mit zunehmender Erfahrung, immer mißtrauischer gegen die menschlichen — und warum also nicht gegen die übermenschlichen Tugenden werden" (365–66).[46] Indirectly, the narrator restates his preference for human heroes over superhuman ones and his advocacy of narration that better reflects real human experience as the literary form most conducive to mediating moral wisdom. In drawing attention to the source of information on Dion's life and to the mode of relating the story, the narrator of *Agathon* establishes a comparison between himself and the eminent, virtuous, and well-intentioned Plutarch, as well as between the respective heroes of the two storytellers. Dion, unlike Agathon, is remarkable in his indifference to sensual pleasures and physical desire. This quality is taken by the people of Syracuse and by others as an indication of his superior virtue, the narrator records. Yet it is misleading to read his austerity as the sign of absolute purity and wisdom, for Dion has other faults, most notably vanity. Even Plato chides his friend for his prudish tendencies, the narrator reminds his readers, a reference that indirectly draws on Plato's authority to support the narrator's generous allowances for his hero Agathon. The narrator, then, refuses to accept Dion as the icon of virtue and qualifies the importance of continence for an assessment of moral probity. This stance taken by the historian of Agathon's life mitigates harsh judgments against his hero's love for Danae and impels the readers to ponder the complexities of the terms "virtue" and "wisdom" as they observe Agathon in Syracuse, touted as the new "meeting place of the wisest and most virtuous men" (337).

Agathon asserts he has learned to distrust the absolute power of good intentions and has recognized the validity in the assessment of moral enthusiasm put forth by Hippias. Still, he approaches Syracuse with a faith in the "beauty of virtue and in the indissoluble binding truth of its laws" (346) that allows him to dream of an active political career truly serving the common good. Agathon's conclusions as to the nature of wisdom and virtue and the feasibility of successfully implementing his noble plans are challenged in Syracuse; his adventures in this setting provide the novel *Agathon* with a new stage on which to explore its Horatian motto.

Agathon attracts the attention of the important and remarkable men of Syracuse by appearing both wise and virtuous. Yet his apparent modesty veils his true hubris: he is lured into the political arena of Dionysius's court by his vain belief that he will be able to impress upon the tyrant the pleasures of a virtuous life. This ambiguous moral position is expressed in the novel by positioning Agathon in relation to both Plato and Hippias as educators. He imagines "how wonderful it would be if Agathon were able to achieve what Plato attempted with no success" (413). By accepting this challenge, Agathon adopts the role previously filled by Plato at court, and thus a position of parity with the most virtuous philosopher. Yet this function also places him, as a sage guiding a misled youth, in relation to Hippias. Just as Hippias exerted himself to lead "Callias" from his Platonic excesses to a life guided by sophistic wisdom, so Agathon approaches the task of influencing the excitable Dionysius to abandon his raucous ways for a life of wise moderation. Hippias recognizes Agathon as the test case for his sophistry and for the validity of his insights into human nature. Agathon likewise encounters a fundamental challenge to his beliefs in the power and truth of Platonic philosophy. Both figures have personal pride as well as ideological conviction at stake, a pride which detracts from their capacity to appraise the possibilities and the limits of their own influence.

Agathon's eloquence also makes him akin to both Plato and Hippias, and the narrator stresses for each of the three figures the enchanting power of his rhetoric, but also its lack of educational efficacy. Despite his mastery of the art of persuasion, Hippias had to concede defeat in his verbal efforts to sway Agathon. Plato's success in impressing Dionysius stemmed from his seductive rhetorical skill — the "eloquence of the Homer among the philosophers" (381) — but proved to be short-lived: Dionysius was soon astonished at how he could let himself be "enchanted by this windbag" (393). Agathon's skill in speaking initially assures him the good graces of the king and the populace of Syracuse. But he too learns the limits of his ability to guide his audiences.

Agathon is presented as a philosophical speaker, one of Plato's students. But this distinction is qualified through irony even as it is constructed, for example in the report that Agathon was once a student of Plato's and was considered one of the greatest speakers in the garrulous republic of Athens (424). Agathon's discursive facility is nonetheless praised as purer and more admirable than the linguistic tricks of the Sophists:

> Man glaubte den Mercur oder Apollo reden zu hören, die Kenner . . . bewunderten am meisten, daß er die Kunstgriffe verschmähte, wodurch die Sophisten gewohnt waren, einer schlimmen Sache die Gestalt einer guten zu geben — Keine Farben, welche durch ihren Glanz das Betrügliche falscher oder umsonst angenommener Sätze verbergen mußten; keine künstliche Austeilung des Lichtes und des Schattens. Sein Ausdruck glich dem Sonnenschein, dessen lebender und fast geistiger Glanz sich den Gegenständen mitteilt, ohne ihnen etwas von ihrer eigenen Gestalt und Farbe zu benehmen.[47] (427)

Agathon's elevated art, then, radiates the light of truth and rejects the recourse to deception ascribed to the Sophists. The Sophists are reproached for enchanting the listeners and thereby disabling their critical facility, for blinding them to the truth through deception, and for manipulating the audience to their own ends through rhetorical agility and persuasion. Greater moral authority is attributed to Agathon: his intent is blameless and his rhetoric has artistic and ethical integrity. Yet the effect his eloquence has on his listeners is precariously similar to that of the Sophists' art. It carries no deceptive aim, yet is said to blind *with* truth. The radiance of his speech "blinds the souls" of his audience (426) and overwhelms even those antagonistic towards him. They are swept up in the movement of his oratory, bound by a "magical power" (427) — the phrase applied throughout the novel to that mysterious force emanating from exquisite art — to applaud his words. Dionysius's intention to implement the program Agathon outlines is the result of enchantment rather than critical judgment. The distinction between seduction and guidance through artistic means is hard to draw. Moreover, Agathon's methods of successfully influencing his target audience are, if not truly devious, still quite calculated. He explains the proximity of his own procedures to sophistic strategies by claiming that his virtuous end justifies even questionable means. Fascination with the noble aim of transforming a treacherous tyrant into a revered and responsible ruler outweighs any self-doubts Agathon might harbor.

Agathon's actions are not, however, motivated by love of virtue alone, for vanity is a compelling agent in his undertakings, as it was, the narrator notes, for Plato. Agathon's inordinate pleasure in the image of himself as the icon of wisdom and virtue and as benefactor of the people persuades him to believe he can maintain an objective perspective on the events at court and on his own role there. His conviction that his integrity will not be compromised, and that he will be able to have a formative and lasting influence on the wayward monarch contrasts starkly with the stance of Aristipp. The sage philosopher chooses to remain primarily an observer. His refusal to become entangled in the affairs at court suggests Agathon might well question not only his true motivations, but also the ultimate wisdom of his own political engagement.

The novel's explorations of Agathon's ability to exert his influence in Syracuse apply to both the private and the socio-political spheres, for personal and political virtue — or lack thereof — coincide in the figure of Dionysius. Agathon's assiduous efforts to edify the tyrant are doomed to failure. Witty eloquence invested with virtuous intent and transmitting philosophical insights is effectively countered by the rhetoric of Agathon's enemies, fueled by flattery and disingenuousness. Agathon had experienced similar limits of his rhetorical arts and thus of his political power in Athens. There he learned that the public served as a seismograph registering the speaker's emotional authority, but that the people's judgment was not an assurance of ethical quality. In Syracuse he must realize that his hold over its inhabitants is equally feeble, for the populace is an incompetent audience, one too easily swayed. Similarly, he has but limited success in establishing a positive and enduring political order from the top by prevailing upon the fickle ruler.

The narrator reveals the questionable aspects of Agathon's comportment and again presents his readers with the critical dilemma of how to evaluate the hero's character. He rejects the role of apologist, for he holds to the "duties of a historian" (434). Yet in his considerations of the essential problems of Agathon's biography, he mounts a moral defense of his hero which is also a defense of the narrative strategies in *Agathon*. Agathon, while not perfect, is certainly estimable, and his intentions in Dionysius's court are honorable. Do not such noble purposes outweigh secondary, nearly accidentally attendant impropriety? The narrator queries his readers: "Was können wir, nach der äußersten Schärfe, mehr fodern, als daß seine Absichten edel und tugendhaft sein sollen?" (435).[48] The narrator's own admirable aim of providing his readers with edifying insights into human nature ought to exonerate it, then, from charges of presenting corruptive material and a fallible hero. This implicit self-defense is immediately buttressed by situating the novel's project to pursue understanding of wisdom and virtue through the story of a psychologically credible figure in relation to positive and negative literary paradigms. Shakespeare's dramas are taken as models of a literature that brilliantly portrays human traits. The charges, similar to those leveled against *Agathon* by its fictive critical readers, that the characters in Shakespeare's plays are inconsistent and therefore unacceptable literary creations are dismissed with the argument that the author is laudably most faithful to real human experience. By contrast, moralistic novels of a Richardsonian cast deny such life experience and the possibility of development: "In moralischen Romanen finden wir freilich Helden, welche sich immer in allem gleich bleiben — und darum zu loben sind — . . . Aber im Leben finden wir es anders. Desto schlimmer für die, welche sich da immer selbst gleich bleiben" (436).[49] The negative paradigm of the moralistic novel contrasts with the undertaking of *Agathon* and argues for the narrative virtue of presenting Agathon's trials and tribulations in Syracuse in their full complexity.

Moreover, the novel is modest in its assessment of the direct moral impact it might have on its readers. The narrative addresses to fictive readers often refer to the limits of its influence, and the story itself raises the issue repeatedly.[50] Despite initial narrative assertions that Dionysius's failings and vices derived from the lack of proper guidance and could thus perhaps be corrected through a concerted educational effort, the conclusions drawn from Agathon's story rest on skepticism about the success of such an enterprise. The determining factor in efforts at moral betterment appears to be personal inclination. Dionysius relapses into his old lascivious habits as soon as the enticement of the newer distractions fades. The same insight applies equally to virtuous characters, however. Dion's inclinations toward austerity are interpreted as manifestations of his great virtue, yet should be recognized as his natural character, the narrator argues. "Dion bewies . . . daß die Philosophie ordentlicher Weise uns nur die Fehler vermeiden macht, zu denen wir keine Anlage haben, und uns nur in solchen Tugenden befestiget, zu denen wir ohnehin geneigt sind" (367).[51]

The queries as to whether or not virtue can be taught, and if so through what means, echo issues debated in Plato's dialogues. In "Protagoras," Socrates challenges the claims of the famous Sophist that his rhetorical art is the skill most indispensable for good statesmen, as it teaches wisdom in one's own affairs and in those of the state, as well as the best means of political influence. Socrates responds with the argument that such virtue is not something which can be taught. The Sophist position, reiterated in Plato's dialogue "Gorgias," that rhetoric is an art in the service of political justice is countered by the Socratic assertion that rhetoric is but a shadow of justice; it aims not at the good but at the pleasurable.[52] Socrates points to the commonalities between the arts of music (specifically musical competitions such as that staged by Danae), poetry, and rhetoric, particularly political rhetoric, in this regard. All approach the soul of their audience with the primary goal of pleasing it through flattery, rather than of mediating moral wisdom, he maintains (500e–503d).

Plato argues the superiority of philosophical dialogue over sophistic rhetoric as a method of wise reflection and as an approach toward recognition of truth and virtue. Wieland's novel, which plays these two ideological positions off against each other and probes the validity of their respective claims, repeatedly reveals the crucial role of "flattery" — even in philosophical guise — in the process of exerting influence over others. Only this flattering, enthralling power of art can fully engage the audience; indeed, it is the condition for impressing it forcefully. If virtue cannot be taught, still moral wisdom can be mediated through aesthetic pleasure, both of which are inextricable qualities, the novel argues, of good art.

The effect of artistic enchantment greatly depends on the stance taken by the audience. In Agathon's experience, those who wished to ensnare him deceptively through aesthetic charms encouraged complete passivity of reception. The seductive efforts of Theogiton and Pythia, each supported by the power of poetry over Agathon's imagination, are attempts to lead him astray in this fashion. Both Hippias and Danae initiate their seduction of Agathon following the strategies of sophistic manipulation of a preferably passive audience, yet each ultimately abandons this position for one of parity with Agathon as an active partner — Hippias does so out of respect, Danae out of love for him. A passive audience is likely to be misled or to be otherwise overwhelmed by aesthetic power. *Agathon* ascribes active interpretive and critical ability to its implied desired readers, and indeed requires it of them. Wieland's narrator plays with the readers, at times teasing their desires with seductive narrative ploys, at times exposing the workings of precisely this ensnaring power. This procedure not only underscores his narrative facility, but also points to reader acquiescence in the seductive literary process. Thus, responsibility for the ultimate effect of the novel is in large part relegated to the readers.

The self-imposed task of revealing, through the example of Agathon's story, "quid Virtus et quid Sapientia possit" is rendered by the narrative as an investigation of the true capabilities of sagacity and virtue rather than as the fabrication of an absolutely moral hero — this, indeed, is forcefully rejected as an impossibility. The two terms of the motto are taken up both individually and in their relation to each other; the tension between wisdom and virtue underlies many of the conflicts and dilemmas marking stages of Agathon's story of identity and self-knowledge. Agathon strives to resolve this tension and to arrive at a harmonious conjunction of wise virtue and virtuous wisdom. The novel *Agathon* endeavors to accomplish a parallel feat and to justify its narrative as an ethical medium of guiding its readers toward better self-knowledge and toward increased insight into the human condition. It places faith in the ability of art to better its audience, in the "correct principle" that "our pleasures, become finer, nobler, and more ethical the more the muses are involved in them" (443). The novel thus insists on art as a medium of edification, yet also scrupulously addresses the danger residing in its particular power. Aesthetic enchantment can also be deceptive and can lead away from, as well as toward, greater recognitions of human truths.

The proximity of guidance and seduction and the difficulties of establishing clear boundaries between the two are constant themes in Agathon's adventures. Hippias attempts to seduce Agathon to the wisdom of his sophistic ideology, and maintains the epistemological stance that knowledge proceeds through such sensual experience and appeal as is found in his seductive arts. Danae's nearly indistinguishable roles as muse and as siren situate the guiding and the seductive arts extremely near each other in the novel, and thereby remind the reader that the guidance toward wisdom ascribed to the muses is also an essential part of the sirens' promise.

They lure Ulysses not merely with enchantingly beautiful song but
also with the prospect of knowledge:

> Komm, besungner Odüßeus, du grosser Ruhm der Achaier!
> Lenke dein Schiff ans Land, und horche unserer Stimme.
> Denn hier steurte noch keiner im schwarzen Schiffe vorüber,
> Eh er dem süßen Gesang' aus unserem Munde gelauschet;
> Und dann ging er von hinnen, vergnügt und weiser wie vormals.
> Uns ist alles bekannt, was ihr Argeier und Troer
> Durch der Götter Verhängnis in Troias Fluren geduldet:
> Alles, was irgend geschieht auf der lebenschenkenden Erde!
> Also sangen jene voll Anmut. Heißes Verlangen
> Fühlt' ich weiter zu hören, und winkte den Freunden Befehle,
> Meine Bande zu lösen; doch hurtiger ruderten diese.[53]

Agathon boldly figures its narrative strategy as one of seduction —
considered by eighteenth-century moralists the most heinous of
crimes against the reader — and then openly defends the ethical
and artistic viability of such a move. The novel insists on its project
of leading the readers to greater wisdom through the pleasures of
its seductive ploys. The readers will truly respond to Agathon's
history and engage in the considerations of virtue and wisdom offered for their enlightenment and enjoyment only if the beauty of
the narrative seduces them to "desire to hear more," like Ulysses.
The responsibility for indulging this temptation and leaving "satisfied and wiser than before" without fully succumbing to its potential dangers rests, in the end, with the readers themselves.

4: A Story of Her Own: Sophie von La Roche's *Geschichte des Fräuleins von Sternheim*

SOPHIE VON LA ROCHE IS acclaimed in literary history as the *grande dame* of eighteenth-century Germany. Her relationships to other famous literary figures assured her consideration as onetime fiancée and "muse" of Wieland, as the grandmother of Bettina and Clemens Brentano, and as the center of a salon that attracted such admirers as Goethe and Jung-Stilling.[1] Her first published novel, *Geschichte des Fräuleins von Sternheim* (1771), was a prominent literary event, celebrated especially by the younger generation of Goethe, Herder, Lenz, and Merck as the epitome of sentimental expression and natural style.[2] The author and her character Sophie were admired and indeed read together as one text of ideal femininity. Throughout her literary career La Roche occupied the role of "praeceptae femininae germaniae."[3]

Two general tendencies can be distinguished in the critical reception of La Roche and *Sternheim* over the last two centuries. First, a biographical interest in La Roche and this approach to her novel dominates (or often obstructs) the readings of the text. Titles of older literature reveal their critical interest: *Sophie von La Roche, die Freundin Wielands* (Assing, 1859); *Sophie von La Roche, die Grossmutter der Brentanos* (Milch, 1935). More recent studies of La Roche also maintain a biographical focus.[4] Secondly, from its first appearance, *Sternheim* was read as a novelty in Germany in terms of form, style, sentiment, and significance. It has been hailed as an early and influential German epistolary novel, sentimental novel,[5] *Frauenroman*,[6] moral novel,[7] socially critical novel;[8] it is considered essential to the tradition of the German *Unterhaltungsroman* and to "trivial literature."[9] Newer criticism has effectively combined the interests of these two strands, asking how the cultural and socio-historical situation of the author accounts for the novelties of her writing.[10] The advent of methodological orientations that take account of gender as a category of analysis has particularly reinvigorated and augmented understanding of La Roche and her works. Critical readings of La Roche informed by theories of gender have elaborated extensively on how her texts figure women and femininity, in the cultural-material context as well as that of literary history. Yet efforts to discuss this particular novel and the genre *Frauenroman* for which it is considered paradigmatic still remain oriented on thematic content and largely neglect inquiries of gender and narrative theory or poetics.[11] The term *Frauenroman* is itself problematic, circumscribing an amalgam of concepts and implying generic unity.[12] The expression "feminocentric novel" favored in studies on the French novel by Nancy Miller and Joan DeJean offers a clearer critical designation of the novel oriented on cultural constructions of the "feminine" as they bear on stories of individual female identity.[13]

Cultural authority over the particular story of female development told in *Geschichte des Fräuleins von Sternheim* long resided with the interpretation that Christoph Martin Wieland, as editor of the novel and instigator of La Roche's career as author, was careful to construct for his readers. Indeed, the success of his venture is ongoing: *Sternheim* is still read as the founding example of the female-authored modern German novel delineated in Wieland's preface as untheoretical, amateur, feminine fiction in contrast to the self-reflective, professional, masculine literature produced by authors like himself.[14] The distinction and distance established between feminine and masculine literary production, and specifically between the feminine and masculine traditions of the novel represented so often through the figures of La Roche and Wieland themselves, have prevented critics from considering similarities between their early novels and hindered recognition of the self-reflective poetic concerns central to La Roche's novel. Like the early novels of Wieland, *Sternheim* self-consciously presents its own innovative narrative of gendered subjectivity within the context of contemporary theoretical debates on the genre of the novel.

The epistolary form of *Sternheim* emphasizes reading and writing as narrative events and blurs the distinctions between readers internal to the novel's fiction and external readers of the novel itself.[15] As Janet Altman puts it, "In letter narratives, characters are created less by what they do than by what, and how, they write" (177). These features of epistolarity, a form associated in the eighteenth century and beyond with femininity,[16] are employed in *Stern-*

heim to structure and motivate the narrative while exploring and expanding generic conventions. *Sternheim* stages its own search for the most commensurate way to tell the history of its unique heroine by developing three competing versions of the protagonist's story. The suitors Seymour and Derby each attempt to script a role for Sophie. The narrative conventions each adopts in their letters characterize these figures (reminiscent of the way that characters are portrayed through generic paradigms in *Don Sylvio*), while the character Sophie, who aims to write and assert her own story of identity, drafts a "new genre of character" that revises the criteria for assessing female virtue as well as the blueprint for the narrative that could relate such a novel character's history. The plots and generic orientations of Derby and Seymour are determined by the anticipated endings of their stories, dependent on the fate of female virtue defined as controlled sexuality. These endings, the narrative closures of marriage or death, are metaphoric ones, in Elizabeth MacArthur's terms: they valorize a conclusive interpretation of the unfolding epistolary development.[17] In contrast, the narrative of Sophie's story told in the letters she writes is metonymic: it focuses on the heroine's practice of virtue in ever new situations, and its openness and continuous development resist determination by the closures inherent in the plots of her suitors. The tasks of resolving the competing claims to interpretive authority over Sophie's story and of integrating its disparate versions into a single narrative that documents the heroine's inner character are explicitly elaborated in *Sternheim* as a metafictional reflection on its own textual status. The composite manuscript of Sophie's story is generated within the novel's fiction, while her own desires and her text are legitimized and contained through the sanction of masculine readers desirous of her and her story.

Wieland's Preface

Wieland adopted the role of literary mentor and editor for La Roche, negotiating the novel's publication and enabling her to enter the public literary sphere despite the handicap of her gender. Wieland's introduction to *Geschichte des Fräuleins von Sternheim*, in which he pretends he has published the novel without the knowledge or assent of the author, deftly employs the literary conventions of such prefaces to position the work in the literary and social landscape. With the cultural authority of the successful writer, he takes on the intricate tasks of legitimizing the creation and the publication of a novel authored by a woman, establishing its sanctioned sphere of influence, and providing a guiding interpretation for the envisioned readers. Wieland defends La Roche's novel not only by characterizing the female author and her writing style, as much scholarship has recognized, but also by situating the novel within the context of the contemporary theoretical discussions on the genre.[18] The arguments which the editor Wieland presents for *Sternheim* and against potential critics link a theoretical concern with the novel as genre to contemporary ideas about gender; he thereby defines and authorizes the new feminocentric novel.

Wieland's preface strongly shapes reader expectations about the feminine nature of La Roche's work. Although the author initially guards her anonymity, her female identity is featured centrally: the primary filter through which to read the novel, Wieland maintains, is the determinant of gender. Wieland interprets how being female affects the conditions of authorship and literary reception. Women's limited skill does restrict the artistic possibilities of the novel, he remarks, yet he also points to the "privilege of the ladies, who are not authors by profession" to justify the greater literary license conceded to feminine folly.[19] Commensurate with the amateur status of the female author is the amateur status of her readers. The appropriate readership, as Wieland defines it, is female and young — that group considered most susceptible to the power of novels and most in need of good advice. He professes he was unable to resist the desire "allen tugendhaften Müttern, allen liebenswürdigen jungen Töchtern unsrer Nation ein Geschenke mit einem Werke zu machen, welches mir geschickt schien, Weisheit und Tugend — die einzigen großen Vorzüge der Menschheit, die einzigen Quellen einer wahren Glückseligkeit — unter Ihrem Geschlechte und selbst unter dem meinigen, zu befördern" (10).[20] Wieland allows that even some men might benefit from reading *Sternheim,* yet he clearly establishes the proper sphere of influence for this work by a woman as a feminine one. In his role as editor, then, Wieland underscores masculine authority over the work, the author, and the readership envisioned. Simultaneously, he shields La Roche from anticipated criticism of vanity and literary ambition. By stressing his own agency, he dispels suspicions that the female author harbors immodest desires for fame, and he sanctions the publication of the novel.

Wieland further justifies the appearance of *Sternheim* by rele-
gating it to a second inferior realm, namely, to Germany, which
has a dearth of good original novels: "Ebenso gewiß ist es, daß
unsre Nation noch weit entfernt ist, an Originalwerken dieser Art,
welche zugleich unterhaltend und geschickt sind, die Liebe der
Tugend zu befördern, Überfluß zu haben" (10).[21] This lament,
familiar in the eighteenth-century theoretical discourse on the
novel, serves here to support Wieland's risky undertaking of presenting a novel authored by a woman to the public. Wieland also
implies thereby that, in the aesthetically impoverished German nation, the artistic inferiority of the feminocentric novel by a woman
writer is acceptable. The limitations of both the female sphere and
the German circumstances paradoxically allow *Sternheim* freedoms
of idiosyncrasy and imperfection which would otherwise not be
granted.

Stipulating La Roche's novel as at once amateur and exceptional, Wieland supports its publication while distancing the text
from other literary production such as, for example, his own. His
preface claims that common aesthetic categories of judgment are
inappropriate tools with which to approach the novel and suggests
that *Sternheim* lies outside the reach of theoretical discourse. This
manifestly theoretical position is the basis on which Wieland claims
interpretive authority over the female-authored text which itself, he
asserts, evinces no theoretical reflection. Ostensibly addressing
concerns of poetic theory only to dismiss them as irrelevant for La
Roche's novel, Wieland redefines central terms of theoretical contention to establish two separate, gendered theories of the novel,
contrasting feminine literary production with the intellectual sophistication of masculine artistic creativity. Engaging the terms of
history, authenticity, and character also crucial in the metanarrative
of *Agathon* to position *Sternheim* within aesthetic and social ru-
brics, Wieland emphasizes the fictionality of La Roche's novel, but
does so in a fashion strikingly different from the way he profiles the
fictionality of his own early novels. Whereas the insistence on fictionality in *Don Sylvio* and *Agathon* underscores a self-conscious,
reflective pleasure in skillful artistic illusion, the insistence on the
fictionality of *Sternheim* is meant to guarantee its status as the
authentic expression of its author's individual imagination and to
attest to La Roche's "beautiful soul."

Didactic efficacy is the prime motivation Wieland advances for his publication of *Sternheim,* although he does note its pleasing aspects in an effort to attract readers. The novel's purpose is to be educational and useful in promoting virtuous conduct. From this morally unassailable premise, Wieland summarily dismisses all dispute on the legitimacy of the genre itself:

> Ich habe nicht vonnöten, Ihnen von dem ausgebreiteten Nutzen zu sprechen, welchen Schriften von derjenigen Gattung, worunter Ihre Sternheim gehört, stiften können, wofern sie gut sind. Alle Vernünftigen sind über diesen Punkt einer Meinung, und es würde sehr überflüssig sein, nach allem, was Richardson, Fielding und so viele andre hierüber gesagt haben, nur ein Wort zur Bestätigung einer Wahrheit, an welcher niemand zweifelt, hinzuzusetzten. (10)[22]

Wieland refers to "a truth" still very much contested in theoretical discussions as if it were self-understood. He not only sweeps aside the doubts about the value of novels per se; he also refuses to engage here in the debate on what constitutes a good novel. Wieland defends the quality of *Sternheim* by placing its author in the company of Richardson and Fielding. The unspecified genre of narrative with which Wieland associates *Sternheim* therefore appears to be that of "history" as indicated in the full title of La Roche's novel and in the titles of Richardson's and Fielding's works, as well as in Wieland's own *Geschichte des Agathon.*

"History" as a generic description was generally emphasized in titles and in prefaces to distance a text from the ignominy of novels and romance and to add dignity to the narrative, all notions explored critically, for example, in *Agathon.* Most crucially, the term was offered as an avowal of authenticity. Wieland's preface to *Sternheim* neither stresses the claim to authenticity nor provides a manuscript fiction as a pretense of truth (although some readers believed that his preface employed just these topoi of editorship in order to cover his own authorship). Instead, the guarantees of authenticity and truth are transposed and transformed, for the theoretical demands of the novel change when the author is a woman. The female author must first and foremost demonstrate her good character, put in question by the very existence of her work. The novel must, then, stage the author's virtue unequivocally. The truth and authenticity sought in writing by female authors in the eighteenth century was that of sentiment and character, rather than of facts. Indeed, claim to factual precision in telling the stories of others amounted to a transgression of the borders of female modesty, which prescribed limitations in knowledge of the world and proscribed speaking for others.

Wieland demonstrates La Roche's authenticity of sentiment and morality in part by inverting the standard rhetoric on the genre in question, and openly presenting *Sternheim* as a work of fiction. Addressing La Roche in the preface, Wieland reminds her that *Sternheim* is "a work of your imagination and your heart . . . written only for your own entertainment" (9). The assertion that the work at hand was meant not for the world, but only for a private sphere, was a common one in justifications of women's writing. Female authors often adopted genres documenting this modest intention, such as letters or personal journals. Wieland's insistence on the fictional status of La Roche's text entails the grave risk of casting the author as a learned woman with literary ambitions, an image which would tarnish her honor.[23] But the recognition of the text as fiction is counterbalanced in Wieland's argument by the novel's lack of artistic skill and sensitivity, for they provide one measure of the author's virtue. The novel's considerable failings — its deficiencies "as a work of intellect, as a poetic composition, indeed even simply considered as a German text" (13) — prove that the author has not overstepped the perimeters within which the feminine is confined and defined:

> Sie, meine Freundin, dachten nie daran, für die Welt zu schreiben, oder ein Werk der Kunst hervorzubringen. Bei aller Ihrer Belesenheit in den besten Schriftstellern verschiedener Sprachen, welche man lesen kann ohne gelehrt zu sein, war es immer Ihre Gewohnheit, weniger auf die Schönheit der Form als auf den Wert des Inhalts aufmerksam zu sein. (13)[24]

As a virtuous woman, well-read but not learned, La Roche cannot be artful enough to construct literary style (unlike the aesthetically accomplished female characters of the male author's imagination, Felicia and Danae). La Roche's sincerity of heart, however, brings forth its own unique and original narrative which the cold-blooded male philosophical spirit could not have produced, Wieland argues. In the scenario Wieland sketches, the novel's flaws attest to the work's authenticity and the female author's virtue, while Wieland insists paternalistically that *he* is transforming La Roche into a writer (10).

Wieland's preface also lends legitimacy to La Roche's novel through the image of its author as mother, as a paragon of ideal femininity whose passion, sexuality, and creativity are controlled within the patriarchal family.[25] Wieland writes that La Roche introduces her protagonist and her work to him as the daughter of her mind (9). *Sternheim* is presented as a feminine product of nature, as opposed to a masculine artistic creation: its genesis is an artless birth (14) and its characteristics are unadorned, unaffected, naive beauty and moral truth. The text is thus offered as a mirror of the author's mind and soul.[26] La Roche's request for criticism and guidance from the male author for herself and her daughter, the novel, is cast as another signal of her proper feminine modesty and clears her from suspicions of literary pretensions or vain claims to authority, for it asserts and supports the hierarchy of the patriarchal order. Wieland, as authoritative male critic and editor, equates *Sternheim* and its heroine Sophie Sternheim and presents them together as a "beautiful moral image" (11) that reflects the moral purity of the author. Thus this fiction, as the manifest — and therefore measurable — product of the author's imagination and heart, guarantees the authenticity of her sentiments and ideology, which in turn provides the sanction for female authorship and even for this text's publication.

Wieland's manner of justifying *Sternheim's* appearance on the literary stage places the novel squarely in the center of disputes over the novel of the early 1770s in which "character" is a crucial point of theoretical contention. Wieland enlists Richardson and Fielding as allies in the paragraph cited above, yet in contemporary criticism the two represented opposing notions of what a novel ought to present. Richardson's model characters were pitted against Fielding's more realistic characters, the direction Wieland championed. Sophie Sternheim's function, Wieland suggests, is that of a model character to be emulated, a heroine whose virtue is rewarded in the tradition of Richardson: "Möchten doch . . . meine Töchter so denken, so handeln lernen wie Sophie Sternheim!" (11).[27] Yet Sophie's character is no mere blueprint of feminine virtue. Her individuality, "die Singularität unsrer Heldin, ihr Enthusiasmus für das sittliche Schöne, ihre besondern Ideen und Launen, ihre ein wenig eigensinnige Prädilektion für die Mylords" (15),[28] Wieland fears, may hinder her positive reception with the critics by breaking with their expectations and biases, yet that indi-

viduality also accounts for the strength of the novel. Precisely because she is a lovable eccentric, Wieland predicts her success in appealing to the readers: "eben darum, weil sie *eine Erscheinung* ist,
unter dem Namen der *liebenswürdigen Grillenfängerin* [sollte sie]
ansehnliche Eroberungen . . . machen können" (16).[29]

Wieland's interpretation of Sophie Sternheim's character reveals the novel's pivotal position in shifting expectations of gender,
the novel genre, and their intersections. Heroines were to be models of virtue or warning examples.[30] The calls for individual character and psychological credibility most strongly formulated by
Blanckenburg, applicable to Agathon and other male protagonists
created by male authors, conflicted with the greater pressures on
the feminocentric novel to be irreproachable and unequivocal, and
to suppress individuality into socially controlled roles. *Sternheim's*
novelty in staking a new character was neither entirely successful
nor fully recognized in its "subversive intent."[31] Yet this character
and her originality are the sanction and description of the work itself. Wieland personifies the novel *Sternheim* as agent and active
subject, conflating it with its author as well as with its title character. "Gutes *will* sie tun; und Gutes *wird* sie tun, und dadurch den
Schritt rechtfertigen, den ich gewaget habe" (17).[32] Rather than
providing the text with an explicit generic description, it is named
and celebrated. This identification between Sophie, *Sternheim,* and
La Roche, a conflation that proceeds initially by not naming the
author and subsuming the author's identity under the profile of
the protagonist, has remained dominant throughout two centuries
of reading the work.[33]

While it is undoubtedly condescending, Wieland's preface is
extremely clever and is successful in introducing *Geschichte des
Fräuleins von Sternheim* to the literary world as one of the first important modern German novels and the founder of a new tradition
of the feminocentric German novel. He finds its feminine style
natural and charmingly original in its artlessness. He defines it as
the product of natural female creativity, a female child born to an
unwitting author and the spitting image of her virtuous mother.
Wieland, as male authority, offers it to a predominately female
audience. As editor, he supervises and sanctions the exchanges
between the author and her female readers, defined in their roles as
mothers and daughters. He intervenes in the text with footnotes
when a female authorial voice threatens to become too strong or

when he wishes to apprise readers of his controlling presence. And Wieland reminds the readers that he has engendered this work as literature in the public sphere: the female author's figurative child is legitimized through him and bears his authoritative name.

The Female Editor

Sternheim tells the story of a female protagonist, Sophie, related by a female narrator, Rosina, to a female audience, "my friend" (19).[34] This feminocentric structure is repeated on the level of plot, for the heroine's letters are addressed to her female soul mate and confidante, Rosina's sister Emilia.[35] Sophie's audience is, however, not exclusively female. It is significant that her letters are also subject to the approval of an authoritative male figure. She explicitly requests judgment of her letters not only from Emilia, but also from Emilia's father, a preacher, who thus becomes her second, male reader. The distant father figure observes, evaluates, and sanctions her character represented in her letters, while also monitoring the potentially exclusive female intimacy the private letter might hold.

In her role as fictional editor, Rosina serves the narrative self-reflection of *Sternheim* (that Wieland denied the novel) by presenting a conventional manuscript fiction. She casts herself as a scribe who copies and compiles authentic letters of the heroine and her acquaintances: as stated in its title, the novel tells Sophie Sternheim's history "Von einer Freundin derselben aus Original- Papieren und andern zuverläßigen Quellen gezogen."[36] The public availability of the heroine's texts in Rosina's edition is rendered blameless by the epistolary form that vouches for the authenticity of the story and its original private intent, while the individual letters and journal entries written by the heroine attest to her modesty and her natural, virtuous femininity. Rosina structures the implied readers' expectations further by anticipating the story's "happy end" and describing its moral lessons. Sophie's history will show the readers: "diese liebenswürdigste junge Dame in Schwierigkeiten und Umstände verwickelt . . ., die den schönen Plan eines glücklichen Lebens, den sie sich gemacht hatte, auf einmal zerstörten, aber durch die Probe, auf welche sie ihren innerlichen Wert setzten, ihre Geschichte für die Besten unsers Geschlechts lehrreich machen" (61).[37] The publication of the private documents of Sophie's life is justified here by their value as didactic moral example.

The outward pose of *Geschichte des Fräuleins von Sternheim* as a text marked by gender would appear to correspond with Wieland's introductory reading. Yet the specular moments of the novel go beyond the initial editor fiction. The epistolary structure of *Sternheim* foregrounds the processes of reading and writing and informs the novel's metafictional considerations. By juxtaposing the letters of different characters, La Roche experiments with various narrative paradigms for relating the heroine's history. The tensions arising from the desire to control Sophie Sternheim and *Sternheim* within established generic conventions reveal narrative cruxes of La Roche's work and reflect the literary and social pressures of late eighteenth-century Germany that bear on female stories of identity.

Virtue Rewarded or Virtue Betrayed?

Sophie's adventures are told primarily from her own perspective, through her letters and her journals, yet other characters' letters also convey information about central events in the novel. The reader must interpolate the shape of the whole from these various renditions. Much has been made of this multi-perspectivism in *Sternheim*.[38] What has not been recognized is how the letters of various characters vie not only for the dominant interpretation of her story, but indeed for its very narrative construction, and thereby mediate metafictional reflection on the construction of the novel itself. The battle over Sophie's story is waged most directly between the two English suitors for her affections, Seymour and Derby, who each cast Sophie as heroine and themselves as her appropriate partner. Their expectations and their interpretations of her behavior are strongly influenced both by literary conventions and by their own desires: their letters present conflicting plots revolving around a virtuous or a fallen heroine. Furthermore, Seymour and Derby each explicitly present their stories as unfolding works of literature that follow generic patterns and constraints. They themselves adopt roles in the versions of Sophie's tale they champion and they attempt to shape her into the heroine who best accords with the literary trajectories that mirror their subjective desires.

Seymour desires Sophie as the pure and virtuous sentimental heroine. The literary form which frames his imaginative scripting of her is the drama. This reflects his personality and his image of Sophie, for he admires her from afar, choosing to place himself off-stage as a passive spectator, as it were, until the last act, in which he

would claim the triumphant heroine as his own "to crown her virtue" (92). When Sophie's virtue is under duress and is in doubt at
court, Seymour's fleeting impulse to intervene actively in the plot
against her by marrying and thereby rescuing her from the clutches
of the lustful prince is easily countered by the arguments of his uncle, who reminds him of the exigencies of the dramatic situation.
The sentimental heroine must publicly enact her virtue to prove it
true, the uncle insists: "Alle Züge des Charakters der Fräulein geben mir Hoffnung zu einem Triumphe der Tugend. Aber er muß
vor den Augen der Welt erlanget werden" (93).[39] Seymour adopts
his uncle's conventional notions with hopes of a good performance
that would humiliate the prince and vindicate his own love in the
male battle for the heroine. "Mein Oheim erregte in mir die Begierde, den Fürsten gedemütigt zu sehen, und ich stellte mir den
Widerstand der Tugend als ein entzückendes Schauspiel vor" (93).[40]

   Seymour's letters repeatedly render Sophie's story through figures of the theater. For instance, he relates the events of the even-
ing at the court's theater as a competition between two dramatic
performances, one on stage and another in which Sophie has the
leading role. "Heute, mein Freund, heute wird sie in der Hofko-
mödie dem Blick des Fürsten zum erstenmal ausgesetzt; ich bin
nicht wohl; aber ich muß hingehen, wenn es mir das Leben kosten
sollte" (93).[41] He awaits the performance with anticipation and,
once at the theater, anxiously observes Sophie for outward signs of
her inner emotions. His review of her acting highlights her defi-
ance of the role assigned to her by the court. All eyes are on her
theater box rather than on stage, yet she demurely chooses a seat
which protects her from so much unwanted attention. Sophie further accentuates her rejection of the "comedy" in court by disap-
proving of the comedy on stage. The spectacle of the court is
associated with drama, superficial perception, and exteriority; it
stands in clear contrast to the values of modesty and interiority that
define Sophie's individuality and independence. In his judgment
over Sophie, Seymour relies too greatly on the conventions of the
theater which she herself finds so distasteful. Since he views her as
an actress who must dramatize her virtue, he is misled into reading
her virtue as nothing more than an act. Seymour's lack of interpretive acumen, due in part to his self-centered desires for her, becomes evident in his description of the lottery of images, one of the
entertainments for the courtiers. When Sophie draws the card de-

picting Daphne fleeing Apollo, Seymour initially delights. He takes the card as a sign supporting his image of Sophie as the embodiment of virtue. "Meine Freude war nicht zu beschreiben; . . . die Freude des Fräuleins bekräftigte mich in der Idee, daß sie durch ihre Tugend eine neue fliehende Daphne sein würde" (144).[42] Seymour soon reinterprets Sophie's demeanor: "Aber wie schmerzhaft, wie niederträchtig hat mich nicht ihre Scheintugend betrogen, da sie sich gleich darauf dem Apollo in die Arme warf!" (144).[43] When coincidences lead to the appearance that Sophie and the prince have had a private rendezvous together, Seymour assumes that the prince's seductive plot was successful. Proving himself a poor critic, he condemns Sophie for a duplicitous, merely theatrically adopted mask of virtue. Referring to Seymour, Derby writes: "Die heftigste äußerste Verachtung belebte seine Anmerkungen über ihre vorgespiegelte Tugend, und die elende Aufopferung derselben; über die Frechheit sich vor dem ganzen Adel zum Schauspiel zu machen, und die vergnügteste Miene dabei zu haben" (136).[44] Preoccupied by his own grief and self-pity, Seymour realizes too late that this interpretation was wrong. He reflects on his passive spectatorship and laments his expectations that Sophie demonstrate her virtue by enacting it through conventional paradigms: "Wie grausam war meine Eigenliebe gegen das liebenswerte Mädchen! Erst wollte ich nicht von meiner Liebe reden, bis sie sich ganz nach meinen Begriffen in dem vollen Glanz einer triumphierenden Tugend gezeigt haben würde. Sie ging ihren eigenen schönen Weg, und weil sie meinen idealischen Plan nicht befolgte, eignete ich mir die Gewalt zu, sie darüber auf das empfindlichste zu bestrafen" (208–9).[45]

Seymour's incompetent interpretation of the scenes at the costume ball is one place where the narrative directs attention to issues of how to judge and how to portray the novel's protagonist. Seymour learns that he misconstrues Sophie's actions through the lens of his subjective passions; his mistakes point to the difficulties of reading outward signs of inner character, but also indicate that those who are most self-aware and who can critically judge their own expectations of a text will be superior readers. In the metafiction of the novel, Seymour's misjudgments serve to emphasize the author's aesthetic challenge of staging her heroine's virtue convincingly. Sophie's letters are one means of doing so: the letters (as legible signs of her virtuous character) gain force as convincing documents of Sophie's authentic emotion in contrast to her appearances in public, the signs Seymour misreads. Seymour's letters describing events at court show him primarily as the melancholy audience of an unfolding drama and reflect his limitations as a spectator or reader of Sophie's story. Derby, in contrast, adopts an active authorial role and aims to make Sophie fulfill the script he writes for her. Seymour's facile interpretation alerts Derby to be more cautious in his own judgments, for Seymour's idealistic projections of Sophie's role blinded him to the secret truth Derby discovers: surprisingly, she proves to be acting independently. Still, he underestimates the heroine's capacity to "make fools" (137) of those who wish her to enact a role they dictate. Sophie ultimately foils Derby's plans by again following her "own pretty path."

Derby's ambition to seduce Sophie is kindled specifically by jealously of Seymour and generally by the spirit of male competition. He writes to his friend B* in Paris that he is tired of hearing the stories of his exploits, for he has something better to offer:

> Bald werde ich Deinen albernen Erzählungen ein Ende machen, die ich bisher nur deswegen geduldet, weil ich sehen wollte, wie weit Du deine Prahlerei in dem Angesichte deines Meisters treiben würdest. Auch solltest Du heute die Geißel meiner Satire fühlen, wenn ich nicht im Sinne hätte, Dir den Entwurf einer deutsch-galanten Historie zu zeigen, zu deren Ausführung ich mich fertig mache. . . . Also prahle mir nicht mehr, mein guter B*, denn von Siegen wie die eurige, ist kein Triumphlied zu singen.[46] (99–100)

With masculine bravado, he promises to author and enact a novel of seduction. His pride insists, "Für mich soll sie geblüht haben, das ist festgesetzt" (101).[47] The story he imagines is one of villainous corruption of a virtuous heroine and his aim is to educate and convert Sophie from her enthusiastic sentimentality to his own sensual pleasures: "gewiß, sie soll neue Entdeckungen in dem Lande des Vergnügens machen, wenn ihr aufgeklärter und feiner Geist alle seine Fähigkeiten dazu anwenden wird" (101).[48]

The "love story" (119) Derby plots actively intervenes in the intrigues of the court. Derby ridicules Seymour's weak stance and allows himself double-edged commentary at Seymour's expense as the latter languishes for Sophie: "Sie wären der schicklichste Liebhaber für sie gewesen, und ich hätte ihr Vertrauter und Geschichtsschreiber sein mögen" (106).[49] Derby's image of himself as the narrator of the lovers' story is an ironic and vicious joke, for the novelistic narrative in which he is casting Sophie is drafted directly against Seymour's dramatic expectations and hopes. Derby describes to his friend his plans to wrest narrative control over the development of the plot: "Die Komödie des Fürsten mit meiner Sternheim, wovon ich Dir letzthin geschrieben, ist durch die romantischen Grillen des Vetters Seymour zu einem so tragischen Ansehen gestiegen, daß nichts als der Tod oder die Flucht der Heldin zu einer Entwicklung dienen kann; das erste, hoffe ich, solle die Göttin der Jugend verhüten, und für das zweite mag Venus durch meine Vermittlung sorgen" (184).[50]

Derby relishes his role as the villain and pursues his goal of overpowering Sophie's virtue, yet he is at times led astray from his own story by the power of her conduct. While he aims to convert her to his pleasures, he himself faces the danger of being converted to hers. His increasingly heartfelt passion for her is, in itself, out of character for him. She captivates him and, he claims, very nearly makes an enthusiast of him too. Sophie's influence over his passions also leaves an immediate mark on the shape and style of Derby's narrative. His taste for sensual, erotic literature initially guides the tale he wishes to tell himself. Yet he soon begins to write in a different tone, one more likely to come from Seymour's pen than his own. Derby stops short in his first letter to B* to note the change in his narrative register with shock: "Halt einmal: Wie komme ich zu diesem Geschwätz? — So lauteten die Briefe des armen Seymour, da er in die schöne Y** verliebt war: Sollte mich diese Landjungfer auch zum Schwärmer machen?" (102).[51]

Derby decides to incorporate this new role into his repertoire of deceit and to don the guise of enthusiast temporarily, insofar as it serves him to seduce Sophie. Indeed, he appropriates the image of himself as enthusiast to figure his seductive strategy: "Wie Schwärmer, die in den persönlichen Umgang mit Geistern kommen wollen, eine Zeitlang mit Fasten und Beten zubringen; muß ich dieser enthusiastische Seele zu gefallen, mich aller meiner bisherigen Vergnügungen entwöhnen" (141).[52] In his letters to B*, Derby recasts such slips in voice and attitude as a conscious enactment. Yet despite this show of authorial control, Derby realizes that the test of character in his developing story applies to himself as well as to Sophie. Just as he aims to lead her from her path of virtue, she threatens (albeit unwittingly, but surely in accordance with her ideology of the power of good example) to lead him from his infamous career as villain. Derby catches himself in yet another narrative inconsistency, as he actually considers changing the direction of his story's plot even as it unfolds:

> Indessen ist ihr Verderben deswegen nicht beschlossen. Wenn sie mich liebt, wenn mir ihr Besitz alle die abwechselnden lebhaften Vergnügungen gibt, die ich mir verspreche; so soll sie Lady Derby sein, und mich zum Stammvater eines neuen närrisch genug gemischten Geschlechtes machen. . . . Wie zum Henker komme ich zu diesem Stücke von Hausphysik! Freund, es sieht schlimm aus, wenn es fortdauert; doch ich will die Probe bis auf den letzten Grad durchgehen. (195–96)[53]

Derby can imagine a plot that begins with a successful seduction of the virtuous protagonist and ends in marriage. He fantasizes about the novelty of a union between his "wit" and her "sentiments" (196), figured in their legitimate descendants. But the story of the sentimental protagonist Sophie cannot accommodate such radical narrative innovation. Sophie is bound to a conventional narrative of virtue mocked here by Derby: "Sie schrieb einen großen Brief im gigantischen Ton der hohen Tugend" (196).[54] Sophie cannot love Derby as he desires; his dream and her virtue are mutually exclusive. Her pure love, the only viable one as heroine, is instead inspired by the "magic sympathy of enthusiasm" (142) which she shares with Seymour. Derby must be faithful to his role as villain as Sophie must be to hers as heroine, yet he ascribes the necessity of maintaining this role only to Sophie's stubborn, idealistic virtue, which has led to costly developments in his novel: "dieser närrische Roman war ein wenig kostbar; doch, sie verdiente alles. Hätte sie mich nur geliebt, und ihre Schwärmerei abgeschworen!" (230).[55]

There are striking parallels in characterization, plot, and theoretical interests between *Geschichte des Fräuleins von Sternheim* and *Geschichte des Agathon*.[56] The conflicts in *Sternheim* between the idealistic, enthusiastic heroine and the hedonistic, sensualist seducer are not unlike central conflicts between the idealistic enthusiast Agathon and his sensualist seducers in Wieland's novel. As Sophie is bound in love to Seymour, Agathon's love for Psyche is likewise an expression of "magic sympathy" between souls. Psyche figures as a virtuous competitor and contrast to Danae, as Seymour does to Derby. Sophie, like Agathon, arrives as an outsider to a society of luxury foreign to her taste. She, like Agathon in Smyrna, is much admired for her talents (including her gracefulness and her lute playing, qualities she shares with Agathon) and she elicits much irritation, bewilderment, and ridicule with her ideology of virtue. She is, like Agathon, disdainful of the sensual temptations surrounding her and dismissive of the art forms, such as the play at court, which cross the border between tasteful artistry and artful seduction. Sophie Sternheim herself is marked for seduction by the powerful prince and by Derby, as Agathon is by the powerful Hippias and by Danae. Sophie's dilemma, like Agathon's, is figured in a critical moment through the myth of Daphne and Apollo, and the relation of this myth to her situation is subject to several contending interpretations within the narrative, as is also the case in *Agathon*. In each case the subjective receptive stances motivating the conflicting interpretations are an express theme within the fiction of the novels, as well as an occasion for metafictional considerations. Derby, like Hippias and Danae with Agathon, is convinced that he can rechannel a sensibility for sensuality from Sophie's imagination, which is passionate about moral ideals, to her physical senses and to more worldly pleasures through seductive aesthetic representation. The most successful seductive ploys of both Derby and Danae rely on them each becoming the vehicle of such representation, that is, on artfully embodying the ideals the naive enthusiasts hold most dear. And like Danae, Derby is in danger of having his own aesthetic and ethical principles tempered and even transformed under the influence of the unwittingly seductive ardor of the object of his desires.

The authors of *Sternheim* and *Agathon* each offer metafictional reflection on their own generic innovations and thus elaborate on their efforts to narrate original stories of subjectivity adequate to the changing demands of modern society and its new understandings of gendered behavior. Both novels integrate scenes of narrative production and reception centrally into their plots to explore available paradigms for stories of identity modeled through generic narrative conventions, as they engender their own tales and engage in specular assessment and theoretical self-positioning within the contemporary aesthetic and social discourse. Both texts show the primary importance of their novel concepts of self-love and independence, delineated according to the protagonist's gender, for the successful development of a coherent individual history, and both

Agathon and *Sternheim* make the complex and delicate relationships between aesthetic styles and ethical comportment central to their narratives.

The possibilities for the literary elaboration of these fundamentally similar issues differ radically, however, in the two novels. The gender difference between the two protagonists and the gendered signatures of the novels' authors dictate the options. While the true love between Danae and Agathon might soften the hero's fall from virtue and lead to positive mutual influence of the characters, such a resolution (which Derby at times imagines) is out of the question for the protagonist Sophie. Agathon's love with Danae can be seen as an enrichment of his experience and character, but for the heroine, such a liaison can only be interpreted as loss. *Agathon* experimented with a narrative form of mediation between sensualism and idealism and considered critically the terms of wisdom and virtue, yet such narrative experimentation is not open to the feminocentric novel that courts legitimacy. Were Sophie to modify the ideals that guide her actions, it would mean the abandonment of her upright inner character entirely, in turn the ostensible reflection of her creator's soul and the legitimation for female authorship. Agathon's pure love for Psyche can be recast as a sibling relationship. For Sophie, Seymour *is* her fate. The many similarities to Agathon also suggest a reading of Sophie herself as a kind of sibling of his, a Psyche, as it were. Psyche remains, in *Agathon,* a cipher, an image of a moral ideal guiding masculine desire, a beacon for Agathon as he navigates his course in life and constructs a viable story of male identity. Part of the poetic dilemma of *Sternheim,* staged through the competing letter narratives about its protagonist, is the imperative for Sophie to enact both these roles. She must represent, like Psyche, a steadfast feminine image of virtue attracting and guiding masculine desire, while simultaneously serving, like Agathon, as a vehicle through which the novel explores the challenges inherent in constructing an individual history. Sophie's letters attempt to negotiate these often conflicting demands and to create and realize her own story of female identity.

As will be shown, the novel attempts to resolve the narrative disjunctions occasioned by the need to tell at once the story of ideal virtue and the credible story of true individual character by legitimizing Sophie's written narrative of her life, the compilation of her letters, through the appeal it holds for a competent masculine reader. Lord Rich desires Sophie herself as his wife, an unattainable goal, since she is promised to his brother Seymour. As the individual figure Sophie disappears, transformed into the perfect image of the model wife and mother who symbolically bears the children of both desiring brothers, her text, the manifest record of her character, is bequeathed to Lord Rich, who sublimates his desire for its author and transfers it onto her story.

In the two stories which Seymour and Derby sketch, Sophie is expected to follow the feminine role defined by the narrative conventions each employs to represent either virtue triumphant and rewarded or virtue betrayed and overcome. These binary possibilities, the euphoric and the dysphoric plots of the heroine's text defined by Nancy Miller, are both present in *Sternheim,* for Sophie enacts each of these roles in turn as the stories are imposed upon her.[57] Her decried stubbornness lies in merely "enacting" these roles as the narrative strands of the novel require, while persistently resisting their validity for her story as a whole. As will be shown, Sophie defies both men and the limitations each wishes to dictate with his script by writing her own story as an alternative to the conventional patterns they propose. The novelty and strengths of *Geschichte des Fräuleins von Sternheim* lie in no small measure in suggesting a new model of the feminine story which projects an alternate assessment of female virtue and identity and imagines new narrative possibilities in the telling of a heroine's tale.

"A New Genre of Character"

Sophie resists both the genres favored by Seymour and Derby and the roles the men draft for her. As Derby exclaims: "Das Mädchen macht eine ganz neue Gattung von Charakter aus!" (142).[58] The phrase "new genre of character" captures the tensions between individuality and the pressures of conformity placed on the heroine that surface in Wieland's preface and underlie the narrative.[59] The characterization of Sophie is novel, as is the mode of telling her story, but the constraints limiting the extent of these narrative innovations in a new novel of female moral character remain powerful.

In many respects Sophie represents the conventional feminine ideal: she is virtuous, full of sentimental emotions, unaffected, natural and an exemplar of charitable love of others. Sophie is unusual, however, for the conviction with which she expresses these

qualities and in the forms such expression take. She has a pedagogical zeal to enlighten and thereby improve the society she is
part of, and a "masculine courage" (92) in pursuing this ideology.
Seymour describes her individual character, the perfect sentimental
balance between heart and head, as an inherited blend of maternal
English and paternal German attributes. Sophie herself honors
both her parents as models of behavior and ideology. Yet she particularly worships her deceased mother and attempts to emulate
her in all respects. Her father fosters this identification to extremes:
"Herr von Sternheim [führte] das zwölfjährige Fräulein bei der
Hand zu dem Bildnis ihrer Mutter, und sprach von ihrer Tugend
und Güte des Herzens mit solcher Rührung, daß das junge Fräulein kniend bei ihm schluchzte, und oft zu sterben wünschte, um
bei ihrer Frau Mutter zu sein" (51).[60] Sophie greatly resembles her
mother and even wears her mother's clothes at her father's behest,
as she aims to fashion herself after her completely. On his deathbed, Sophie's father sees but one image, in Sophie, of both
women: "meine Sophie!" (56).

Sophie's identification with her mother thus places her on the
border between life and death, for her desire to become just like
her mother at least partially implies self-extinction. Her idiosyncratic bond with her unearthly maternal model becomes particularly evident in contrast to the worldly court. Sophie writes to
Emilia that her first appearance at court earned her the distinction
of being thought an apparition. Sophie's aunt has insisted she re-
place her favored clothes, namely those of her mother, with a more
fashionable white dress. Yet this change of costume has the effect
not of weakening, but rather of strengthening the association with
her dead mother, for it gives her the pale mien of a ghost. The image of Sophie Sternheim as spirit to be conjured and carried off is
coined by a young cavalier in banter. Sophie counters with a different image of herself as ghost to emphasize her distance from the
courtly mores, her embrace of the guiding spirits of her parents,
and her trust in heavenly protection. She believes, she asserts, "daß
für jedes Gespenst eine eigne Art von Beschwörung gewählt werden müsse, und die Entsetzung, die ich dem Grafen bei meiner Erscheinung verursachte, läßt mich denken, daß ich unter dem
Schutz eines mächtigern Geistes bin, als der ist, der ihn beschwö-
ren lernt" (65).[61] The figure of Sophie as apparition remains a central means of characterizing the protagonist throughout the novel.

The image of immateriality underscores the nature of the protagonist's existence as fiction, the power of La Roche's narrative to
conjure up the spirit of Sophie and to provide the imaginary shape
through which she communicates with the reader. Wieland reiterates this image by choosing the term "Erscheinung" (appearance)
to describe the idiosyncratic novel *Sternheim* itself, as well as its appearance in print (16). Likewise, Sophie's rival suitors wish to convince the ethereal heroine to materialize in the shape most
favorable to them. But it is Derby who discovers the magic incantation with which to charm her and bring her into his power: "aber
das Wort Tugend, welches ich etlichemal aussprach, war die Beschwörung, durch welche ich ihren Zorn besänftigte" (172).[62]

Sophie manipulates her figurative position between life and
death, corporeity and disembodiment, to write in letters her own
"new genre of character" that endeavors to hold fast to moral ideals despite the imperfect, real conditions beyond the control of the
female protagonist. The image of "the heart," at once physical and
metaphorical, comes to stand for bodily and spiritual integrity in a
fashion that allows for greater flexibility in the assessment of female
virtue and, correspondingly, for new plots in female stories of
identity. By dissociating female virtue from an exclusive depend-
ence on sexual purity or indeed male sexual control, Sophie can
avoid the polarity between the plots of "virtuous" or "fallen"
woman; she can subsume them both into her own self-image as a
suffering, but not defeated, virtuous protagonist.

Sophie's recasting of virtue's essence begins in the course of
Derby's efforts to cajole her into sexual submission. When Derby
cannot win Sophie's heart or her acquiescence to his advances, he
forces himself upon her. This scene of violence is crucial in appreci-
ating the novel's complications and in assessing the elaborate efforts expended in *Sternheim* to control the narrative.[63] Derby
relates his behavior through figures of rape: "ich drang in sie"
(222).[64] He rends her clothes from her body "to achieve my aim
even against her will" (222). He wishes to see Sophie nude in the
image of Milton's Eve, a reference that places Derby in the position of Satan preparing to seduce Eve. It also recalls the role Derby
had once imagined for himself as Sophie's first and legitimate mate,
since he had envisioned playing Adam to her Eve. The dual roles of
Adam and Satan reflect the confusion Sophie has brought into
Derby's story and the conflict between his "new sentiments and his

old principles" (122) previously revealed in similar images — for example, while Derby pines with love, the mirror shows him a "satanic figure" (122). Derby wishes in part for love and moral legitimacy, but he fulfills his part of devilish seducer. He complains that he has found no satisfaction with Sophie, "since much is missing from the idea of pleasure"(219), yet he comments dryly, "I have enjoyed my rewards" (224). Sophie is now "my half lady" (228) and "one of the loveliest flowers to wilt on your friend's fiery breast" (300). After being thus abused and abandoned by Derby, the heroine longs for death. But she simultaneously reveals a vigorous desire for earthly absolution. She insists that her heart is innocent and yearns for corroboration of this sentiment as well as for compassion from her friends. Sophie's friends do support her struggling sense of herself as virtuous: "ich sah, daß sie mich unschuldig glaubten, und mein Herz bedauerten; ich konnte sie als Zeugen meiner Unschuld und Tugend ansehen" (235).[65]

Sophie's heart represents her innocence and her sensibility, as it stands metaphorically for her soul and her virtue. Yet it also represents her physical integrity which Derby violated. In response to his assaults she cries: "Sie zerreißen mein Herz, und meine Liebe für Sie; niemals werd ich Ihnen diesen Mangel feiner Empfindungen vergeben!" (222).[66] "Herz" as figure, then, moves between synecdoche, metonymic identification with the body, and metaphor, identified with the incorporeal soul. Using the image of the "heart" in her discourse of morality allows Sophie to suspend and subordinate the importance of the body, to acknowledge it only euphemistically and indirectly. The confirmation of her heart's purity by her friends enables her to rebuild an integral sense of a virtuous self not fully predicated on the sexual fate of her body. Sophie self-assuredly enumerates her positive spiritual qualities not tainted by her misadventures with Derby:

> Ich kannte den ganzen Wert alles dessen, was ich verloren hatte; aber meine Krankheit und Betrachtungen zeigten mir, daß ich noch in dem wahren Besitz der wahren Güter unsers Lebens geblieben sei. Mein Herz ist unschuldig und rein; die Kenntnisse meines Geistes sind unvermindert; die Kräfte meiner Seele und meine guten Neigungen haben ihr Maß behalten; und ich habe noch das Vermögen, Gutes zu tun. (236–37)[67]

This catalogue of virtues removed from the physical self provides her with a renewed foundation for her identity as an "innocent and pure" woman.

A similar fluidity between various inflections of "heart" as a figure that simultaneously acknowledges and denies the body informs the discussions of marriage in *Sternheim* and provides the foundation for envisioning an alternative female destiny to marriage also viable in the social order. Frau Hills asks Sophie to convince the widow Frau von C* to remarry, as four honorable men are asking for her hand. Yet Frau von C* asserts: "Ich wähle nicht; ich will meine Freiheit genießen, die ich durch so viele Bitterkeit erkaufen mußte" (254).[68] Given Sophie's own dreadful experience of matrimony and her subsequent social freedoms as Derby's "widow," she surprises even herself in agreeing to argue against Frau von C*'s decision to remain single. Sophie's arguments for marriage are those of virtue and duty: she chides Frau von C* for resisting the opportunity to make other people happy. Frau von C* insists she too first married with this motivation and belief, but has learned that one's own happiness may instead be the cost of such charitable action: "ich habe so sehr erfahren, daß man andere glücklich machen kann, ohne es selbst zu werden; daß ich nicht Herz genug habe, mich noch einmal auf diesen ungewissen Boden zu wagen" (267).[69] A marriage based on the idea of charity requires a "heart" that is giving as well as courageous, one that Frau von C* feels she can no longer muster. Sophie wishes to believe in matrimony as the most honorable and virtuous life course for women. Yet she must also concede to Frau von C*: "die Seite, welche Sie von meinen Vorschlägen sehen, hat in Wahrheit viel Abschreckendes" (268).[70] Sophie's efforts to resolve her internal conflict hinge again on dissociating "Herz" as a figure for the body from "Herz" as a figure for spiritual generosity towards others. Although Sophie still feels the primary dictates of female duty and the heart are to marry, she can accept Frau von C*'s alternative to marriage as legitimate because it, like marriage, is built on a foundation of charitable good works and allows for the fulfillment of feminine duty towards others. By educating young girls according to the demands of their social classes, Frau von C* will compensate for her negative example of deciding not to marry. Providing legitimacy for Frau von C*'s choice to stay single acknowledges that the institution of marriage can be an abusive one towards women, since she explicitly gives this experience as the reason for her decision. A woman's virtue and social function can, in this scenario, be demonstrated independently from men. The emphases of Frau von C*'s educational program reflect this broadening conception of feminine identity and virtue and suggest new possibilities for stories of female subjectivity and character.[71]

The novelty of narrative that *Sternheim* represents, like the novelty of the heroine's character, is sketched in metafictional passages in *Sternheim* in part as a function of various national influences and is developed through the novel's thematic interest in national traits. Although willing to recognize the status of *Sternheim* as one of only few good German novels, contemporary critics lamented La Roche's "anglophilia" and "gallomania." Wieland admonishes La Roche for this fault in the preface to *Sternheim* and in his footnotes. Gottlieb Konrad Pfeffel, claiming to be speaking for "many of my friends" as well as for himself, complains in 1783 of La Roche's predilection for English heroes; he believes her influence on national taste ought to be employed to propagate "German" ideals.[72] Such critiques show a misunderstanding of the novel. The heroine's unreflected bias for England and the English is one of the faults she must overcome in the course of the plot, for she must learn to distinguish between positive and negative representatives of the nation. Rosina underscores what has led the protagonist astray, namely her "desire for England" (199): her passion for England blinds her to Derby's machinations, while he ensnares her by manipulating her prejudices for his country. The blind love for England is not only a personal shortcoming of the heroine, but is rather shown to be a national one which Sophie learns to recognize and resist. *Sternheim* thus advocates measured judgment over the merits and faults of neighboring nations, both England and France, as compared to German conditions.

The national characteristics defining the heroine and the novel are configured through positions of gender in familial constellations, but also through attributes of class. Sophie's "English" characteristics are inherited from an aristocratic mother and her "German" ones from her bourgeois father. Her noble English sentimentality and her German bourgeois earnestness, honesty, and patriotism mutually influence each other. Her notions of practicing virtue are markedly class-conscious: while she does not advocate revolutionary changes in the German social structure, she strongly promotes social charity and responsibility of the upper classes for their inferiors.[73] La Roche depicts social differences and engages in social criticism from the moral standpoint of sentimental sincerity in original and explicit manners in the novel. In this sense *Sternheim* is a German novel, located in the German context, long sought by critics in eighteenth-century letters; its overt English ancestry, particularly Richardson, ennobles it, as it were, as the English ancestry of its protagonist ennobles her.[74]

Traits defined in *Sternheim* as English and German thus complement each other in the heroine and in her history. A further national comparison shapes the novel and its metafictional self-reflection. German bourgeois values of modesty, thoughtful scientific inquiry, and independence are juxtaposed with French aristocratic vanity, superficiality, and fashion explicitly as a cultural conflict that influences the literary production of stories about the protagonist Sophie.[75] Not only the dramatic plots against Sophie, but also Derby's courtly novel of intrigue against her are associated with France. Derby addresses his letters to his friend and confidant in Paris, figured as the locale of decadence and easy sexual conquests celebrated in the stories they trade. Sophie rejects the court's dramatic orientation toward spectacle and intrigue and turns rather to solitude with her German books. When her aunt takes these from her, Sophie responds with the determination to write texts for herself. Her own sentiments, instead of her stolen books, guide her textual resistance to the courtly customs and language foreign to her.

While Sophie rejects the German aristocracy's "slavish bias" (129) for French literary style and for all things French, she does laud the way learned Frenchmen interact with their ladies. The French are more willing than the German men to recognize and to foster achievements of women, Sophie asserts. She laments the irresponsibility and poor judgment of the German men as cultural mediators:

> Warum brachten seit so vielen Jahren die meisten unserer Kavaliere von ihren Pariser Reisen ihren Schwestern und Verwandtinnen, unter tausenderlei verderblichen Modenachrichten, nicht auch diese mit, die alles andere verbessert hätte? Aber da sie *für sich* nichts als lächerliche und schädliche Sachen sammeln, wie sollten sie das Anständige und Nutzbare *für uns* suchen? (131)[76]

The German novel and the debate on its moral status similarly suffers from German men's double standards of propriety and their misjudgment in matters of cultural exchange. Sophie insists that if one is to forbid girls to read novels, men will have to speak less of their amorous adventures and exotic experiences: "unsere Väter, Männer, Brüder müßten nicht so viel von ihren artigen Begebenheiten und Beobachtungen auf Reisen usw. sprechen; sonst machte auch dieses Verbot und die Gegenübung wieder einen schädlichen Kontrast."[77] Speaking specifically of positive models for novels to be read by young women, Sophie explains: "Moralische Gemälde von Tugenden aller Stände, besonders von unsrem Geschlechte, möchte ich gesammlet haben; und darin sind die Französinnen glücklicher als wir. Das weibliche Verdienst erhält unter ihnen öffentliche und dauernde Ehrenbezeugungen" (272).[78] She turns, then, to a positive aspect of French culture to imagine a new literary form for Germany. Such a perfected genre, offering stories of virtuous and accomplished women as models for young female readers appropriate for their class status, is rarely found in German, she claims. The cry for the German "original novel" in novel theory is reiterated here in terms specified by gender and class.

Sophie's own tale is an example of the narrative she would have adolescent German women read. It demonstrates the introspection, sincerity, and modesty attributed to Germany as well as the feminine sentimentality of England. She herself relates those parts of her story appropriate to her younger charges as educational material from which they may benefit, to encourage them to employ their talents to the best of their capacity, in the service of practicing the virtue of charity. Thus the heroine's virtuous character portrayed in *Sternheim*, joining bourgeois and aristocratic, German and English qualities, and associating itself with the French manner of recognizing female accomplishment is itself the defense and the definition of the new genre her "history" offers.

Compiling Sternheim's Story

Rival narratives of Sophie's life, offering alternate readings of the protagonist and of the relationships of genre and gender, vie for dominance in *Sternheim;* the tensions between them invigorate the novel's plot. Wieland in the preface and the footnotes established expectations of how to interpret the work as a feminine novel. The fictional editor, Rosina, offers a similar interpretation of the exemplary qualities of her mistress and her story, outlining the contours of the epistolary narrative about a heroine for a female audience. The suitors for Sophie's affections adopt conflicting narrative conventions for writing about a heroine, "virtue triumphant" and "virtue betrayed," to pen their versions of the heroine's tale. Sophie's own narrative of her adventures resists these projections as she strives to embody and write a new "genre of character" that confounds the plots of Derby and Seymour. *Sternheim* incorporates these many strands and nascent definitions of the feminocentric novel explored here, directing reader attention to such theoretical problems as genre, character, authenticity, and interpretation through the epistolary multi-perspectivism and emphasis on the subjective practices of writing and reading. The metafictional reflection on the novel's own status and its relation to its readers culminates in an elaborate presentation of the way in which the story it offers is, literally, constructed as a material object, a written text to be read and possessed. The process of bringing the individual private letters of the novel's figures into the public domain and of transforming them into a composite "History of Fräulein von Sternheim" is traced in the novel as it approaches its end.[79] This process is linked within the novel's fiction to the conclusions of the competing plots: as each of these plots is resolved, the author of each one ceases to write and his or her narrative is subsumed under that of another writer. It is useful, therefore, to examine what happens to the letters of Derby, Seymour, and Sophie, the three principle writers.

On rediscovering Sophie as "Madam Leidens" at Summerhall, Derby begins a second volume of his novel. In a letter to Lord B*, the recipient of his earlier letters about Sophie, Derby stylizes her yet again as his "my heroine" (300). Irritated that she has not yet succumbed to his plot, he continues the written contest between them, thereby overthrowing Sophie's own plans. A letter from Derby to Lady Summers reestablishes his link to Sophie: "Was für ein Grauen überfiel mich, meine Emilia, als ich die Hand des Lord Derby erblickte" (294–95).[80] Derby takes offense at Sophie's "audacity" (299) in being in England and again aims to crush her independence. He resolves to reproduce the plot of kidnapping and isolation he had imposed on an earlier victim, Nancy. Once in Summerhall, his dire deed accomplished, Derby enacts the role of confidant for Lord Rich, just as he had done earlier for Rich's brother Lord Seymour. Derby had interpreted the previous story he projected for his heroine as a warning example for young girls, thinking her fate sealed; now too he swears to educate *his* daughters in the dangerous designs of the likes of him and again reads her tale as a closed text with one clear meaning.

Derby's interpretation and his confidence in his narrative dominance is, however, again premature, for Sophie finds the means of writing a resistant subplot to the one he constructs. Sophie's letters, like those of Derby, describe how elements of their previous conflict resurface in their continuing battle. She figures the power Derby has over her in this second trial in terms strikingly similar to the circumstances of their first violent conflict: "Tugendlehre, Kenntnisse und Erfahrung sollen also an mir verloren sein, und ein niederträchtiger Feind soll die verdoppelte Gewalt haben, nicht nur mein äußerliches Ansehen von Glück wie ein Räuber ein Kleid von mir zu reißen, sondern meine Gesinnungen, die Übung meiner Pflichten, und die Liebe der Tugend selbst in meiner Seele zu zerstören?" (305–6).[81] To communicate the extent of Derby's brutality, Sophie employs the image of him tearing off her clothes as he did in the rape scene, robbing her of honor and happiness. The multiple meanings of "Ansehen" as appearance, reputation, and respect underscore the reference back to the false marriage and the losses she suffered through it. Here again, Sophie gradually reasserts her inner virtues as antidote to the violence Derby inflicts upon her. By writing to Emilia, and later in her journal, she affirms her own story of identity based on her moral principles.

The primacy of writing as a site of conflict, a form of power, and a means of asserting agency is dramatized repeatedly. As her paper runs out, Sophie resolves to stitch letters on cloth to continue writing. When Derby's cohort John appears with yet another twist of Derby's plot, Sophie refuses even to read Derby's letter. John must verbally communicate the choice that Derby, anticipating a relapse of Sophie's "earlier peculiarities" (317), offers to his victim. Should she refuse his offer of making her an honest woman through marriage, she will surely face death. For the first time, Derby accords her some active role in the construction of her story, while radically accentuating the poles "death" or "marriage" of the conventional heroine's plots. Yet again he is confounded by Sophie's refusal to accept the terms as he conceives them. Sophie chooses death over marriage with the villain, but she insistently rejects the role of the fallen heroine that death would imply. Even on what she believes to be her deathbed, she writes strongly against her nemesis, refuting his plot by dictating to Emilia which story to tell of her: "Sage: daß ich der Tugend getreu, aber unglücklich, in den Armen des bittersten Kummers, meine Seele . . . ihrem Schöpfer zurückgegeben . . . habe" (321).[82] The rebuttal of Derby's story extends to particulars; for example, Sophie reclaims the image of the blooming and then wilted rose to figure her own fate. Sophie also takes care that her letters and journal, the written documents of her resolute character, come into the possession of the priest so that she might be publicly vindicated. The resistance to Derby, the determination to remain true to her ideology of virtue and to affirm her own worth even in the midst of despair, is thus explicitly a textual resistance that seeks an audience.

Derby's voice in the novel, in contrast to Sophie's, becomes ever weaker as Sophie asserts herself. The last letter directly from Derby's pen is that in which he describes the kidnapping. Thereafter, as Sophie extricates herself from his plot, his voice is mediated and is finally fully silent. In a scene not presented through his own letters, but rather in a letter Seymour writes to Doktor T*, the ailing Derby tells Seymour and Rich of his actions and his remorse. Derby believes Sophie is dead. As a final rewriting of their story, he plans to erect an expensive tombstone "worauf die Beschreibung ihrer Tugenden und ihres Unglücks neben den Merkmalen seiner ewigen Reue aufgezeichnet werden soll" (326).[83] In their contest, Sophie has triumphed. Through her supposed death she has converted the villain to a celebration of her virtue. Moreover, Sophie has of course *not* died. She has symbolically enacted the role demanded by the plot of Derby's tale and brought that strand of her story to a close, only to resurface in the narrative, resurrected and purified of the disgrace Derby brought upon her.[84] Sophie's prediction that she will "enter into the company of the virtuous in transfigured form" (321) proves accurate for the narrative of *Sternheim*. The "angel" Sophie, as she is repeatedly apotheosized, fulfills, yet undermines, Derby's plot and then reappears transfigured in a new version of Seymour's tale. Hence it is not coincidental that Derby's voice becomes subordinate to that of his arch-rival Seymour.

Seymour himself, meanwhile, is so emotionally overwrought that his brother Rich must take over his narrative. The letters Rich writes to Doctor T* tell the two brothers' versions of Sophie's story, which are similar and parallel, yet fundamentally in conflict, since each man desires Sophie as wife. "Wenn es billig ist, daß der Stärkere nicht nur seine eigene volle Last, sondern auch die Bürde des Schwächern trage, so erfülle ich meine Pflicht, indem ich nicht nur unter dem gehäuften Maß meiner Empfindungen seufze, sondern auch das überströmende Gefühl von meinem Bruder zusammenfassen muß. Meine Briefe an Sie sind die Stütze, die meine Seele erleichtert" (335).[85] Rich as the stronger of the two has the capacity to adopt the roles of observer and chronicler, despite his personal desires. He renounces his love for Sophie and even agrees to speak to her of his brother's love, since Seymour insists, as Rich relates: "O Gott! — ich muß sie erhalten oder sterben — wer wird für mich reden: wer? Ich kann nichts sagen" (339).[86] The weak Seymour remains a passive spectator in his own drama. He is incapacitated by his passion while Rich, the most mature of Sophie's suitors, the least preoccupied with himself, and the most consistently attentive to her, reads the signs of her love for his brother and accepts the position as mere friend and intermediary between the lovers.

In mediating between Seymour and Sophie, Rich relies predominantly on their letters; here desires are repeatedly secreted, yet also disclosed, in written form. Their tangibility and accepted veracity allows the exchange of letters to perform the exchange of love. The role of letters in the courtship of Sophie and Seymour is reminiscent of the courtship of Sophie's parents — her mother fell in love with her father through his letters and her own writing served as outlet for her secret passion. Rich negotiates between these privileged material texts and their authors and thus becomes the conduit for the exchange of epistolary confirmation of character. When Sophie's papers come into Rich's hands he reads them with Seymour, and the expressive power of her writing that mirrors her soul once again conveys to Rich the extent of his brother's future happiness, as well as of his own renunciation. Rich then requests Seymour's letters be returned from Doctor T*, for they too must be read and must speak for him, as Sophie's letters speak for her: "Sie müssen gelesen werden, und für ihn reden" (339). Through Rich's orchestration of their reading, Sophie and Seymour are united as couple. Rich, then, not only advances their story toward resolution in marriage, but also brings their individual narratives together through his activities and status as "Super Reader," to borrow Janet Altman's term.[87] Rich, the philosophical nobleman appropriately characterized, in part, by his extensive library, often presents the privileged interpretations of stories about Sophie. Furthermore, in his role as compiler of the diverse narratives, Rich becomes what one might term, in analogy, the novel's "Super Writer": that is, the direct voices of Sophie and Seymour recede as their recorded, written voices demand renewed consideration within the story, and Sophie Sternheim's tale passes into Rich's narrative control.

The title figure of *Sternheim* herself underscores and confirms Rich's position as privileged observer/reader and as dominant voice/writer at the end of the novel. Like Rich, Sophie also gathers together the disparate narratives of the characters prominent in her adventures. Her own collected papers are ceremoniously handed over to Lord Rich and literally pass into his possession with the sanction of Sophie herself. The heroine's process of compilation and comparative reading of her own story — that is, of various narratives constructed around the common fabula — is traced in her last three letters. Simultaneously, each letter brings an aspect of her story to narrative resolution. Sophie marks these closures with the different signatures given each of the three letters: Madam Leidens, von Sternheim, and Lady Seymour. Each of her names corresponds to a plot told of her and each can be associated with one of the three rival suitors wishing to include himself most prominently in her story.

Sophie signs the first of her final three letters after her "resurrection" as "Madam Leidens." Here she tells Emilia what remains to be done in order to finally free herself of this name and identity as sufferer, adopted to signify her unhappy relation with Derby.[88] To restore her external image which Derby has indeed robbed from her, she must publicly exonerate herself from the doubts cast on her character. Not surprisingly, she attains this vindication through writing, as the emphasis on written documentation again reveals the paramount importance of narrative authority over her own tale for Sophie's successful self-assertion. Emilia receives excerpts from Sophie's journal that represent both figuratively and in their material form the harsh conditions the heroine suffered: "Die Auszüge von meinen mit Reißblei geschriebenen Papieren werden Ihnen zeigen, wie hart und dornigt der Weg war, welchen ich in dem letztern Jahre zu gehen hatte. Aber wie angenehm ist mir der Ausgang davon geworden, da ich von der Hand der leutseligsten Tugend daraus geführt wurde!" (330).[89] Sophie provides Emilia with a suggested reading of the materials she sends. Similarly, she wishes to influence the way her rescuers read her character. Lady Douglas and particularly Count Hopton must be convinced of Sophie's virtue. He reads Sophie's exterior with probing glances: "seine Blicke durchspürten zugleich meine ganze Person mit einem Ausdruck, als ob er abwägen wollte, ob ich mehr die Nachstellungen eines Liebhabers oder des Mitleidens einer tugendliebenden Dame verdiente" (331).[90] Sophie is concerned to provide the proper interpretation of her situation still open to conflicting views. She therefore creates a different text to read, a letter (although the addressee is in the same house) which counteracts the external appearance of her circumstances with a statement of her inner principles and clarifies the confusion about her relationship to little Lidy. She offers proof of her written testimony with reference to Lady Summers as character witness. "Ich . . . verlangte Schreubzeug und Papier. Ich schrieb den andern Tag der Lady die Erklärung ihrer Zweifel wegen der kleinen Lidy, und zeigte die Beweggründe an, warum ich mich des Kindes angenommen hätte" (332).[91] The written word is staged as the foundation of Sophie's story even when she speaks directly to Lady Douglas about her adventures. Sophie relies on the letters she wrote as an outline for their conversation, leafing through them with her listener and providing explanations of the contents. The materiality of the letters, as well as the reason for not presenting them as text to be read, are emphasized by the reminder that they are written in German, which Lady Douglas cannot read.

Sophie's next letter to Emilia is signed "von Sternheim" and opens with the basic question about her fortunes and identity that the novel *Sternheim* itself elaborates: "Was wird die Vorsicht noch aus mir machen?" (340).[92] The first news for Emilia is that of Derby's death, which has freed Sophie of the name "Leidens" completely, leaving her at a point of uncertain transition. She again takes on her paternal name as she reviews her adventures and weighs her future. Her considerations are guided by her literal reading of the competing versions of her story given by Derby and Seymour. She sends their letters, along with her own journal entries from Tweedale, to Emilia as documents of the two men's characters: "Hier, lesen Sie seine Briefe, mit denen vom Lord Derby, und senden Sie sie mir mit allen den meinen an Sie zurück" (340).[93] Sophie thus requests their return together with her own letters sent to Emilia. The transfer and exchange of letters grows with each mailing, and slowly the epistolary mosaic presented to the external readers of *Sternheim* takes physically contiguous shape within the fiction of the novel. Each primary character reads increasingly larger portions of the "History of Fräulein von Sternheim" and delivers an interpretation and a judgment about the continuation of the story, such as the one Sophie desires from Emilia: "Sie werden bei Derbys Briefen über den Mißbrauch von Witz, Tugend und Liebe schaudern. Hätte ich nicht selbst böse sein müssen, wenn ich seine Ränke hätte argwöhnen sollen? Was ist Seymours Herz dagegen? Ihren Rat hätte ich gewünscht, durch einen gemeinsamen Geist erhalten zu können" (340).[94] Sophie opts to marry Seymour and thereby to privilege his narrative projections of her story, but this choice will silence her own authorial voice.

Sophie's choice for Seymour's "heart" figuratively unites physical and spiritual love in their marriage. She thus embraces Seymour's story, fulfilling the role in which he cast her as virtue triumphant. Yet an ultimate interpretive reliance on the polarization between the stories of the two men Derby and Seymour and Sophie's position of choice between them, as she constructs it, is too facile a reading of *Sternheim* itself, for it obscures the complexities of Sophie's own written construction of her story, reducing the narrative of the heroine explored throughout the novel to that of a choice between two conventional plots. Moreover, as Sophie is well aware, Rich's role as third rival for her hand and heart complicates the final closure of marriage between Sophie and Seymour, as well as the narrative resolution of the novel. *Geschichte des Fräuleins von Sternheim* contains these threats to its ordered, ideological, metaphorical closure in part by integrally linking the fate of Sophie's own written tale and the position the figure Rich occupies.

Metaphoric closure with insistence on the selective axis of narrative, in Elizabeth MacArthur's terms,[95] is in constant tension with the metonymic movement propelled by ever-restless desires. Unfulfilled desire is most explicitly manifest in the character Lord Rich. The letters Rich writes attest to his constant struggle to repress his passions for Sophie. Sophie's penultimate letter, signed

"Sternheim," recounts the transference of his desire, which causes her apprehensions about her marriage decision, onto her writing. She tells Emilia:

> mit einer rührenden vielbedeutenden Miene trat er zu mir, küßte die Blätter meines Tagebuchs, drückte sie an seine Brust, und bat mich um Vergebung, eine Abschrift davon genommen zu haben, welche er aber mit der Urschrift in meine Gewalt geben. "Aber erlauben Sie mir," fuhr er fort, "Sie um dieses Urbild Ihrer Empfindungen zu bitten; lassen Sie, meine englische Freundin, mich diese Züge Ihrer Seele besitzen, und erhören Sie meinen Bruder Seymour." (341)[96]

Rich alone expressly accords Sophie authority over the narrative she has written of herself that he desires to possess. By granting him what he so desires, as the image of whom he desires, Sophie Sternheim in turn authorizes his reading of her story and his figurative control over the narrative that reflects *Sternheim*. The manuscript version Rich receives from her is markedly the "original" copy, figured pointedly by Rich as the "original image" of Sophie's soul. The mark of authenticity is again inscribed in the way the material narrative is figured within *Sternheim*. As with the letters between Seymour and Sophie, writing becomes the locus and containment of erotic desire. Yet this gift of friendship is one-sided rather than an exchange. Rich becomes the archivist of her self under the name Sternheim, while she becomes Lady Seymour: "Da war ich und weinte, und entschloss mich Lady Seymour zu werden" (342).[97] The signature "Sternheim" to this letter underscores the connections between Rich's possession of her story as Sternheim, told by the novel we read, and the effort to resolve the disruptive dynamics of his desire for the narrative as a whole.[98]

Sophie writes her final letter as "Lady Seymour." She recapitulates her ideological principles and imposes an unequivocal reading of her adventures as a triumphantly withstood trial of virtue. She paints a picture of familial happiness and virtue, in which marriage is the highest form of charity and piety. Sophie has apparently brought Seymour's plot for her to a satisfying close. Yet there are strains on the narrative's endings. It must disavow or conceal many of the qualities defining the figure of its heroine: her individual, unique character must be subordinated to the profile of the ideal, maternal Woman. Such resolution into the image of perfect virtue is problematic for the "genre of character" the novel has attempted to define and represent. A particularly disturbing force in the story of female virtue is sexuality, and elaborate measures are required to bring it under narrative control.

The Legitimation of Desire

Desire in *Sternheim* is regulated closely to insure clarity and stability between the public and the private spheres. The process of compiling and establishing the "History of Fräulein von Sternheim" within the novel entails mobility between these public and private realms. Sophie's virtue and character must be ascertained communally and publicly, and her personal letters serve as open textual basis for this recognition in which the external readers participate. However, once her reputation has been cleared and her marriage bond has been socially sanctioned, the heroine moves away from the public forum of her letters into the private sphere of the family. Her voice fades into the tableau painted by Lord Rich in the final letter of the novel. Her distinction from the materiality of the letters that Rich took as an image of herself is thereby underscored: "ihre schönen Briefe sind nicht sie selbst" (347).[99] *Sternheim* as narrative possession of Rich and the external readers is clearly marked as separate from Lady Seymour as Seymour's wife, inscribed in her proper familial realm. Thus the heroine is increasingly distanced from the readers at the end of the novel. Her position in a private sphere is emphasized as her roles of wife and mother are extolled.

At the end of the novel Sophie is hailed by Rich as the sanctified mother she has always sought to become. An increasingly abstract paragon of virtue, Sophie merges with the ghostly image of her mother she has long idolized. She is strikingly disembodied. The figuration of her purity rests on the subordination of her body and of sexuality, even as the power of the image is measured by the strength of erotic passion it evokes in the male observers. Rich leaves the readers with this image of the family: "Mein Bruder ist der beste Ehemann und würdigste Gebieter von etlichen hundert Untertanen geworden; Seligkeit ist in seinem Gesichte, wenn er seinen Sohn, an der Brust der besten Frau, Tugend einsaugen sieht; und jeder Tag nimmt etwas von dem lodernden Feuer hinweg, welches in alle seine Empfindungen gedrungen wäre" (348–49).[100] The signs of Sophie's female body are simultaneously featured and desexualized through abstraction: her son is nourished at her breasts by her virtue. Seymour's desires have found a channel

in the family unit, while Rich's passion, also responding to Sophie
as mother, has no legitimate place: "Auf unserer Rückreise wurde
sie Mutter; — und was für eine Mutter! O Doktor! ich hätte mehr,
viel mehr als Mensch sein müssen; wenn der Wunsch, sie zu meiner
Gattin, zu der Mutter meiner Kinder zu haben, nicht tausendmal
in meinem Herzen entstanden wäre!" (347).[101] Male desires repeatedly serve this function in the text of substantiating Sophie's
virtuous character, which must, however, be figured as spiritual.
One of the struggles between the rivals for the possession of
Sophie (a struggle motivating much of *Sternheim's* overall narrative
as well as the individual narratives within it) is precisely the contest
to conjure the ghostly Sophie into material form to the satisfaction
of their desires. Derby's villainy stemmed from the focus and insistence on the primacy of Sophie's body, while her resistance relied on transforming the figures of the body into spiritual signs and
in separating her virtue from her physical fate of rape. Seymour desired to see Sophie enact dramatically his notion of virtue, but
Sophie crossed his plot by subordinating external appearances to
inner ideology and motivations, the physical to the spiritual. The
"magic sympathy" linking the sentimental couple tacitly incorporates the physical desire into a spiritual ideology. Rich's narratives
approximately figure Sophie as the spiritually pure ideal she wished
to become, as "female angel," yet he suffers from being unable to
possess this unattainable, eroticized image. Her material narratives
are all he can hold of her and these do not pacify his mature masculine desire — rather, they are the sign of the unbridgeable distance between intangible figuration and Sophie's "real self."

The children in *Sternheim* are the central vehicle for acknowl-
edging sexuality and physical desire which, to be legitimate, must
be articulated through the figurative denial of Sophie's erotic corporeity. They are metaphorical proof of the masculine desire for
Sophie which validates her character, as well as signs of her own
sexuality. Yet they allow for Sophie's dissociation from her physical
self even in the roles of abused heroine and virtuous mother most
dependent upon it, for the children represent Sophie's female body
while appearing as figures distinct from her. Further, the three
children in *Sternheim* are the figurative resolutions of the plots
shaped by the three men's desires competing for Sophie.

The adoption of Derby's daughter Lidy, which, for Sophie, marks
the "recovery of my soul" (309), figures doubly for her self-under-

standing. Lidy is the embodiment of Derby's illicit desire and, by association, of Sophie's humiliation. Her physical humiliation is, by extension, that of women in general reduced to the body. Derby's narrative of his many conquests underscores the iterative nature of this structure and the interchangeability of the women. Lidy is Nancy's child but, since fathered by Derby, stands for his sexual exploitation generally, to which Sophie was also subject. Yet Lidy also represents the "unhappy innocence" that Sophie nurtures in herself (310–11). Sophie's own childlike innocence is again remarked in her garb — at the time of the kidnapping she wore "a pure white linen dress" (312). Sophie's insistence on charity as the primary virtue finds expression in her relation to the child who is a sign of her sexual transgression. By taking Lidy into her care, Sophie recasts the script Derby's desire would force upon her, replacing virtue understood only as chastity with her conception of virtue as charity.

While the offspring of proscribed desire is figured as female, the product of legitimate union is male. The first son Sophie bears to Seymour affirms their marriage and constitutes a harmonious family unit. Sexuality is contained in the marriage: Seymour's desire finds expression through fatherhood and Sophie's female sexuality and creative power is brought safely under patriarchal control. However, the image of Sophie as mother inflames Rich's passion anew and thereby threatens the stability of the family. His desire must also find expression and material shape. The second son of Sophie and Seymour is the acknowledgment of this desire as legitimate and is symbolically fathered by Rich. The child's presence enables Rich to possess his beloved Sophie, for he bears the "features of his mother — this similarity brings me great happiness" (347). The child's presence moderates Rich's passions: "Dieses Kind ist die Stütze meiner Vernunft und meiner Ruhe geworden" (348).[102] Finally, as "son of his heart" (344) he bears Rich's name. The final tableau of this extended family has been read as a "feminine utopia" and a matriarchal realm in which the male rivalry for the woman is dissipated and patrilineal succession is "softened,"[103] but the constellations offered at the end of the novel appear more problematic than this reading allows. The demand for patrilineal succession as sign of the male claim to the mother is not suspended, but is indeed doubled, revealing the novel's controlled, but not resolved, conflicts.

There is yet another child/father pair to be examined in the discussion of the novel, involving possession, representation of friendship and desire, and the image of model motherhood as sign of patriarchal control over female creativity. As discussed above, the novel itself is stylized as the female child of its author. This child also manifests her mother's features, but bears the patronymic of its symbolic father Wieland on its title page. The circulation and transference of desires and the symbolic importance of male potency at the origin of female creativity is repeatedly marked in Wieland's preface through references to the "real" children and family spheres of the novel's two "parents," while the familial sphere is invoked to mitigate the public appearance of female productivity. Wieland wishes to impart the spirit of Sophie Sternheim to his own daughter Sophie. La Roche is implicated in the parenting of Wieland's "real" child as well; she is called "unsre[r] kleine[n] Sophie (denn Sie sind so gütig, sie auch die Ihrige zu nennen)" (11).[104] The pretext of *Sternheim's* narrative birth is overdetermined and integrally related to concerns about female virtue, precariously situated on the border between private and public realms and defined through control of female sexuality and, by implication, of female creativity. The texts of Sophie Sternheim's story rest "safely," in the end, in the possessive male editorial hands of Lord Rich and of Wieland and are publicly legitimized through their ability to attract and hold the masculine desires of these critical readers.[105]

While the endings of *Sternheim* elide narrative possibilities imputed to its heroine during the development of her story and seem to reject the implications of social and narrative mobility the protagonist explored in her own writing, the novel does incorporate and stage these conflicts as one crucial basis of its narrative dynamics. The epistolary form of *Sternheim,* so conducive to a focus on writing and reading, on narrative communication, and on multiperspectivism, resists the ideological metaphoric closure of the novel in favor of a metonymic, open structure. As such it features issues of agency, of who writes, reads, and interprets according to disparate ideological grids, ones that are critical to the intersections of gender and genre.[106] If the power of conventional plots is reaffirmed in the closure(s) of the novel, the struggle to construct alternate scripts of female identity remains fundamental to the generic experiments and new character of Sophie Sternheim.

5: Narrating Nothing: Maria Anna Sagar's *Karolinens Tagebuch ohne ausserordentliche Handlungen, oder gerade so viel als gar keine*

> O was wird das für eine matte Geschichte von uns beyden wer-
> den? Siehe in zwei Zeilen kann man unsere ganze Begebenheiten
> bringen. Es wird heißen: Nanette und Karoline zwey Schwestern
> von ehrlichen Aeltern sind, die eine Anno 1761, die andere Anno
> 1763 geboren worden, haben gegessen und getrunken, sind
> groß gewachsen, haben beyde an einem Tag Anno 1771 gehey-
> rathet, und sind Anno — das weis ich jezt noch nicht, gestorben.[1]

KAROLINE, THE TITLE FIGURE OF Maria Anna Sagar's novel *Karolinens Tagebuch ohne ausserordentliche Handlungen, oder gerade so viel als gar keine* (1774), despairingly wonders how the few events of a woman's life can possibly be narrated as a compelling story. After writing three hundred pages of a "journal" for herself and for an audience, she still suspects that the sole aspects of the tale to be told about her, rather than by her, remain the punctual facts of birth and parentage, maturation, marriage, and death. The extant biographical information about Karoline's author prove these suspicions about how female identity is construed to be justified. Maria Anna Sagar, the daughter of the government official Roskoschny [Rozkosny], was born in Prague on July 24, 1727. She married the playwright and "Prager Schloß-hauptmann" Johann Sagar. She died on the fourth of June, 1805, in Vienna.[2] *Karolinens Tagebuch* is the second of Maria Anna Sagar's two novels published in Prague with the publishing house Wolfgang Gerle. Her first novel, *Die verwechselten Töchter* (The Switched Daughters), appeared the same year as Sophie von La Roche's *Sternheim,* in 1771.

Sagar's work stands at the nascence of the German feminocentric novel, yet has been almost fully forgotten.[3] Her two novels tell richer stories of female identity than that told of her.[4] Both are remarkable in their self-assurance and their humor, contradicting notions of female authorship in the eighteenth century shaped by the dominance of La Roche in literary history. Like La Roche, Sagar had to contend with the constrictions placed on the woman writer and with dominant social constructions of femininity. And like La Roche, Sagar claimed a feminine authority for her texts by citing conventional configurations of femininity. Sagar, however, engaged these social and aesthetic issues in diametric opposition to sentimental ideology. *Karolinens Tagebuch* directly challenges the genre of the sentimental novel and its claim to moral and literary authority over a female audience by incorporating and critiquing its conventions. Sagar's second novel in particular offers an alternative version of the relations between literary authority and female authorship: it self-assuredly proclaims its feminocentric bias while exploring questions of feminine subjectivity in tandem with narrative conventions and the activity of writing as a woman.

Metafictional considerations of the nexus of genre and gender, as mutually determining forces, are at the center of *Karolinens Tagebuch*. Writing, specifically authorship of novels, is established as a commonality between the author, her heroine Karoline, and the two heroines of the novel that Karoline writes.[5] The structure of *mise en abyme* mirrors and multiplies the activity of writing, while also building on the often iterated figurations of writing as mirror. The mirror is evoked as contradictory agent for the constitution of feminine identities. It can be both corrective tool and dangerous incentive to female vanity, but it also provides the frame for experimentation with multiple images and roles. Gendered role playing is a fundamental narrative strategy in *Karolinens Tagebuch*. Thematically it underscores how posturing in public and private realms is a measure of identity and how the roles demanded in specific situations are social constructs. Faithful performance of these roles, with emphatic attention to their demands and contours as prescriptions, can paradoxically allow the actors freedom to circumvent their limitations. In terms of poetics, role playing is the basis of fictional experimentation and in particular expands the authorial possibilities of the woman writer. It entails a doubleness which is exploited openly as a strategy of remaining irreproachable while traversing restricted terrain. The novel *Karolinens Tagebuch*, in which such extravagant narrative exploration takes place, is described by the author as an empty space which, like the mirror, allows for ever-changing reflections.

The defining frame for writing is figured in the preface to the novel through one recurrent image Woman sees of herself in the cultural mirror: the text is "nothing." The preface offers a stark contrast to Wieland's presentation of La Roche's novel. Here the anonymous female author assertively introduces her own work to her audience, playing with expectations of female authorship. After examining Sagar's preface, I will turn to Karoline who, as writing heroine, will be the focus of this inquiry into the novel's metafiction. An analysis of Karoline's novels, shaped by gothic and sentimental conventions, will be followed by a discussion of Karoline's multifaceted profile as an author. Karoline not only writes novels; she also writes about herself as writer and about her maturation and expected marriage to Karl. These two plots in her journal are mutually threatening yet complementary, as both circle issues of identity and the forces which shape it. The conflicts between the strands of Karoline's narrative, as well as between the generic conventions offered in the sentimental novel and the alternative Sagar presents, become most clear in the novel's dilemmas of closure, with which my discussion of *Karolinens Tagebuch* will end.

Defining the "Nothing" of the Novel

Maria Anna Sagar — or rather her authorial persona — is the first in the progression of female writers introduced in *Karolinens Tagebuch*. In the preface, she stakes out her position as author, defining a space from which her voice can claim authority. The preface fulfills many familiar functions: it is an authorial legitimation for novel writing, a poetic program, an introduction to the main text, and an advertisement for it. Sagar alludes to the standard topoi of preface writing without accepting their authority and she independently outlines the contours of her own literary enterprise with humor and spirit. Introducing a work she unabashedly claims as her own, rather than drawing on a manuscript fiction or other distanced editorial stance, she counters the proscriptions against female authorship and establishes an unassailable defense for her expression by cleverly delineating, with solid boundaries, a space she declares to be empty. "Nichts," "nothing" becomes the central figure for her narrative.[6]

Sagar proclaims the emptiness of her narrative in the full title of the novel, *Karolinens Tagebuch, ohne ausserordentliche Handlungen oder gerade so viel als gar keine*. This assertion of insignificance is further explicated at the outset of the preface, as she captures and guides the attention of her readers:

> Wie meine lieben Leserinnen, Sie haben das Titelblatt gelesen, und wollen doch im dem Buche noch weiter umblättern; hat es sie nicht gewarnet, das Werkchen gleich wieder wegzulegen; wollen sie mit Nichts — und was ist ein Tagebuch ohne ausserordentliche Handlungen anderst — ihre Zeit versplittern? Ich sage Ihnen noch einmal, es ist Nichts. Was können Sie sich von einem böhmischen Frauenzimmer versprechen; wie kann die nur auf den Gedanken verfallen ein Buch zu schreiben. Was kann es seyn, als . . ."[7] (i)

The initial questioning admonition to the female readers refers first of all to the specific novel at hand — the title suggests that the particular work is unexceptional and therefore a waste of time. The prejudices that reading novels in general is a frivolous activity and that women often waste their time this way also reverberate in the warning. Rather than engaging moralistic arguments for and against the genre to defend her writing (as occurs in *Sternheim*), the female author draws on topoi of female self-disparagement to deflect objections against her text, insisting on "nothing" as its defining quality and essence. The *Nichts* emphasized in the preface circumscribes central dilemmas of female authorship which surface throughout the novel: concerns of personal and literary virtue; the relations between gender and literary genre and style; the source of narrative authority. It is offered as a woman's journal, a form which modestly cedes claim to literary value. As one assumes from the title, it records an uneventful life. Yet events, usually the supporting structure of entertaining narrative, are what appeal to readers. The text defines itself initially by what it is not, it is uneventful, it is not a man's life. The "nothing" of content thus joins the "nothing" of form. The third central issue addressed by the "nothing" is the dilemma of authority for the marginalized female, Bohemian author.[8] What, Sagar insists, what can one expect from a woman who lights on the absurd idea of writing a book?

The author's apparent modesty and candid warnings prove to be a ploy. The intimated answer to the last question, "Was kann es seyn als . . ." reiterates the claim of "nothing" graphically with the ellipsis, but thereby also transposes the valuation of that lack. While the answer is not provided, the missing information is secreted in the punctuation and this secret becomes the appeal of the text for the readers. Insistence on the obvious reading of the title and the initial authorial claims has the effect of guiding the readers to skepticism and curiosity, to a reconsideration of the overt message and a search for the subtext. Thus, the insistence on "nothing" is revealed to be an effective advertising strategy designed to arouse feminine curiosity about precisely the nothing of the text:

> Doch gefällt Ihnen vielleicht meine Offenherzigkeit? Nu . . . es kann seyn, daß manches auswärtige Frauenzimmer die Leser vor ihrem Werkchen — wäre es auch noch so unbedeutend, nicht so aufrichtig warnen würde, wie ich; vielleicht aber kenne ich auch mein Geschlecht besser, und verstehe es, ihre Neugier zu reizen: so schliesse ich nach mir selbst. Denn je mehr man mich von etwas abhält, desto begieriger bin ich darauf. Aber nur still! das bleibt unter uns Frauenzimmer im Vertrauen gesagt.[9] (i–ii)

Sagar's authorial persona is self-assured about her knowledge of her female readers and reformulates her national identity from a sign of provincialism to one of positive particularity. She sets herself up as a female author who employs her subjective, personal, and therefore authoritative knowledge of feminine traits to engage and captivate the intended female audience.[10] Thus Sagar offers her work, through the introduction in the preface, as a novel by a woman for women. She develops the figure of "nothing," used disparagingly by others to define women, into a secret, positive foundation for this genre.

The preface reveals a further characteristic of Sagar's writing strategy in her feminocentric novel: it discloses how playfulness with multiple feminine roles informs her authorial stance. Sagar fulfills the requisite clause of feminine demureness about her work and lauds herself on her ingenuousness about its failings. Yet she refers to a further trait defined as feminine, curiosity, to unveil the hidden motive behind her initial self-fashioning, thus exposing her tactical duplicity as frankly as she declared her literary incompetence. The dual authorial roles rely on a split between general wisdom and specifically feminine insights into feminine characteristics. This second knowledge is conspiratorial and confidential; it is figured as a constituent of female identity to be guarded by insiders. By adopting multiple roles simultaneously, Sagar creates the space within which she may write and defines it as both empty and brimming with secret significance. She adopts feminine roles, but refuses to be trapped within their strictures and instead takes the liberty of moving fluidly between them.

The Writing Heroine Karoline

Karolinens Tagebuch, not surprisingly, places Karoline's identity at its center. Sagar's work considers the forging of a female self which must negotiate multiple expectations of femininity and it links this process with concerns of textual production: the novel concentrates primarily and frankly on writing as a woman. The spirited heroine Karoline, like the authorial persona presented in the preface, must contend with prejudice against female authorship. Thus her initial task is to justify her activity of writing, the fiction which engenders Sagar's novel. Its title already serves as a character reference for the heroine. Her uneventful life implies her virtue and the genre "journal" gives her writing a shape appropriate to (feminine) literary propriety. The authorial pose Karoline first adopts is confessional. She casts her project as one of writing an open, honest account of her ordinary life with the aim of self-scrutiny and self-improvement. This first-person narrative form in its stated function was one granted to women writers in the eighteenth century, since it modestly claimed knowledge of and significance only for a limited and private sphere.

And yet, this humble genre also disquietingly bore within it the danger of unseemly self-absorption. As journal author, Karoline must walk the tightrope between requirements of female modesty and suspicions of female vanity. She must discover a way to write "I" self-critically, unassumingly, while subtly documenting and asserting her virtue, the necessary condition for approbation of her writing. Karoline cleverly attends to potential reproaches of narcissism by markedly distancing her writing from expressions of female vanity. She explains and justifies her desire to write by identifying it as an alternative to idle preening in front of the mirror: "Nur werfe mir nicht vor, daß ich so viel Papier und Zeit verderbe: denn es dünkt mir doch, daß ich besser daran thue, als wenn ich die leeren Stunden vor dem Spiegel zubrächte, um zu forschen, welcher Blick, oder welche Stellung mir besser lassen? Zu dem weist du ja, daß meine meiste Arbeit nur in nichts bedeutenden Knötchenmachen bestehet, wobey ich wieder Zwirn oder Seide statt des Papiers verderbe, ohne doch die Zeit nützlicher angewendet zu haben" (6–7).[11] Karoline counters the anticipated reproach that writing is itself a waste of time with a double gesture of parallelism. She degrades her typical occupations with which writing is competing as themselves insignificant, and she raises the practice of writing to the same status of "work" and legitimacy as her other feminine tasks. By figuring her writing as "making knots signifying nothing" she repeats the preface's show of belittling female writing as insignificant while drawing on this image to assert and justify her writing and its style as properly feminine. Moreover, writing as tenable activity is contrasted with frivolous feminine faults. The emptiness in her life, the lack of "extraordinary events," threatens to misguide her towards fascination with the mirror and her own image.[12] Her writing, although admittedly focused on her self, is presented as a mode of distracting her from this "I" she might begin to value too highly. Writing as mirror of the soul is thus presented as an activity which will prevent her delight in vain reflections.

Further criticism of impropriety in Karoline's writing is deflected by breaking with the formal self-reference of the private journal. Her "journal" takes on communicative, epistolary form as Karoline addresses her writing to her sister Nanette and, secondarily, to her "writing-master" Cyrilli. Ostensibly the epistolary form is more adequate to Karoline's virtuous desire for moral guidance from these two authorities, and it highlights her touted sincerity and candor. This assertion stresses the function of epistolarity as direct documentation of character and its proximity to the journal, while countering suspicions of secretive seclusion. Karoline, in other words, amends the questionable moments of the journal form and sketches her writing project as a cooperative and communicative enterprise. Yet a second and ultimately more important aspect of the epistolary form, namely its focus on the acts of writing and reading, soon takes center stage: through letters, Karoline gains an audience for her texts.[13] Karoline requests a response from her readers to the tone as well as the content of individual letters and articulates her desire to adjust her style according to her critics' counsel. Her readers accept their task as audience and sanction her efforts; they, and with them the external readers, are thus implicated in the responsibility for her resulting text.

There are two, gendered poles in the readership Karoline addresses. The primary intended reader is her older and wiser sister. The second implied reader is Cyrilli, the figure of male authority standing watch in the background over the potentially threatening written exchange between women.[14] "Mein Richter eine liebvolle Schwester; mein Oberrichter unser sanftmüthiger Schreibemeister!" Karoline exclaims (10).[15] A split readership defined along gender lines, also seen in *Sternheim*, is a typical trait of the eighteenth-century German female-authored feminocentric novel.[16] However, the apparent centrality of the patriarchal hierarchy established here is deceptive.[17] Although Cyrilli does remain a controlling instance in the background, it is the loving sister Nanette who occupies the position of the most privileged reader. Cyrilli's critical approval of Karoline's narrative is imperative for her writing project, and his expectations and standards must be met by her as author. Yet Nanette's specifically feminine concerns, expectations, and shared experience with Karoline, as well as her entertainment, prove the most important criteria shaping Karoline's multiple narratives.

Karoline parades honesty as a main feature of her writing addressed to herself (as journal) and her sister (as letters). Karoline insists that she has no secrets, for she trusts in the good-natured forgiveness of her negligible moral and literary faults by her judges: "Was können die zwey Leute nicht ihrem Günstling alles verzeihen?" (10).[18] Nanette, however, in her sole letter of *Karolinens Tagebuch,* imposes a limitation of this honesty as the very condition upon which she will accept Karoline's activity of writing. Even though the sphere Karoline claims to address is both private and feminine, Nanette insists on the necessity of protecting it and warns her sister against revealing the secret essence of this realm to outsiders. In her admonition, Nanette draws on the figure of "nothing" presented in the preface to denote this shared female knowledge: "Ich lege es dir so gar im Namen unseres ganzen Geschlechts auf, gewisse uns allen gemeine Sächelchen hinter eine Falte zu schieben, damit man nicht in deinem ganz offenen Herzen das wichtige Nichts des gesammten Frauenzimmers entdecke, sonst sollst du auch an mir eine eben so unerbittliche Richterin finden, als ich jezt noch bin Deine wohlmeinende Schwester" (9–10).[19] The female readers and writers become a conspiratorial community protecting the precious "nothing" which is common to all women. It must remain unnamed, unspecified and hidden, yet understood as the essence of womankind. Karoline's exploration of female identity must proceed without naming or revealing its core.

The patriarchal paradigm of femaleness and femininity as deficiency and lack is called upon in figuring women's essential qualities as "nothing."[20] Women's physical and intellectual essence was thought to be biologically determined as the lack of male and masculine traits.[21] The prescriptions of ideal femininity relied on either maintaining or overcoming these female deficiencies. The defining basis of woman's virtue was to safeguard her "emptiness" — chastity and innocence, her lack of sexual experience and lack of knowledge. In Nanette's exhortation, this paradigm of male dominance and superiority over women and the prohibition on (women's) articulations of sexuality is transformed to designate precisely a realm which defies male control. "Nothing" — still following the pattern of female virtue as virginity — is a possession to be well guarded. Yet contrary to the notion of female virtue as innocence and ignorance, it is emphatically transformed from nothing into something, into a positive entity: a specifically female knowledge to be kept secret, inaccessible to men.

The conflation of "nothing" with the promise of a secret knowledge hidden in the text develops the connection between nothing and secrecy from the preface. Nanette's admonishment to her younger sister alerts the initiated, female readers of *Karolinens Tagebuch* to look for the substance of that secret banned from its pages which are offered as empty.[22] Karoline as author faces a twofold task of pleasing both her judges, the male authorities represented by Cyrilli and the women readers represented by her sister. Her text must be open, honest and guileless; it must bare (and assert) its insignificance to be acceptable women's writing for the male critics and it must assuage male fears of a feminine realm which eludes male control. Yet to be successful for a female audience, it must refuse to yield to men the secret essence of the "nothing" it proclaims. The "nothing" thus delineated captures and outlines dilemmas of female authorship at the outset of the feminocentric novel(s) of *Karolinens Tagebuch:* if Karoline's writing is to be credible, virtuous, and legitimate in the eyes of her diverse audiences, a "nothing" defined doubly along gender lines must be the center of her text.

Like Sagar's authorial persona of the preface, Karoline celebrates her duplicity openly and with increasing pride as the text develops; she too enacts multiple authorial roles and moves freely between them. Karoline initially presents herself as the docile journal writer and capricious young woman addressing her more sedate sister. Yet Karoline's own life seems unlikely to entertain her readers and engender the praise for her writing she truly seeks. Therefore, she invents a fiction fashioned on sentimental and gothic novel conventions. Karoline employs an obvious manuscript fiction, itself a constant in the genre she imitates, to justify her novelistic adventure story of a virtuous heroine. Posing as scribe, which allows her to pursue her literary ambitions, she relates the adventures of Eleonora Lusani, who in turn relates the story of a certain duchess. Karoline frames this tale with her own comments on the story and with other segments of her journal. She thus simultaneously takes on the position of passive scribe, active literary critic, novelist, and indeed, as first person narrator, of the protagonist Eleonora herself, as well as of whimsical journal writer.

Karoline thus creates and delineates her relationship to her audience at the outset of her work. She expressly requests *written* response to her own writing, placing value on the letters' materiality. Yet her readers are not only, or even primarily, partners in written communicative exchange — most crucial is their participation as readers of her narrative. They are explicitly to stand judge over her writing, over its quality as well as its message. Karoline's letters to Nanette alternately tell her own story — her journal — and the tales of her heroines told from Eleonora's perspective. Karoline's own story has two central strands at once parallel and mutually threatening: her maturation from girl to woman, marked by marriage and the new role of wife, and her development as author. Although Karoline emphasizes the discrepancies between her own life and the stories she creates, her fictions clearly facilitate her experimentation with various guises and models of femininity. As she writes her heroines Eleonora and Henriette from girlhood to womanhood, she explores what she cannot write expressly in her own tale of maturation. The embedded texts cite various models of female authorship and feminine narrative available in the 1770s but also take issue with them as adequate literary forms in which to address dilemmas of feminine identity and narrative authority.

Stories of Silence: The Adventures of Eleonora Lusani

The manuscript fiction which officially covers (for) Karoline's authorship of Eleonora's story shifts the burden of defending the narrative style of Eleonora's letters, as well as her moral character, onto the figure herself. An eighteenth-century novel heroine, generally, is ethically suspect, but a heroine who tells her own tale is particularly so. This predicament, similarly faced by Hyacinthe in Wieland's *Don Sylvio,* is promptly addressed in Eleonora's introduction to her own adventures, in the first "letter" to Karoline:

> Wie ungereimt, wirst du vielleicht denken, vielleicht auch zweifeln, wie es möglich sey, daß ein Mädchen, in so jungen Jahren, bey einer so ziemlichen Denkungsart, unter der Aufsicht und dem Schuz einer vernünftig- und tugendhaften Mutter, auf Abentheuer gerathen könne. . . . ja noch befrage ich mich oft, ob es wirklich wahr seye, daß ich bey meinem kaum entwickelten Alter die jenige Romanenheldin bin, deren Begebenheit ich dir hier beschreibe. Jezt höre mir zu: . . .[23] (43–44)

"Wie ungereimt" (how incongruous), she exclaims. The categories of poetics and propriety intersect as interdiction against Eleonora's leading role in her own narrative. Eleonora relies on the topos of being an unlikely "novel heroine" as her first line of defense. Novels stand here for implausibility; she insists that, in contrast, *her* story as told in letters to her friend Karoline, is true. Thus both manuscript fiction and epistolary genre are called upon in the adventures of Eleonora Lusani as conventional topoi of authenticity and feminine narrative virtue.

The following account which Karoline ascribes to Eleonora details the process of becoming such a novel heroine. Unlike the heroes of the adventure novel or the Bildungsroman, whose inner development to maturity and social integration is shaped through a series of experiences they encounter on their wanderings through foreign spheres, the heroine's inner development and maturation must occur without endangering the prospects of her successful socialization, that is, without tainting her virtue through experience. Karoline protects her heroine's reputation while both following and satirizing the model of the sentimental novel by constructing an isolated, buffered, and specifically feminine sphere as the arena of her inner adventures. Eleonora's experiences are pointedly the adventures of non-adventure. Always a model daughter, Eleonora is torn violently and inexplicably from the protection of her mother's arms and the comfort of her sister's company and is sequestered in an remote villa, where a woman of astounding beauty and aura assures her she is safe. She is kidnapped by women in order to protect her from a similar fate of kidnapping at the hands of a dastardly man who would threaten her chastity and virtue. She must endure being wrenched by women from her familiar, secure, feminine realm of sister and mother in order to escape a forced separation and alienation from this realm, placing her under male dominance. The central feature of Eleonora's trials is the need to survive nothingness: absolute isolation, absolute ignorance, and, in the crucial test, absolute silence and solitude. Eleonora comforts herself with reading, imagining herself to be a novel heroine. Her sole companion, the mysterious duchess who calls herself Fani, educates her in the virtues of the sentimental heroine — primarily unquestioning submission, obedience, and self-denial — and warns her particularly against the fault of vanity. Eleonora has nothing on which to ground her experiences; nothing, that is, but lack. She is secluded in a labyrinthine house in a place unknown to her, isolated from the outside world, from her family, from nearly all companionship. All information about her situation is withheld from her. The captivity and adventures of Karoline's heroine Eleonora delimit new spaces of emptiness in which to explore constructions of feminine identity defined as nothingness.

Eleonora's initial response to the brutal kidnapping is a proud, self-assured appeal to her rights and her integrity: "ich will wissen, warum ich hier seyn muß, und wer sich unterstehet, mir als einer freygebohrenen Person Gewalt anzuthun? und warum man mich meiner Mutter entrissen, die allein, nach Gott, das Recht hat mich mit Zwang zu behandeln? Ich will doch nicht vermuthen, daß man hier keine Gesäze kennet?" (64–65).[24] Her independent sense of self is offended by the treatment she is receiving, and rightly so. But instead of answers, she is admonished to stop asking. The laws governing her have changed. Now she may not ask questions, nor may she express her fears, her loneliness, or her curiosity about her own situation. Her kidnapper tells her stories to distract her from her own misery, and gradually Eleonora resigns herself to her fate: "ich ergab mich endlich etwas ruhiger in mein Schicksal; denn sie hatte so was einnehmendes an sich, woraus Erziehung, Belesenheit mit den reizendesten Tugenden vereinigt hervorschimmerten, daß man ihr nicht widersprechen konnte" (74).[25] The duchess embodies the silent, virtuous, modest feminine authority considered "proper" according to eighteenth-century mores. She radiates a comforting feminine aura, even without words or information, which reassures Eleonora and leads her to trust her kidnapper as a substitute mother, the epitome of female authority. Obedient daughter that she is, Eleonora soon strives to win the approval of the duchess.

Even after Eleonora accustoms herself to the lonely existence in the labyrinthine house, she must endure yet another test of her ability to accept powerlessness. This test is framed precisely as a test of feminine virtue (on which Eleonora prides herself). She is to lose Fani's companionship for an unspecified period of time, "a few days . . . eight days at the most" (104), during which she may not speak or interact with anybody. She has already learned to swallow her questions and her demands, and has become docile and obedient to the duchess. But this is not yet enough: her substitute mother now also abandons her with no explanations, and imposes the immense burden of total isolation and silence. Eleonora is naturally distraught and fearful: "Aber mein Gott Frau Fani! Was werde ich denn hier alleine und sprachlos machen?" (104–5).[26] Fani frames this further trial of lack as one honing feminine virtues of silence: "Nun Fräulein Eleonora, versuchen sie einmal das Vorurtheil, das alles Frauenzimmer ohne Ausnahm geschwäzig seye, und beym Mangel an Gelegenheit dazu, nicht leben könne, zu Schanden zu machen" (105).[27] The requirement of silence in spite of an innate need to talk is presented as an elemental, existential conflict. The sinister suggestion, and certainly Eleonora's fear, is that she indeed will *not* be able to live in total silence and isolation, that her very nature makes this impossible. The task she faces, then, is to overcome what is defined as female nature and to prove through her exceptional character that another feminine identity is possible.[28] The new identity envisioned, however, is founded centrally on self-denial and on severing all extant connections from the female realm. The virtue of silence implies not only no chatter, but also a total lack of communication and a female identity defined in opposition to itself, as anomaly from all other women. Eleonora recognizes this implication. She is fully prepared to fulfill her own desires for female community at the risk of not being considered a paragon of virtue, if only her isolation could be broken thereby and her happiness returned: "ich gestund ihr vielmehr frey, daß ich lieber in den Armen meiner Mama und Schwester schwäzen, als diesen Ruhm verdienen wollte" (106).[29] Unfortunately for Eleonora, this is not an option; she is abandoned by her jailer friend and is fully alone.

Eleonora's story is thus one of violently enforced ignorance about her fate, silencing, and disempowerment.[30] The process of accepting these conditions is the test of her virtue and proper femininity. To mature from girl under the protection of her mother to individual — if not independent — woman she must experience and endure powerlessness and learn to embrace proudly this lack as a definition of the self. Her new identity lies, then, in bravely suffering the tests of nothingness as feminine virtue. Karoline, in contrast, refuses to be silenced as Eleonora is in her tale. Instead, she and her author Sagar articulate the burdens of such enforced silence, and let the fictional Eleonora also do so after having survived the trial.

Eleonora's maturation entails a rupture from the female community which had provided protection from the outside, masculine world and a primary sense of her identity as dutiful and loved daughter. The event of her kidnapping demonstrated the fragility of the mother, who was unable to protect Eleonora. Her substitute mother, the last bond to the female realm, also abandons her. Yet after this rending, Eleonora becomes privy to the knowledge that she is not quite as cut off from the other women as she had feared. She becomes part of a new female community, larger than the familial sphere and defined as "other" to masculinity. In Eleonora's enforced isolation during the absence of the duchess, she is suddenly, unexpectedly confronted with a man in the house, the embodiment of a figure whose portrait hangs on the wall. This apparition terrifies her; she screams and he disappears, like a ghost. The female servants, otherwise invisible beings, rally to her cries and calls, appearing with expressively worried looks in their eyes, if not with words of comfort. Despite their silence and limited means of communication, Eleonora is enormously relieved at their mere presence: "O wie froh war ich, mich wieder von Menschen, und zwar von meinem Geschlecht umgeben zu sehen; wir sahen einander wie 4 stumme Bildsäulen an" (110).[31] Eleonora is rewarded for her successful completion of the trial of silence and isolation with an even more striking reinduction into the female community. Upon her return, Fani says: "sie haben mir ihr Wort gehalten und sich der Prüfung gedultig unterzogen; sie verdienen für diesen Zwang eine Schadloshaltung, die ich ihnen bald zu geben verspreche . . . bereiten sie sich zu den seltsamsten Erzählungen vor, worüber ihr ohnedem empfindsames Herz gerühret werden wird"

(112–13).[32] Eleonora's silence is finally compensated with narrative and information. The story she hears provides knowledge Eleonora has long sought about her captor. Furthermore, it quite exactly mirrors Eleonora's own experience. After being initiated into a new feminine identity defined by lack and by overcoming female nature, Eleonora may now break out of her isolation and ignorance to gain the knowledge that she is not alone after all, and that her fate is one shared with other women.

"The History of the Duchess v. ***"

The duchess's story, purported by Eleonora to be the authentic rendition of the first person narrative told to her, introduces yet another female story and voice into *Karolinens Tagebuch*. In content and style, it offers an elaboration of the contrasting forms of female authorship and authority already presented in the novel. This new story is remarkable in that it is an exaggerated, even more extreme version of the fate the duchess, Henriette, imposed upon Eleonora. Eleonora must face enforced separation from her mother, but Henriette's mother and father are dead. The orphan Henriette was sequestered by her uncle-guardian in the same labyrinthine house in which Eleonora is held hostage. Here she is enclosed during her entire girlhood. Eleonora has no knowledge of the outside world while she is kidnapped, whereas Henriette never has any experience outside of the house, nor any companionship but that of her servant Fani (whose role she adopts toward Eleonora). Her uncle (otherwise an "upright" man) betrays his responsibilities toward Henriette by marrying her off at age fourteen to a false friend of his in a fit of misjudgment. Always dutiful, she accepts this fate automatically, "like a machine" (119), though it is to ruin her life. Her uncle admits on his deathbed, "Du bist ein unschuldiges Schlachtopfer einer übereilten Freundschaft geworden" (122).[33] Her husband seldom visits his bride in her fortress, still keeping her imprisoned there after impregnating her. After the uncle's death, Henriette is fully at her husband's mercy. He robs her of the son she bears, and denies her very existence to the world, claiming she died in childbirth. Henriette shoulders her fate with the stoicism of Rousseau's ideal heroine.[34] She would rather suffer the injustice of her unloved, evil husband than transgress the borders of female virtue by protesting actively against such treatment.

The violation of her integrity and rights which she must endure proves, indeed, integral to the constitution of her sense of identity: "Ein bis dahin mir noch unbekannter Stolz ward in mir rege, . . . ein natürliches Licht zeigte mir meine Würde, die ich vielleicht bey einer gleichförmlichern Behandlung von meinem Gemahl nicht so bald erkannt haben würde; ich dachte nach, mein Bewußtseyn erwachte, und ich fand, daß man mich beleidigte" (128).[35] Henriette follows her faithful servant Fani's advice and "takes refuge in the consciousness of her innocence" (129). She shapes an identity out of the nothingness and emptiness of her life through the experience of her self-denial and of her husband's denial of her existence, which paradoxically communicates to her the existence of a self. Like Eleonora, who must withstand the trials of lack to prove her feminine virtue and construct an adult feminine identity, Henriette must demonstrate her feminine worthiness by keeping her marriage vows and suffering twenty-eight years of imprisonment in an existence disavowed by her husband. Despite this overwhelming indication of feminine "heroine-ism," Henriette confesses to Eleonora that, even in her seclusion, "feminine weaknesses" threatened her. She succumbs to vanity, for her isolation leads her to preoccupation with her image. The "nothing" she must fill daily to keep herself distracted from her circumstances leads her automatically, again "almost like a machine" (136), to ponder her image in the mirror and to ask, for the first time, who she is:

> was will sie denn da, wer ist sie, hätte ich beynahe gefragt; so beschäftigte mich das erstemal das Ich! Sonst hatte ich nur die Ordnung meines Anzugs darinn gesucht, und mein mir erst wichtig gewordenes Ich noch nicht bemerket. O wie viel Betrachtungen fieng ich jezt nicht an, über das liebe Ich anzustellen? und vielleicht nicht ohne der Vorsiz meiner Eigenliebe, wozu das Lesen einiger eben nicht der ausgesuchtesten Bücher vieles beygetragen haben mag. Ich hatte sie mir selbst aus der Bibliothek gewählt, und was für Waare wählt nicht ein sich selbst überlassenes unerfahrenes Ding.[36] (136–37)

Although an awareness of her dignity and of her innocence is appropriate for her, further considerations of her self are not tolerable in the sentimental heroine's moral code. The awareness of herself as independent subject, "das liebe Ich," reflecting itself in the mirror is questioned and condemned as vanity.

The feminine failing of vanity is said to be encouraged through misguided reading. Isolated as she is, the only positive figures Henriette can find to help her comprehend her own identity stem from books. Like Eleonora, she too wishes for reassurance that the "nothing" has been transformed into something of value. Eleonora sought aid in interpreting her own situation from the novels she read, pitying the heroines and thereby herself, and attempting to find positive models of identification in those figures. "Bey den traurigen Stellen, die ich las, hielt ich mich immer am längsten auf, und ich fand eine gewisse mit Thränen abwechslende Anmuth darinnen, weil sie mir das sonderbare meines Abentheuers in einem gewissen Lichte der Prüfung, die mich vollkommener zu machen versprach, vorstellten" (107).[37] Eleonora's reward for her trial of self-denial is to have her newly shaped identity mirrored and thus confirmed through the duchess's more authoritative narrative. The story told acknowledges her ordeal and affirms her heroic behavior. It provides for self-recognition and support of the identity constructions she has been forced into. Henriette too turned to narrative for reflections of her self and her own situation, and thus conceitedly fancied herself a virtuous heroine. This fault is ironic, for as a figure of Karoline's tale, she is precisely such a stereotypical heroine.[38] However the duchess cannot acknowledge this identity and still maintain her virtuous profile. A contradiction thus arises here in the theories of those who claim that novels with virtuous heroines are edifying and useful for their female readers, as they provide models to be emulated. Novels, like the mirrors they are compared with, must serve as vehicles for female self-criticism and improvement without risking vanity by offering overtly a positive identification or consciousness of self. Virtue, often equated with beauty, must be strived for and maintained, but it may never be acknowledged. In front of a book, as in front of the mirror, the primary demand on the female audience is ignorance of her laudable self, a receptive stance of negative reflection.

The duchess instructs Eleonora in the proper use of such tools for self-reflection while also warning her of the dangers lurking within them. The older woman first praises her for her beauty and for her virtuous obliviousness to it and warns her against overlong contemplation in front of the mirror. Eleonora's response to this enlightening commentary is an inordinate horror of the mirror: "So, sind das unsere Feinde? — von heute an, soll mich kein Spiegel mehr beschäftigen, o fort fort alle aus meinem Zimmer . . . das verwünschte Glas!" (77–78).[39] The duchess chides her now for this impetuous exclamation, and attempts to moderate her overzealous, even enthusiastic, ardor for virtue, as Eleonora reports to Karoline:

> der Spiegel hätte keine Schuld, wenn ihn unser Eigensinn zu Erregung verderblicher Leidenschaften mißbrauchte. Er ist vielmehr unser Freund, versezte sie wieder, wenn wir ihn wohl zu gebrauchen wissen. Er zeiget uns unsere Unvollkommenheiten, die uns auch die besten Freunde, aus Furcht uns zu betrüben, gar oft verschweigen. Unter diesen und mehr dergleichen lehrreichen Anmerkungen, mit denen ich deine mir bekannte Lebhaftigkeit und Ungedult nicht reizen will, legten wir uns schlaffen.[40] (78)

Henriette aims to correct Eleonora's vision by offering her own experiences as an warning example. Her story offers a clear reflection of Eleonora in that the faults she describes are generally feminine rather than individual. The narrative ought to be employed like the mirror to aid in recognition of faults and perception of imperfection, yet emphatically not as mediator of affirmative self-knowledge or identification. Eleonora demonstrates the "good" response of the heroine by taking this exhortation to heart. The fundamental conflict between individual character and the generic character of the "virtuous woman" familiar from La Roche and from the general debates on the novel resurfaces in the embedded sentimental novels of *Karolinens Tagebuch:* the individuals are to emulate and embody the generic character, rather than to distinguish themselves individually. But in reference to herself, Karoline emphasizes the dullness of these moralistic lessons and furthers her satire against them.

The duchess traces for Eleonora the inevitable trajectory of her breach of this command, from imagining herself a novel heroine to exploring these fantasies by writing. She moves from an inappropriate reading stance to the greater transgression of attempting to capture and preserve the new-found image of herself in the mirror of writing. The novel in which the duchess presumptuously fashions herself as the ideal sentimental heroine appears in her mature autobiographical narrative as a foolish literary effort. She criticizes herself for her inadequate youthful attempts at authorship, revealing the true motivation for her writing as self-captivation. Thus Henriette tells the story of her attempted epigonic authorship to her young charge Eleonora as a warning against the dangers of "idle gazing in the mirror" (135). She criticizes her own satisfaction in the images she harbored of herself as heroine, virtuous victim, and author. This pleasure in self-affirmation through identification with a self-sacrificing woman led her to further forbidden admiration of herself: "[ich] fiel . . . in keine geringe Verwunderung, an mir mittels des Spiegels alle die Züge zu bemerken, die ich auf dem Papier meiner Heldinn gegeben" (137–38).[41] Henriette so enjoys the image of herself as author of such a noble heroine, reflective of her own character, that she commissions a portrait of herself pondering her next words with quill in hand. This portrait mirrors the equation of women's writing with a mirror serving female vanity and captures the fantasy image first glimpsed in intangible, fleeting reflections of the glass in a substantial, permanent form. The portrait as mirror proved her undoing, the duchess laments: "Wie manche Stunde brachte ich vor meinem Bildniß in recht thörichten Betrachtungen zu, und so zehrte ich mich mit Klagen über das elende Leben des Urbilds dergestalt ab, daß ich endlich krank wurde" (138–39).[42] She falls into a depression and melancholy which lasts "twelve full years" until her youth and beauty are devastated and she can no longer be, as she once imagined, an attractive object of pity.

The autobiographical narrative of Henriette's life told to Eleonora offers a criticism of her efforts as author and of the novel genre she chose to emulate. Yet this criticism is disavowed by the story she now tells. As figure, she remains bound to the conventions she claims to reject, for she is the heroine she vainly imagines herself to be. As reader, she also follows generic conventions by responding to her own fate with pity. The sentimental "reading" of her portrait which encapsulates her story is the transgression which ultimately leads her to her mysterious illness. The cause of her illness is attributed to her self-pity rather than to the dire circumstances which make the heroine pitiful. Yet her misconduct and the ensuing twelve-year melancholy are themselves the continuation of her stellar career as sentimental heroine. The typical phase of illness as punishment for failings (or the "feminine weaknesses" (134), as Henriette understands them, which found her even in the midst of her isolation) is yet another topos of the sentimental feminocentric novel.[43]

The narrative style of the confessional autobiography Henriette tells is equally caught in the constraints and contradictions of the sentimental novel. She offers her story as warning and presents herself as fallen heroine with outpourings of the very emotions of pity she once wished to elicit through the novel she so "foolishly" began. By telling this story of her own weakness and fate to Eleonora as admonition, she fulfills her earlier wish to narrate her own story in a sentimental vein. The reception of her story that she expects from Eleonora, namely *Rührung,* also corresponds to this desire. She follows the generic paradigms of justification for her mature authorship (educational, moral purpose) and of the source of her authority (moral reflection on the lessons of trying personal experience). Her narrative overtly criticizes the young self and her earlier attempt at writing novels, but also affirms them through its formal conventions and style. Conversely, the story she tells disavows its own narrative style and condemns the type of novel she narrates. In essence, she offers her own story to Eleonora as the mirror she warns against, showing the novel as reflective tool to be of equivocal value, as is the mirror. The virtues of her narrative thus depend greatly on the interpretive competence and conduct of the audience.

Karoline's Authorial Profiles

Karoline's novelistic fictions centrally employ figures of "nothingness" and the mirror in order to approach questions of feminine identities and Sagar's theoretical concerns of how to read and write feminocentric narratives. Eleonora and Henriette attempt to fill the emptiness defining their lives with a sense of identity constructed from the void. Each fully isolated, they seek to endow the images spied in the reflecting mediums of the mirror and of literature with some substance, as in the duchess's portrait and the production of their autobiographical narratives. Eleonora and Henriette each tell the story of striving to embody exemplary feminine virtue, as construed by sentimental ideology. Karoline recounts these limiting stories and concocts their leading characters as props in her own narrative of female identity, also written in part to break the isolation she feels. As mirrors within Karoline's journal and *Karolinens Tagebuch,* they reflect and refract her own, and Sagar's, narratives of Karoline as heroine.

Karoline draws her figure Eleonora, as both heroine and author, as a stark foil to herself. A comparison between the two friends is explicitly demanded, as Karoline addresses her reader: "Aber liebe Schwester! Meine Meynung ist, nebst meinen eigenen Nuzen, auch dich zu unterhalten. Indessen ist das vorhergehende, wie ich selbst gewahr werde, eine viel zu frostige, wenn ich nicht sagen soll, abgeschmackte Unterhaltung für dich. Doch warte . . ." (40).[44] The account of Karoline's life, justified through the purpose of education for the writer, cannot hold real entertainment for her reader. This is the pretext for complementing her own "uneventful story" with the novel of Eleonora's more exciting adventures, designed to hold the reader captive. The aim of entertainment, one half of the eighteenth-century poet's maxim, stands alone as the reason for inserting this story of allegedly greater literary merit into her journal. Although Eleonora is undoubtedly a virtuous heroine, Karoline does not suggest she is to be emulated and does not offer her story as an edifying one, either for her readers or herself. She accentuates the differences in character between herself and Eleonora, but more to endear herself to her readers than as admonishment or self-criticism. Eleonora is the ideal sentimental heroine striving for good and obediently bending to the violent treatment she receives, as well as to the catechism of female virtue. Karoline has no patience for "educational comments" such as those of the duchess (78). Karoline, however, has the virtues of being authentic and spirited in her emotions. She also has the appealing qualities of spunk, cleverness, and a good measure of self-confidence.

In Eleonora's voice, Karoline points out differences between the two of them as audience of the duchess's story. Karoline also accentuates her own character by offering a precise, critical reading of "Eleonora's" text. The commentary on her own fiction occurs in the context of asking for criticism from Nanette and Cyrilli as a sign of their interest. Although she would prefer praise, she writes, she would welcome even reprimands as a sign of their consideration rather than suffer being ignored: "Einwürfe oder auch noch so bittere Anmerkungen kann man immer eher vertragen" (54).[45] In her double pose as journal writer and copyist-reader, Karoline's critique of Eleonora's narrative draws the readers' attention to peculiarities of her figure's language and sharpens her own multifaceted profile as author:

> Anmerkungen — o die schrecken mich gar nicht ab, dafür kann ich mich ja selbst schadlos halten; kann ich mir nicht auch über andere das nämliche erlauben? und das will ich gleich versuchen: siehe in der vorlezten Zeile des Lusanischen Briefes — den Ausdruck: sie will der Mutter *mit Vorsaz* nicht ungehorsam werden. —

Was will sie damit sagen? ist es nicht ein schalkhafter Vorbehalt
im Fall einer Ueberraschung des Herzens? oder bin ich vielleicht
selbst schalkhaft das Wort, mit Vorsaz so auszulegen.[46] (54)

The criticism Karoline offers distances her as journal author from
the narrative style she ascribes to her figure Eleonora. Eleonora's
sentimental exclamations conceal insincerities, Karoline suggests,
and appear psychologically suspect. In contrast, Karoline's own
persona as character, reader, and specifically as journal writer is presented as direct, authentic, and psychologically credible. Karoline's
suggestion that this reading discloses her "mischievousness" is a
further clue to the authorial role-playing and duplicity hidden in
her interpretations and language. She points to her own clever
authorial devices and strategies: she illuminates Eleonora's status
and function in her novelistic narrative as a citation of a feminocentric genre contrasting in style with the writing that Karoline
openly acknowledges as hers. Her comments simultaneously underscore for her readers the importance of reading critically, if they
are to apprehend her games. The citation of the feminocentric
sentimental novel within Karoline's journal as but one of the forums for her writer's voice discredits the authority of the genre as
the prototypical narrative of feminine virtue. In stark contrast to
her heroines, Karoline braves the female, feminine dilemma of
"nothingness," also a reiterated figure for her life and her narrative,
through playfulness and mobility. Rather than striving to enact
flawlessly a single role of perfect femininity defined through negativity, Karoline adopts strategies which enable her to avoid the constrictions her heroines face in asserting their identities. Rather than
fixating the *Nichts,* she exploits it. Rather than attempting to capture one positive image the mirror offers, she uses the mirror to
experiment with many different feminine roles. As author, she ex-
ercises her writing as a mirror which has the capacity to accept and
reflect multiple images without holding Karoline to the constraints
of any single one.

Karoline initially contrasted her writing, ostensibly prompted
by the virtuous desire to account for her character, with the seductive shine of the reflecting glass. Yet she is quick to annul this opposition and readily admits to pleasure and vanity as motivations
for her writing. She is enraptured by her own affairs and character
as she writes and captivated by the writing itself as mirror. Her
"will to write"[47] is, like the female preoccupation with the mirror,

ultimately motivated by a desire for affirmation and approval and is plagued by its same tensions. In Karoline's education, she reports, female virtue and beauty were always equated. The task she faced in her efforts to please her mother was to be virtuous and thus praised as beautiful, while virtuously not taking vain note of this and thereby annulling the validity of the appellation. The impossibility of pleasure in one's own beauty and the concurrent requirement of beauty as the reflection and proof of virtue together lead to an insatiable narcissistic preoccupation with the self in front of the mirror (16).

In the absence of the authoritative mother, Karoline looks for affection and affirmation from her older sister, her reader, as she attempts to find and fashion the self through her writing. Her real aim, she admits, is a two-fold one of winning the attention and favor of her readers and of satisfying her own desire to write. This holds true for her many authorial personas of naive, chattering girl; sincere, self-reflective bride-to-be; editor and copyist of Eleonora's letters; self-ironic female author; and professional novelist. Her original "desire to write" (6) becomes her "favorite work" as she is "fully in love with writing" (39). Her infatuation waxes into a true obsession, an "addiction to writing" (53), she writes, and one that is ultimately self-centered.[48] Her narcissism, which she remarks and mildly criticizes, is itself a feint to distract from (and also guide to) her literary creativity, her playground for fantasies in the construction of the self and thus a further reflection and image for which she desires approbation.

> Heute, glaube ich, hätte ich meiner Schreibsucht ziemlich Genüge gethan, oder soll ich nicht vielmehr sagen, ich bin müde fremden Kramm zu Markte zu tragen, da ich selbst in meine eigene Plauderey verliebt bin. — Aber das gestehe ich dir, meine liebe Schwester, allein durch das Abschreiben fremder Begebenheiten, ich kann es nicht verhelen, suche ich nur deine Aufmerksamkeit zu erkauffen, weilen das Register von meinem Thun und Lassen, oder meiner Gedanken, dich wahrscheinlich oft zum Gähnen bringen muß, obschon es für meine Einbildung manchmal sehr wichtig scheinen mag.[49] (53)

Karoline unites the poses of writing as dutiful confession, as passive copying, and as capricious chatter with the show of her sincerity and spontaneity. Her pleasure in her own affairs and image, as well as other faults which overstep the confines of "femininity," are for-

givable and forgiven since she readily admits them, as a still innocent, if self-indulgent, maiden.

The strategy of self-criticism demands recognition of such proclaimed authenticity as a positive value which also counterbalances
her trespasses in narrative style. Karoline offers her thoughts as un-
calculated chaos, writing as the words occur to her. She repeatedly
stresses the fragmentary nature of her writing, employing ellipses as
sign of conceptual and narrative confusion or of prudent prohibition of particular thoughts. Describing her narrative style as incho-
ate superficially conforms to the formulas of modesty and self-
disparagement expected from writing women, while also meeting
the guidelines for proper, feminine letter-writing. Yet Karoline's
reflections on this score are less a criticism of herself than a assertion of her situation as woman:

> Nein, das geht schwerer her, als ich geglaubt habe, dir auch von
> meinen Gedanken Rechenschaft zu geben. Es sahe in meinem
> Kopf damit oft so aus, wie mit einem zerrütteten Bund Zwirn,
> wo man keinen Anfang und kein Ende findet, es waren nur lauter
> unzusammenhangende Fragmenten von Gedanken, nur Halbe-
> oder Viertelanfänge eines Gedanken, von welchen immer einer
> den andern verdrängte, mit einem Wort: mein Kopf fasste nichts
> als flüchtige Ideen. Warum — ich hatte auf nichts bestimmtes zu
> denken. (14–15)[50]

Her contemplations on "feminine" style, figured with images from
the household sphere, point to opportunity, or rather the lack of it
in female lives, to learn the skill of concentration. She laments her
lack of training in the exercise of formulating ideas and makes it responsible for the chaos in her thoughts, a fault considered
prototypically feminine: "Herr Cyrili sagt immer, man muß denken
lernen. Gut, das kann ich schon, er soll mich aber lehren den Gedanken zu gebiethen, daß sie sich nicht so verwirrt, sondern or-
dentlich darstellen" (15).[51]

The tactical advantages Karoline draws from sometimes
adopting this female role and feminine style as one of her authorial
positions, namely freedom from certain formal constraints, are underscored for her readers by her awareness of writing as activity requiring skill. Remarks on the challenges of composition refer to
Karoline's pose as journal author attempting to communicate her
daily reflections, yet also apply to and illuminate her more sophisticated pose as author of the novels embedded in her journal. The

faculties necessary for competence in her métier as author of novels are those of strategic planning and shrewd decisions: "Ich will es dem klugen Minister nachmachen, der selbst zu rechter Zeit einen geschickten Fehler zu begehen weis, um daraus zu schliessen, was man von ihm urtheilet — O mache kein satirisch Gesicht darzu, Schwesterchen! was weist du von der Staatsklugheit? Nur uns Schriftstellern ist sie bekannt" (164–65).[52] Not only must an author be a clever, political strategist, she must possess the self-confidence, resolution, and authority to implement the decisions made. The images Karoline constructs to describe her authorial dilemmas aptly express her difficulties in asserting such an authoritative position. Tellingly, she chooses to ponder her quandaries as writer through images of powerful male figures — the political minister, the army commander, the ruler — who must make difficult strategic decisions: "Heute aber . . . [ist] meine Einbildungskraft so voll mit unbestimmten, und flüchtigen Bildern beladen, daß ich nicht weis, wie, oder wo ich anfangen soll. . . . Das herrschen gefiel mir, ich empfinde es, wäre nur nicht meine eigene Freyheit der Preis meiner Herrschsucht! Ich streite immer, und thue nichts; tausend Entschliessungen folgen auf einander, und eine jede macht mich unentschlossener, als zuvor" (81).[53] Practicing authority entails suppression and the limitation of possibilities, Karoline discovers, as well as risks. Authoritative writing, she suggests, demands a masculine exertion of power, of which Karoline purports herself incapable given the feminine confusion of her ideas. She claims to relinquish the position of command by comparing herself to a gambler who vows to give up his addiction to the game; she will no longer write her own thoughts, but will instead turn to the task of copying someone else's story — a claim clearly serving her game of duplicity and emphasizing her skill in playing it. The resignation is a ruse, for her strategy, as she writes, is to keep the game as open as possible while remaining in control. The feigned distinction between her creative writing and mere copying is one of the ploys in the narrative tactics she forges allowing her to rule without giving up her freedom, since she hesitates to narrow her narrative options through authoritative gesture. By adopting multiple roles, she reigns over her literary enterprise and grants herself "feminine" possibilities of flexibility and evasiveness. Ultimately she constructs a specifically female authorial persona and narrative strategy in which she renounces the authority to write in order to (be allowed to) reclaim it. Her strategy further entails anticipation of reader expectations and preventative self-criticism, particularly of her own profile as female author:

> Heute z. E. saß ich, wie gewöhnlich bey meinem Schreibpult — lache nicht, daß ich mein kleines Tischchen so nenne, vor unsern Hausgenossen nenne ich es nie anders, es giebt mir ein wichtiges Ansehen, denn die Dienstboten erzählen es ausser dem Hause, und bringen mich dadurch als ein gelehrtes Frauenzimmer in Ruff — Hm!. . . schon wieder eine Satire über mich selbst? Je nun es ist schon geschrieben, doch — glaube nicht Schwester, daß ich es deswegen thue, damit ich andern diese Lust beraube. O nein, sie mögen sich immer über mich lustig machen, wie sie wollen, ich gönne es ihnen. Ich bin ein frommes Kind, ich hole mir selbst die Ruthe: aber wer kann denn hernach so ungezogen seyn, und mich schlagen wollen, da ich mich so gehorsam bezeige. Siehest du? wieder eine neue Politik?. . . Aber ich bin ja völlig aus meiner Erzählung gekommen.[54] (268–69)

Karoline employs "political" self-irony framed as unreflected openness, but immediately revealed as strategy, to defend her chosen role as female author. She is stubborn and self-assured in her insistence on this role, standing up to her brother Leopold's teasing on this account even when he threatens to publish her writing.

Sagar uses the conflict between Leopold and Karoline to engage in humorous response to the critics of her earlier novel, *Die verwechselten Töchter,* and to take issue with the theoretical preoccupations of the male critics.[55] Leopold imagines the publication of Karoline's nonsense would earn her the "nice nickname of a miserable chatterbox" and her work would be found "even more improbable" than Sagar's first novel (197). Karoline's response debunks such criticism, first through the apparent docility of the female writer, claiming the work was not "serious" literature but only intended for other women, and secondly by questioning the male critics' ability to read the work and ask of it the appropriate questions. Karoline is irritated when the criterion of "probability" is raised to attack the novel. She suggests that it adheres to patterns of its genre and that it is as such fully legitimate. Furthermore, she claims the genre as a feminine one, at least one for which "feminine logic" is also essential. The male critics seem blind to the implications of the genre and their cries of "improbability," she suggests, miss the point of the fictional narrative entirely. The arguments she launches against Leopold recall those of the prefaces to *Die verwechselten Töchter* and *Karolinens Tagebuch* on the ability of female readers to comprehend the merits and secrets of women's writing, which male critics cannot perceive. She tells her impudent brother to go ahead and publish her writing; as long as it is reviewed, it will please her. While apparently discrediting the import of her work (and of *Die verwechselten Töchter*) as female products, Karoline continues to derive delight and pride from her role as female author.

Karoline's Conflicting Plots of Authorship and Marriage

Karoline's journal entries about herself tell two parallel and mutually threatening tales. She writes about her development as author of novels and of her own journal account of her life, and she writes about her anticipated marriage. Karoline's elliptical narrative strives to articulate for her sister and for herself the confusion in her responses to being a "bride" and her efforts to prepare for her new role of wife. She is sure to find a sympathetic female reader in her sister Nanette, also betrothed. Although she wishes to account fully for her emotions, Karoline has no need to articulate all her anxieties and anticipations to be understood: "Gegen dich habe ich keiner Zurückhaltung, noch Verstellung nöthig; du bist ja meine liebste und vertrauteste Schwester, du magst es frey wissen, daß ich meiner Freundinn [Eleonora] Schlaf beneide. Es ist nicht mehr jene Zeit, wo auch ich — du weist schon, was ich sagen will" (79–80).[56] Karoline's sense of identity is in transition from her familiar status as sister and daughter to the ominously unknown identity as Karl's wife. Though by no means opposed to the marriage, Karoline is apprehensive about what will happen to that self she knows.[57] The transformation of the very self she is at pains to construct in her tale is figured as a potentially violent dissolution and recasting: "Je nun ich kann mir nicht helfen, ich möchte mich gerne umschmelzen oder, wenn es nicht wehe thäte, in einem Mörser, wie ein Harlekin zerstossen lassen, auf das ein neues Geschöpf herauskäme. Doch das ist auch nichts, denn es würde immer wieder nur ein Harlekin kommen. Lasse mich also lieber so, wie ich bin" (274).[58] This image reflects Karoline's passive position in the change of status to be effected through marriage, for the terms of melting down and refiguring by bestowing a new name on Karoline recur in describing her future relationship to Karl. The similarity of names of the betrothed suggests either proximity, some preservation of Karoline's independent identity or, conversely, the absolute erasure of it.

Karoline describes for Nanette how she practices replacing her current self-image, her natural playful airs, with the wifely poses demanded by her new role: "Meinen Spiegel habe ich schon gebetten, mir alle jungfräuliche Sünden zuverzeihen, und mich Hochachtung anziehende, oder bußfertige Frauenmienen zu lehren. Ein Paar dergleichen hat er mir schon mitgetheilt: aber vor dem feyerlichen Genickbrechen will ich noch keinen Gebrauch davon machen. Erlaube mir also liebe Schwester, noch bis dahin zwangfrey zu bleiben: denn ich habe dir noch eine Menge Erzählungen in meiner Natürlichkeit zu machen" (267–68).[59] Though humorously inserted, the image she chooses for herself of sacrificial lamb again emphasizes her passive position and communicates many of the anxieties she associates with the marriage ceremony — vulnerability, violence, and sexuality.[60] The mirror is again her trusted ally in experimentation and exploration of identities. Karoline plays to discover how she might fill the outer contours of the roles prescribed for women with inner, personal substance.

Writing likewise facilitates such investigation of feminine identities. Here she clearly aligns her "natural" narrative style with her youthful and as yet single status and places her stories in this vein at odds with her future role. Karoline's writing is defined in opposition to her role as Karl's intended bride throughout. Her brother Leopold ridicules her activity and preoccupation with writing generally, and specifically implies that it improperly competes with what should be her priority, diverting the attentions she should be giving Karl: "hören Sie einmal, Karl kommen Sie nur herein, thun Sie alles was ihnen beliebt, meine Schwester wird nichts gewahr, sie ist ganz in Wichtigkeiten begraben" (95).[61] Karoline's journal persona also upholds this opposition, telling the story of her upcoming marriage as one of confusions and contradictions which negatively affect her journal writing. "Mein armes Hirn" (169) she complains, "in meinem Kopfe sauset und brauset das verwünschte Wort *Braut* so entsezlich, daß es mir von Herzen eckelt" (168).[62] Her fixation on the alienating term is said to prohibit all coherent narrative production and even threatens her normally unrestrained desire to write of herself. She laments: "Ist das etwa das Loos aller Bräute? O so möchte ich lieber in meinem Leben nie eine Braut seyn!" (278).[63] The embedded novelistic narratives, Karoline claims, distract her from her distracted and anxious self as she anticipates marriage with Karl. The act of "copying" someone else's tale calms her by hindering her own reflections. She attempts to banish all thoughts of men from her mind and to direct her attention solely to her "good and kind" sister's entertainment: "Dem ganzen Mannsvolk hingegen . . . nun . . . was denn . . . ach nichts . . . Nein gar nichts will ich mit diesen ungestümmen Geschöpfen zu thun haben — fort mit ihnen; ich will lieber fortfahren, meiner Freundinn Abentheuer dir zu beschreiben" (103–4).[64] The contrast Karoline builds between her marriage and her writing skills serves her management of multiple authorial roles as well as the manuscript fiction of Eleonora Lusani's adventures. The tale she claims to copy as a mindless diversion from the menace of marriage is creatively generated out of the conflicts in identity with which she contends. Ultimately, however, the two plots of Karoline's narratives, marriage and writing, are indeed contradictory. Her duties as wife will demand all her time: "Jezt aber muß ich auf einige Zeit diesem Vergnügen entsagen. Ernsthafte Betrachtungen nehmen mich ein. Hauswirthschaft und Sorgen zeigen sich mir fast in einer fürchterlichen Gestalt" (303).[65] More fundamentally, the marriage will erase her personal signature and her authority over her own story.

Disclosing the Fiction of Marriage as Closure

Thus it appears as if *Karolinens Tagebuch* disavows its heroine's "feminine" narrative strategies of multiplicity by accepting the conventional culmination of the feminocentric novel and channeling the heroine's search for identity into an answer of "wife." Marriage is a favored event with which to close stories of heroines. The heroine's enclosure in the identity of "wife" is reassuring for the larger society: it fixes inconstant woman under the control of man and bridles dangerous currents of female desire into patriarchal social structures. Yet such resolution often strains the narrative it ends. The difficulties in forcing the protagonist's experience and the novel's narrative queries together into the rubric of "wife" are apparent even in works considered most representative of this genre, as in *Geschichte des Fräuleins von Sternheim*. Sagar's text highlights both these classic quandaries while distancing itself from the conventions of the feminocentric novel by emphatically refusing marriage as thematic and formal closure.

The closure of marriage is denied even to the sentimental novels Karoline authors. The embedded stories seem to demand resolution in multiple marriages, as the plot developments of Karoline's double tale reveal. Eventually, the duchess Henriette and her son, who was taken from her at birth, are reunited and the danger to Eleonora appears no longer imminent. The stage is thus set for the resolution of the heroine Eleonora's fate. Through her trials Eleonora has left the haven of female community, of her mother and sister, and has matured in "feminine virtues." Karoline recognizes marriage is the only way out of her authorial dilemma of how to close her novel. She must adopt the paternal role and see her heroine through to the safety of matrimony. However, this outcome of her text is foreclosed by the writing master Cyrilli's intrusion into Karoline's narrative plans. His warning that she attend to the needs of what he has recognized as her fiction interrupts her presentation and causes her to abandon the project altogether, loose ends and all. Cyrilli's comments mock the novel genre being mimicked, while the elaborate fictional construct and the difficulties of its containment are openly made a theme: "Ich nehme mir die Freyheit sie zu warnen, ein wenig behutsamer zu seyn. . . . Sie haben sich ziemlich verwicklet, wie werden sie sich heraus helfen, und wo haben sie alles das Zeug hergenommen?" (258–59).[66] Cyrilli raises theoretical concerns which decisively expose the relevance of Karoline's extravagant fictions for the narrative of *Karolinens Tagebuch ohne ausserordentliche Handlungen* and its author Sagar:

> wo zielen sie mit dem Wust der irrenden Ritter und ihren komischen Heldinnen hin? Soll es etwa eine Satire auf die Recension der verwechselten Töchter seyn, wegen dem Vorwurf, das Werkchen hätte zu wenig Handlung? Ich meines Theils lächelte zwar, als sie jüngsthin sich über die Gelehrten ärgerten, daß sie noch immer ausserordentliche Auftritte in Romanen zu lesen begehren: aber nach mir müssen sie nicht alle beurtheilen. (258)[67]

Among male critics, Cyrilli is an exception. Still, his authority sanctions the female author's challenge to the established scholars, underscoring the targets of the satire as, primarily, the male critics whose elaborate theories on the novel are clearly ludicrous and inappropriate to a feminocentric text. Women like Karoline are housebound and their stories are not adventurous. If novels are to be eventful, they must necessarily be either improbable (as Eleonora remarked) or "immoral," featuring a "fallen" heroine. Sagar's title of this, her second novel, suggests that it is the continuation of her work in opposition to the critics of her first novel, as she warned in her preface to *Die verwechselten Töchter:* "ich rathe es Ihnen noch einmal, meine Herren Leser! tadeln sie nichts an meinem Werkgen; den Kopf sollen sich nicht einmal darüber schütteln! oder ich werde mich mit einer Forsetztung an ihnen rächen."[68] The outlandish tales of Eleonora and Henriette are the inverse of Karoline's own, a further satiric barb to the theoreticians.

Karoline addresses her reply to "Mein Herr und Meister!" and begins her letter with a commentary on the address as conscious literary flair: "Der Titel, hoffe ich, wird wohl so recht seyn; denn er gefällt mir — Nur weiter; warum übereilen Sie mich? ich hätte ihnen mehr Gedult zugetrauet, verzeihen sie mir, mein bester und liebster Lehrer. Ich hatte meiner Geschichte eine unerwartete Entwicklung zugedacht. Sie bringen sich selbst um die Ueberraschung. Oder gefällt ihnen ihr Entwurf besser, so seye es, ich will nicht klüger seyn als sie" (263).[69] Karoline's self-assured explanation of her novelistic plans to marry off her characters indicates her sound knowledge of the narrative conventions she is employing as caricature. While she defers to Cyrilli, she does so with playful emphasis on her own authority over the text she is writing: witness the title she bestows on him, the style of which is as important to her as the respect it shows; the teasing suggestion that the reader ought to submit to the author's judgment with patience; the difficult authorial decision that the *Hofmeister,* the probable figure of identification for Cyrilli, must die to accommodate the narrative economy: "Den ehrlichen Hofmeister o um den ist mir wohl leid; aber ich kann mir nicht anders helfen. Er muß auch sterben, sonst reiche ich mit allen meinen Schäzen nicht aus, weil ich schon im Anfange zustark angegriffen habe" (265).[70] The exchange between the writing master and Karoline about the design and exigencies of the narrative replaces the closure of her novel and reveals in exaggerated fashion the novel's artifice and that of its projected endings.

Karoline closes her letter to Cyrilli with as much flourish as it began. While she dismisses her literary undertaking as a rather frivolous flight into fancy and thanks her teacher for not letting her imagination stray too far afield — "Wer weis, wie weit auch mich mein Gernwiz geführet hätte" (265)[71] — her signature reasserts her profile as female writer. She ends: "Leben Sie indessen wohl, und

glauben sie, daß ich unveränderlich bin ihre gehorsame Lehrlinginn Karoline. P. S. Merken sie sich das Wort: *Lehrlinginn,* das ist
von mir neu erfunden" (266).[72] Her neologism with its linguistic
marker of gender pointedly underscores the terrain she has con-
quered. She is a confident *female* apprentice in the craft of writing;
her literary output is the product of her active, creative imagination
and her clever implementation of strategy.

Karoline's pending task as literary strategist according to the
narrative paradigms she knows and the expectations she has raised
is now, she knows, to see herself as heroine through to the closure
of the long-anticipated marriage with Karl. Yet this need poses peculiar problems for the author. *Karolinens Tagebuch,* as shown,
consistently sets marriage and Karoline's writing at odds. The roles
she must soon take on as wife do not allow for her literary pursuits — these were an exorcism of her youthful energy: "ich habe
schon ausgetobt, und ausgeschwärmt — und das mußte ich doch
wohl vorher, ehe ich eine gesezte Matrone zu machen anfange. . . .
Itz soll ich heyrathen, und der modificirende Gedanke, eine ehrba-
re Frau zu heißen, vertilget alle Franzereyen aus meinem Kopfe"
(267).[73] Her writing is the vehicle for explorations which men find
in their adventures. Writing and reading, for Karoline, are diver-
sions from her own condition of boredom. The sentimental novels
she writes allow her "tears": "Ich hatte mir ernstlich vorgenom-
men, Bäche von Thränen fliessen zu lassen, und hätte, vielleicht
mir zu gefallen selbst geweint" (264).[74] Her ironic tone does not
deny the sentimental genre the functions of entertainment and
emotional release she ascribes to it. But she surmises that they have
no place in her future life. As wife, she will be fully occupied with
her household duties and her emotional focus will be the husband
and family. Indeed, her secret tears when Karl becomes ill are a
sign of this new orientation.

Furthermore, the marriage itself threatens to undermine the
very possibilities of Karoline's authorship, for it challenges both her
identity and the sovereign right she claims as the author of her own
story. She has no say in the patriarchal system which negotiates the
transformation of her self: "Karl R** soll mich umschmelzen, er
soll mir seinen Namen geben; er hat schon von unserm guten Va-
ter die Erlaubniß hierzu. Siehe das weis ich alles: aber in was vor
einem Rath ist es denn beschlossen worden? mich dünkt, ich hätte
wohl in diesem Rath auch eine Stimme haben sollen; doch ich bin

nur ein Kind: wider den Spruch meines Vaters werde ich nicht appellieren dörfen" (142).[75] Karoline learns to incorporate this subordinate role into her repertoire and to enact it (and within it) with a degree of independence. She is initially at a loss in her new role as bride: "Zu dem heutigen Lustspiel aber seye ich gar nicht vorbereitet worden, deswegen müßten mich die Herrn nicht tadeln, wenn ich nicht nach der Anlage des Stückes geschickt antworte, denn es seye bekannt, daß die extemporierten Vorstellungen selten gut gerathen" (99).[76] But soon she sketches the scenes she will enact at the family "engagement dinner" in exaggerated-satirical style, and prepares her sister for the show. Her models for these fantasies are the novels she and her sister share. They teach her the power of her (the heroine's) beauty and her gaze over her intended groom and tutor her in her preparation for her dramatic performance. Karoline also relates, for her sister, the drama of a later discussion with her father on her upcoming marriage, complete with script and stage directions, asking Nanette to judge "ob ich meine Rolle gut gemacht habe?" (291) and she ends, "Hier hast du die versprochene Komödie" (302).[77] Such open and playful performance of prescribed gendered roles that contain possibilities of subverting them (as the father in Karoline's script well recognizes) is a crucial, defining moment of *Karolinens Tagebuch,* enacted both narratively, most ostentatiously through the dramatic form, and thematically. But this strategy of open duplicity and multiplicity, of a mobility between constructions of the feminine that counters reduction and allows for redefinition of the construction from within, is one the figure Karoline cannot apply to the unknown entity "marriage" and the role of wife. She must, then, write herself up to marriage, to this point of relinquishing both the authority over her tale and her occupation as author.[78]

While musing on the approaching end of her narrative, Karoline again, as so often, contrasts her story with other heroines' adventurous ones and wonders if her uneventful plot can really support the grand closure of marriage, since there were no unusual obstacles to overcome which could thereby be resolved. "Und jezt soll ich schon aufhören zu schreiben; soll denn unsere Hochzeit so einfach weg ablaufen? nichts ausserordentliches vorfallen? Kein Zweykampf, keine Prüfung der standhaften Tugend. . . O was wird das für eine matte Geschichte von uns beyden werden?" (302).[79] She summarizes the two sisters' story woefully, yet ironically, as cited at the beginning of this chapter. Karoline's recapitulation of her story "without events" accentuates the inadequacy of the paradigms she cites for the substance of what she has been writing. Marriage as station in the sequence birth, growth, marriage, death, is a most significant event, indeed one of the few events told about a woman's life, yet it is inexpressive as a term; it remains to be defined and explored. Thus the true obstacles to Karoline's writing marriage as closure of her own tale are too great to be overcome. The fixed role of "wife" the closure of marriage offers is an inadequate solution to the open questions of feminine identity and narrative. Karoline's own expectations of being fully recast as wife and fully dependent on Karl are indeed one source of the impossibility of marriage as resolution, for they engender new conflict. Sagar's novel ends instead with the anticipation of marriage. In the face of the unknown future, Karoline begs for continued female companionship and compassion: "O Schwester verlaß mich auch alsdann nicht! ich beschwöre dich. Arme Karoline, wie wird es um dich aussehen, wenn der Karl nicht der beste von allen Männern ist . . ." (303).[80] As Karoline suspends her narrative, she underscores the contradictions of her position and leaves her audience with fundamental questions of identity which have consistently guided her literary production: "werde ich mir denn immer selbst ein Widerspruch seyn? Lache mich nicht aus, Schwester, doch wenn du mirs gar nicht schenkest, so weine auch dann und wann über mich. Beydes verdiene ich. Lebe wohl" (304).[81]

The denial of formal closure through marriage in *Karolinens Tagebuch* emphasizes the lack of thematic resolution in the anticipated marriage. And by refusing thematic resolution through marriage, the text discloses the fictionality of this narrative convention in the sentimental novel against which it polemically positions itself. Reflections on this refusal to employ the fictions of closure close Sagar's novel and illuminate the structure of the feminocentric novel it offers as alternative to the models it satirizes. In the terms employed in discussing *Geschichte des Fräuleins von Sternheim,* Sagar's novel privileges metonymic openness rather than unified metaphoric closure. The narrative strategies of multiplicity and play found in Sagar's work resist the final enclosure in feminine roles (of mother; of *Schöne Seele*) which legitimizes La Roche's text and her authorship. If *Sternheim* attempts to meet the challenge of how to narrate female and feminine identity by creating a new and exemplary "genre of character," *Karolinens Tagebuch* approaches the same dilemma with recourse to another cultural construct of femininity as changeable and elusive "nothing." *Karolinens Tagebuch* proposes to define this "nothing" and its narrative articulation in prose by revealing its manifold possibilities rather than by solving the enigma it claims as a collective female possession.

Epilogue: Caveat Lector

THE PRECEDING CHAPTERS HAVE EXPLORED how the multifaceted, passionate discussions about narrative and reading in the
eighteenth century are taken up in the fictional discourse of the
new German novel of the 1760s and 1770s, crucial decades of the
novel's transition from a defensive position external to the poetic
canon to literary prominence at the end of the century. Just as
many of the efforts of moralists, social critics, and literary theorists
to define the novel and its reception converge on the question of
human desires in relation to narrative, so this issue is at the heart of
the novels under consideration here. While theoretical discourse is
often at pains to categorize and control the forces of desire, fictional discourse exploits its properties of ambiguity and fluidity in
creative inquiries into the pleasures of literature.

Wieland, La Roche, and Sagar met with radically different critical fates. Wieland was enshrined in the pantheon of German clas-
sics, La Roche was relegated to the "inferior" sphere of women's
literature, and Sagar was almost fully forgotten. This discrepancy
in academic reception obscures the fact that men and women together, and through reciprocal definitions of narrative using terms
of gender, shaped the novel as the genre which would become the
perennial favorite of the emerging middle class: the two German
traditions of the developmental novel and the feminocentric novel
are fundamentally related. The texts by Wieland, La Roche, and
Sagar that stand at the beginning of the tradition(s) of the modern
German novel all elaborate metafictions that take up and contribute to the contemporary theoretical discourses on the novel to
proclaim their own generic innovation. The metafictional defense
of the novel as a viable literary genre, as both serious and enjoyable
fiction, is developed in each of these texts through categories of
gender which reflect differences in the social and literary roles
available to men and women and employ and stylize these differences in their legitimations of the novel. The articulation of the
relationships between gender and generic conventions affects the
way each of these texts delineates issues of poetic theory and con-

siders the relationships between aesthetic, ethical, and social concerns.

The social valuation of individual passions and the differentiation between various expressions of desire are explored in the early novels of Wieland, La Roche, and Sagar through the characterization of fictional figures as readers and as storytellers. This narrative tactic emphasizes the powers of the imagination and the passions in relation to aesthetic consumption and production. Wieland and La Roche cast their protagonists as *Schwärmer*, whose unbridled desires are expressed through enthusiastic reading, in the case of Don Sylvio, or the enthusiastic embrace of moral ideals, in the cases of Agathon and Sophie, while the desires and imagination of Sagar's heroine Karoline are manifested in her "addiction" to fiction writing. The aesthetic tastes of these characters that both reflect and shape their emotions are revealed in their own narratives of identity, elaborated within the fictions of the novels that tell their histories. Metafictions presented through plots of reading and storytelling are underscored in Wieland's novels by the detailed profiles of the characters as narrators and in the texts of La Roche and Sagar by their epistolary form.

The transformations of the hitherto disparaged genre of the novel that generate new narrative models for stories of identity in accordance with new notions of character and agency, authenticity and narrative authority, also entail transformations in the conceptions of readers and their consumption of literature. The texts contribute to the understanding of historically and culturally specific mentalities of reading through their imaginative representation of readers and reading practices. The characteristics of the capable reader are explored through the plots of these novels, which are built on the social functions and individual uses of narrative paradigms, and in their metafictional reflections on the interpolation of fiction into interpretations of experience. The most qualified readers, profiled as characters of these novels as well as in projections of the ideal readers, evince both aesthetic and social competence. They can recognize and appreciate the narrative strategies and self-conscious fictionality of the texts and their implications for the artistic profile of the author (differently constructed in each of the novels analyzed here) and are capable of integrating literature appropriately into their life so as to foster social stability. Both an attitude of desire toward the text and the ability to regulate this desire in accordance with social precepts are presented as prerequisites for attaining interpretive competence and the attendant privilege of pronouncing culturally recognized aesthetic judgment. The independent ability to regulate desire is a sign of the reader's intellectual and social maturity, while the ability of the narrative to attract readers with this capacity reflects its aesthetic, intellectual, and ethical worth. The relation between the novels and their readers is structured through an implicit contract that the narrative strategies appealing to the readers' desires will meet with an acknowledgment of their effectiveness, but also of their poetic and moral legitimacy. Self-conscious and self-disciplining desire as an attribute of the reader's stance that confers legitimacy on the novel's narrative practice is presented in each of the novels analyzed here in gendered terms, yet is figured differently in each according to its tactics of gendered poetic self-definition.

The innate human craving for fiction postulated by eighteenth-century theoreticians of the novel and its readership is ascribed to the desire for wonder and for knowledge, for a particular form of cognition and pleasure derived from stories. The novels of Christoph Martin Wieland, Sophie von La Roche, and Maria Anna Sagar discussed in this study each defend the desire for the pleasures of fiction and court the desiring readers. The novels consider ways in which fictional narrative and its production and reception answer such desires and serve the understanding and construction of "real" experience. These novels develop narrative strategies that provide them the latitude to combine self-critical reflection, assertive aesthetic self-defense, and playful paradox. The focus on reading and on the links between fictional characters' reading styles and their narratives — both those they tell and those told of them — draws attention to the dynamics of the relationships between the novelist, the text, and its readers, and posits that the responsibility for social and moral effects of the text lies to a great extent with the readers rather than solely with the authors. By accentuating the importance of reader acuity and skill in the appreciation of the narrative intricacies they offer, the novels loosen the fetters imposed by moral concerns and increase their aesthetic independence from the strictures defining the genre. The texts raise questions about their own constitution and interpretation. They insist on their legitimacy as epistemological forums. Yet they refuse functional reduction and theoretical containment by celebrating the

ironies, aporias, and rich complexities peculiar to the fictional literary form of the novel, simultaneously eluding theoretical controls
and spurring theoretical reflections on the genre.

Works Consulted

Primary Sources

Blanckenburg, Friedrich von. *Versuch über den Roman.* 1774. Reprint edited and with an afterword by Eberhard Lämmert. Stuttgart: Metzler, 1965.

Bodmer, Johann Jakob, and Johann Jakob Breitinger. *Schriften zur Literatur.* Ed. Volker Meid. Stuttgart: Reclam, 1980.

Campe, Joachim Heinrich. *Wörterbuch der deutschen Sprache.* Braunschweig: Schulbuchhandlung, 1807 ff.

Cervantes, Miguel de. *The Adventures of Don Quixote de la Mancha.* Trans. Tobias Smollett. 1755. New York: Farrar-Straus-Giroux, 1986.

Diderot, Denis. "Paradoxe sur le comédien." In *Oeuvres.* Ed. A. Billy. Paris: Gallimard, 1951. 1003–58.

Engel, Johann Jakob. *Ueber Handlung, Gespräch und Erzählung.* 1774. Ed. Ernst Theodor Voss. Stuttgart: Metzler, 1964.

Gellert, Christian Fürchtegott. *Werke.* Ed. Gottfried Honnefelder. 2 vols. Frankfurt/Main: Insel, 1979.

Gerstenberg, Heinrich Wilhelm von. *H. W. Gerstenbergs Rezensionen in der Hamburgischen Neuen Zeitung, 1767–1771.* Ed. O. Fischer. Deutsche Literatur-Denkmale des 18. und 19. Jahrhunderts, 128, 3. Folge, Nr. 8. Berlin: 1904.

Gottsched, Johann Christoph. *Versuch einer critischen Dichtkunst.* 4th ed. 1751. Darmstadt: Wissenschaftliche Buchgesellschaft, 1977.

Hassencamp, Robert. "Aus dem Nachlaß der Sophie von La Roche." *Euphorion* 5 (1898): 475–502.

Homer. *The Iliad.* Translated and with an introduction by Richmond Lattimore. Chicago: U of Chicago P, 1951.

——. *The Odyssey.* With an English translation by A. T. Murray. Revised by George E. Dimock. 2 vols. Loeb Classical Library 104 + 105. Cambridge, MA and London: Harvard UP, 1995.

Horatius, Flaccus. "Epistulae." *Briefe.* Erklärt von Adolf Kiessling. Bearbeitet von Richard Heinze. Berlin: Weidmannsche Verlagsbuchhandlung, 1961.

Humboldt, Wilhelm von. "Schriften zur Anthropologie und Geschichte." In *Werke in fünf Bänden.* Vol. 3. Ed. Andreas Flitner and Klaus Giel. Darmstadt: Wissenschaftliche Buchgesellschaft, 1980.

Jacobi, Johann Georg, ed. *Iris.* Vols. 1–4. Düsseldorf: 1775.

———. *Iris.* Vols. 5–8. Berlin: Bey Haude + Spener, 1776.

Kimpel, Dieter, and Conrad Wiedemann, ed. *Theorie und Technik des Romans im 17. und 18. Jahrhundert.* 2 vols. Deutsche Texte, 16 + 17. Tübingen: Niemeyer, 1970.

La Roche, Sophie von. *Geschichte des Fräuleins von Sternheim. Von einer Freundin derselben aus Original=Papieren und anderen zuverläßigen Quellen gezogen. Herausgegeben von C. M. Wieland. Erster und Zweyter Theil.* Leipzig: bey Weidmanns Erben und Reich, 1771.

———. *Geschichte des Fräuleins von Sternheim.* Ed. Marlies Korfsmeyer. München: Winkler, 1976.

———. *Geschichte des Fräuleins von Sternheim.* Ed. Barbara Becker-Cantarino. Stuttgart: Reclam, 1983.

———. *The History of Lady Sophia Sternheim: Extracted By a Woman Friend of the Same: From Original Documents and Other Reliable Sources.* Trans. Christa Baguss Britt, with a foreword by Katherine Goodman. Albany: State University of New York, 1991.

———. "Ich bin mehr Herz als Kopf": *Sophie von La Roche: Ein Lebensbild in Briefen.* Ed. Michael Maurer. München: Beck, 1983.

Lämmert, Eberhard, ed. *Romantheorie: Dokumentation ihrer Geschichte in Deutschland 1620–1880.* Frankfurt/Main: Athenäum, 1988.

Lessing, Gotthold Ephraim. *Werke.* Ed. Herbert G. Göpfert. München: Hanser, 1970–79.

Lichtenberg, Georg Christoph. *Schriften und Briefe.* Ed. Wolfgang Promies. Vol. 1. München: Hanser, 1968.

Merck, Johann Heinrich. *Werke.* Ed. Arthur Henkel. Frankfurt/Main: Insel, 1968.

Neugebauer, Wilhelm Ehrenfried. *Der teutsche Don Quichotte Oder die Begebenheiten des Marggraf von Bellamonte, komisch und satyrisch beschrieben; aus dem Französischen übersetzt. Vier Theile.* 1753. Ed. Ernst Weber. Deutsche Neudrucke/ Reihe Texte des 18. Jahrhunderts. Stuttgart: Metzler, 1971.

Plato. *The Collected Dialogues of Plato*. Ed. Edith Hamilton and Huntington Cairns. Bollingen Series 71. New York: Pantheon, 1961.

Review of Wieland's *Don Sylvio von Rosalva*. *Allgemeine deutsche Bibliothek* 1, 2 (1765): 97–107.

Rousseau, Jean-Jacques. *Émile ou de l'éducation*. 1762. Ed. Michel Launay. Paris: Garnier-Flammarion, 1966.

———. *Julie ou La Nouvelle Héloïse*. 1760. Ed. Michel Launay. Paris: Garnier-Flammarion, 1967.

Sagar, Maria Anna. *Karolinens Tagebuch ohne ausserordentliche Handlungen, oder gerade so viel als gar keine. Geschrieben von M. A. S.* Prag: bey Wolfgang Gerle, 1774.

———. *Die verwechselten Töchter, eine wahrhafte Geschichte, in Briefen entworfen von einem Frauenzimmer*. Prag: bey Wolfgang Gerle, 1771.

Schiller, Friedrich. *Gedichte*. Ed. Georg Kurscheidt. Frankfurt/Main: Deutscher Klassiker Verlag, 1992.

Schmid, Christian Heinrich. *Theorie der Poesie nach den neuesten Grundsätzen und Nachricht von den besten Dichtern nach den angenommenen Urteilen*. 1767. Athenäums Reprints. Frankfurt/Main: Athenäum, 1972.

———. *Zusätze zur Theorie der Poesie und Nachricht von den besten Dichtern. Erste bis vierte Sammlung 1767–1769*. Athenäums Reprints. Frankfurt/Main: Athenäum, 1972.

Sonnenfels, Joseph Freiherr von. *Gesammelte Schriften*. Wien: von Baumeisterischen Schriften, 1784.

Sterne, Laurence. *The Life and Opinions of Tristram Shandy, Gentleman*. 1759–1767. Ed. Graham Petrie. With an introduction by Christopher Ricks. Aylesbury: Penguin, 1967.

Sulzer, Johann Georg. *Allgemeine Theorie der schönen Künste in einzeln, nach alphabetischer Ordnung der Kunstwörter auf einander folgenden, Artikeln abgehandelt (Neue vermehrte Ausgabe)*. 4 vols. Leipzig: Weidmanns Erben und Reich, 1786.

———. *Die schönen Künste, in ihrem Ursprung, ihrer wahren Natur und besten Anwendung betrachtet*. Leipzig: bey Weimanns Erben und Reich, 1772.

Voss, Johann Heinrich. *Homers Odüßee übersezt von Johann Heinrich Voß*. 2 vols. Vienna: 1789.

Weber, Ernst, ed. *Texte zur Romantheorie*. 2 vols. München: Fink, 1981.

Wieland, Christoph Martin. *C. M. Wielands sämmtliche Werke*. Ed. Hamburger Stiftung zur Förderung von Wissenschaft und Kultur, Wieland-Archiv Biberach and Hans Radspieler. Hamburg: 1984.

———. *Geschichte des Agathon* 1766–67. Ed. Klaus Manger. Bibliothek deutscher Klassiker, 11. Frankfurt/Main: Deutscher Klassiker Verlag, 1986.

———. *Werke*. Ed. Fritz Martini and Hans-Werner Seiffert. München: Hanser, 1964–1968.

———. *Wielands Briefwechsel*. Ed. Deutsche Akademie der Wissenschaften zu Berlin and Hans-Werner Seiffert. 5 vols. Berlin: Akademie Verlag, 1963–1983.

———. *Wielands Gesammelte Schriften*. Ed. Deutsche Kommission der Königlich Preußischen Akademie der Wissenschaften. Berlin: 1909ff.

Secondary Sources

Abel, Elizabeth, Marianne Hirsch and Elizabeth Langland, ed. *The Voyage In: Fictions of Female Development*. Hanover and London: UP of New England, 1983.

Alter, Robert. *Partial Magic: The Novel as a Self-Conscious Genre*. Berkeley and Los Angeles: U of California P, 1975.

Altman, Janet Gurkin. *Epistolarity: Approaches to a Form*. Columbus: Ohio State UP, 1982.

Apel, Friedmar. *Die Zaubergärten der Phantasie*. Heidelberg: Winter, 1978.

Armstrong, Nancy. *Desire and Domestic Fiction: A Political History of the Novel*. New York and Oxford: Oxford UP, 1987.

———. "Literature as Women's History." *Genre* 19, 4 (Winter 1986): 347–69.

Assing, Ludmilla. *Sophie von La Roche, die Freundin Wielands*. Berlin: Janke, 1859.

Bailet, Dietlinde S. *Die Frau als Verführte und als Verführerin in der deutschen und französischen Literatur des 18. Jahrhunderts*. Europäische Hochschulschriften: Reihe 1, Deutsche Sprache u. Literatur, 409. Bern: Lang, 1981.

Barilli, Renato. *Rhetoric*. Trans. Giuliana Menozzi. Minneapolis: U of Minnesota P, 1989.

Beaujean, Marion. "Das Bild des Frauenzimmers im Roman des 18. Jahrhunderts." *Wolffenbüttler Studien zur Aufklärung* 3 (1976): 9–28.

———. *Der Trivialroman in der zweiten Hälfte des 18. Jahrhunderts.* Bonn: Bouvier, 1964.

Becher, Ursula A. J. "Lektürepräferenzen und Lesepraktiken von Frauen im 18. Jahrhundert." *Aufklärung* 6, 1 (1992): 27–42. [Special issue on "Lesekulturen im 18. Jahrhundert."]

———. "Weibliches Selbstverständnis in Selbstzeugnissen des 18. Jahrhunderts." In *Weiblichkeit in geschichtlicher Perspektive: Fallstudien und Reflexionen zu Grundproblemen der historischen Frauenforschung.* Ed. Ursula A. J. Becher and Jörn Rüsen. Frankfurt/Main: Suhrkamp, 1988. 217–33.

Becker, Eva D. *Der deutsche Roman um 1780.* Stuttgart: Metzler, 1964.

Becker-Cantarino, Barbara. "Freundschaftsutopie: Die Fiktionen der Sophie La Roche." In *Untersuchungen zum Roman von Frauen um 1800.* Ed. Helga Gallas and Magdalene Heuser. Untersuchungen zur deutschen Literaturgeschichte, 55. Tübingen: Niemeyer, 1990. 92–113.

———. *Der lange Weg zur Mündigkeit: Frau und Literatur (1500–1800).* Stuttgart: Metzler, 1987.

———. "Leben als Text: Briefe als Ausdrucks- und Verständigungsmittel in der Briefkultur und Literatur des 18. Jahrhunderts." In *Frauen, Literatur, Geschichte: Schreibende Frauen vom Mittelalter bis zur Gegenwart.* Ed. Hiltrud Gnüg and Renate Möhrmann. Stuttgart: Metzler, 1985. 83–103.

———. "'Muse' und 'Kunstrichter': Sophie LaRoche und Wieland." *MLN* 99, 3 (April 1984): 571–88.

———. "Nachwort." In Sophie von La Roche, *Geschichte des Fräuleins von Sternheim.* Ed. Barbara Becker-Cantarino. Stuttgart: Reclam, 1983. 381–415.

———. "'Outsiders': Women in German Literary Culture of Absolutism." *Jahrbuch für internationale Germanistik* 16, 2 (1984): 147–57.

———, ed. *Die Frau von der Reformation zur Romantik.* Modern German Studies, 7. Bonn: Bouvier, 1980.

Beddow, Michael. *The Fiction of Humanity:. Studies in the Bildungsroman from Wieland to Thomas Mann.* Anglica Germanica Series 2. Ed. Leonard Forster and Martin Swales. Cambridge: Cambridge UP, 1982.

Blackall, Eric. *The Emergence of German as a Literary Language 1700–1775.* Cambridge: Cambridge UP, 1959.

Blackwell, Jeannine. "Bildungsroman mit Dame: The Heroine in the German Bildungsroman from 1770–1900." Ph.D. diss., Indiana University, 1982.

————. "Herzensgespräche mit Gott. Bekenntnisse deutscher Pietistinnen im 17. und 18. Jahrhundert." In *Deutsche Literatur von Frauen.* Vol. 1. Ed. Gisela Brinker-Gabler. München: Beck, 1988. 265–89.

————. "Die verlorene Lehre der Benedikte Naubert: die Verbindung zwischen Phantasie und Geschichtsschreibung." In *Untersuchungen zum Roman von Frauen um 1800.* Ed. Helga Gallas and Magdalene Heuser. Untersuchungen zur deutschen Literaturgeschichte, 55. Tübingen: Niemeyer, 1990. 148–59.

Blackwell, Jeannine, and Susanne Zantop, ed. *Bitter Healing: German Woman Writers 1700–1830: An Anthology.* European women writers series. Lincoln: U of Nebraska P, 1990.

Blumenberg, Hans. *Die Lesbarkeit der Welt.* Frankfurt/Main: Suhrkamp, 1981.

————. "Wirklichkeitsbegriff und Möglichkeit des Romans." In *Nachahmung und Illusion: Kolloquium Gießen Juni 1963: Vorlagen und Verhandlungen.* Ed. Hans Robert Jauss. Poetik und Hermeneutik, 1. München: Eidos, 1964. 9–27.

Boa, Elizabeth. "Sex and Sensibility: Wieland's Portrayal of Relationships between the Sexes in the Comische Erzählungen, Agathon, and Musarion." *Lessing Yearbook* 12 (1980): 189–218.

Booth, Wayne C. "The Self-Conscious Narrator in Comic Fiction before 'Tristram Shandy.'" *PMLA* 67 (March 1952): 163–85.

Bottingheimer, Ruth. *Grimm's Bad Girls and Bold Boys.* New Haven: Yale UP, 1987.

Bovenschen, Silvia. *Die imaginierte Weiblichkeit: Exemplarische Untersuchungen zu kulturgeschichtlichen und literarischen Präsentationsformen des Weiblichen.* Frankfurt/Main: Suhrkamp, 1979.

Bracht, Edgar. *Der Leser im Roman des 18. Jahrhunderts.* Frankfurt/Main, Bern: Lang, 1987.

Brandes, Helga. "Die Entstehung des weiblichen Lesepublikums im 18. Jahrhundert: Von den Frauenzimmerbibliotheken zu den literarischen Damengesellschaften." In *Lesen und Schreiben im 17. und 18. Jahrhundert: Studien zu ihrer Bewertung in Deutschland, England, Frankreich.* Ed. Paul Goetsch. Tübingen: Narr, 1994. 125–33.

————. "Der Frauenroman und die literarisch-publizistische Öffentlichkeit im 18. Jahrhundert." In *Untersuchungen zum Roman von Frauen um 1800.* Ed. Helga Gallas and Magdalene Heuser. Untersuchungen zur deutschen Literaturgeschichte, 55. Tübingen: Niemeyer, 1990. 41–51.

———. "Der Wandel des Frauenbildes in den deutschen Moralischen Wochenschriften." In *Zwischen Aufklärung und Restoration: Sozialer Wandel in der deutschen Literatur (1700–1848): Festschrift für Wolfgang Martens zum 65. Geburtstag.* Ed. Wolfgang Frühwald and Alberto Martino. Studien und Texte zur Sozialgeschichte der Literatur, 24. Tübingen: Niemeyer, 1989. 49–64.

Brenner, Peter J. "Kritische Form: Zur Dialektik der Aufklärung in Wielands Roman 'Don Sylvio von Rosalva.'" *Jahrbuch der deutschen Schillergesellschaft* 20 (1976): 162–83.

Brinker-Gabler, Gisela. *Deutsche Literatur von Frauen.* 2 vols. München: Beck, 1988.

Britt, Christa Baguss. "Introduction." *The History of Lady Sophia Sternheim* by Sophie von La Roche. 1771. Trans. Christa Baguss Britt. Albany: State University of New York, 1991.

Brüggemann, Fritz. "Introduction." *Die Geschichte des Fräuleins von Sternheim,* by Sophie von La Roche. 1771. Ed. Fritz Brüggemann. Leipzig: Reclam, 1938.

Brunkhorst, Martin. "Vermittlungsebenen im philosophischen Roman: Candide, Rasselas und Don Sylvio." *Arcadia* 14 (1979): 133–47.

Campe, Joachim. *Der programmatische Roman von Wielands Agathon zu Jean Pauls Hesperus.* Bonn: Bouvier, 1979.

Cavill, Barbara Maris. *Der verführte Leser. Johann Karl August Musäus' Romane und Romankritiken.* Kanadische Studien zur deutschen Sprache und Literatur, 31. New York and Bern: Lang, 1985.

Chartier, Roger. *The Order of Books: Readers, Authors, and Libraries in Europe between the Fourteenth and Eighteenth Centuries.* Trans. Lydia G. Cochrane. Stanford: Stanford UP 1994.

Craig, Charlotte. "Sophie LaRoche — a 'Praeceptra Filiarum Germaniae?'" *Studies on Voltaire and the 18th Century* 193 (1980): 1996–2002.

Cullens, Chris. "Female Difficulties, Comparativist Challenge: Novels by English and German Women, 1752–1814." In *Borderwork: Feminist Engagements with Comparative Literature.* Ed. Margaret R. Higonnet. Ithaca, NY and London: Cornell UP, 1994. 100–119.

Dawson, Ruth P. "'And this Shield is Called Self-Reliance': Emerging Feminist Consciousness in the Late Eighteenth Century." In *German Women in the Eighteenth and Nineteenth Centuries.* Ed. Ruth-Ellen Joeres and Mary Jo Maynes. Bloomington: Indiana UP, 1986. 157–74.

————. "Im Reifrock den Parnaß besteigen: Die Rezeption von Dichterinnen im 18. Jahrhundert (am Beispiel von Philippine Gatterer-Engelhard)." In *Kontroversen, alte und neue: Akten des VII. internationalen Germanisten-Kongresses Göttingen, 1985*. Ed. Albrecht Schöne. Vol. 6, *Frauensprache-Frauenliteratur?*, ed. Inge Stephan and Carl Pietzcker. Tübingen: Niemeyer, 1986. 24–29.

Dedner, Burghard. *Topos, Ideal und Realitätspostulat: Studien zur Darstellung des Landlebens im Roman des 18. Jahrhunderts*. Tübingen: Niemeyer, 1969.

DeJean, Joan. *Fictions of Sappho 1546–1937*. Chicago: Chicago UP, 1989.

————. "The Politics of Genre: Madeleine de Scudery and the Rise of the French Novel." *L'Esprit Créateur* 29, 3 (Fall 1989): 43–52.

————. *Tender Geographies: Women and the Origins of the Novel in France*. New York and Oxford: Columbia UP, 1991.

DeJean, Joan, and Nancy K. Miller, ed. *Displacements: Women, Tradition, Literatures in French*. Parallax: re-visions of culture and society. Baltimore: Johns Hopkins UP, 1991.

Duden, Barbara. *Geschichte unter der Haut*. Stuttgart: Klett-Cotta, 1987.

Ebrecht, Angelika, ed. *Brieftheorie des achtzehnten Jahrhunderts: Texte, Kommentare, Essays*. Stuttgart: Metzler, 1990.

Ehrich-Haefeli, Verena. "Gestehungskosten tugendempfindsamer Freundschaft: Probleme der weiblichen Rolle im Briefwechsel Wieland-Sophie La Roche bis zum Erscheinen der Sternheim (1750–1771)." In *Frauenfreundschaft-Männerfreundschaft: literarische Diskurse im 18. Jahrhundert*, ed. Wolfram Mauser and Barbara Becker-Cantarino. Tübingen: Niemeyer, 1991. 75–136.

Engelsing, Rolf. *Analphabetentum und Lektüre*. Stuttgart: Metzler, 1973.

————. *Der Bürger als Leser: Lesergeschichte in Deutschland 1500–1800*. Stuttgart: Metzler, 1974.

Fabian, Bernhard, ed. *Deutsches Biographisches Archiv*. München: K. G. Saur, 1986. Microfiche.

Fauchery, Pierre. *La destinée féminine dans le roman européen du dixhuitieme siecle*. Paris: Armand Colin, 1972.

Ferguson, Margaret W. "A Room Not Their Own: Renaissance Women as Readers and Writers." In *The Comparative Perspective on Literature: Approaches to Theory and Practice*. Ed. Clayton Koelb and Susan Noakes. Ithaca, NY and London: Cornell UP, 1988. 93–116.

Flessau, Kurt Ingo. *Der moralische Roman*. Köln: Böhlau, 1968.

Frenzel, Elizabeth. "Mißverstandene Literatur: Musäus' Grandison der Zweite und Wielands Die Abenteuer des Don Sylvio von Rosalva — zwei deutsche Donquichottiaden des 18. Jahrhunderts." In *Gelebte Literatur in der Literatur,* ed. Theodor Wolpers, 110–33. Göttingen: Vandenhoeck & Ruprecht, 1986.

Frevert, Ute. *Frauen-Geschichte Zwischen Bürgerlicher Verbesserung und Neuer Weiblichkeit.* Frankfurt/Main: Suhrkamp, 1986.

———. *Mann und Weib, und Weib und Mann: Geschlechter-Differenzen in der Moderne.* München: Beck, 1995.

Friedrichs, Elisabeth. *Die deutschsprachigen Schriftstellerinnen des 18. und 19. Jahrhunderts.* Stuttgart: Metzler, 1981.

Fries, Ursula. *Buhlerin und Zauberin: Eine Untersuchung zur deutschen Literatur des 18. Jahrhunderts.* München: Fink, 1970.

Gallas, Helga, and Magdalene Heuser, ed. *Untersuchungen zum Roman von Frauen um 1800.* Untersuchungen zur deutschen Literaturgeschichte, 55. Tübingen: Niemeyer, 1990.

Gallas, Helga, and Anita Runge, *Romane und Erzählungen deutscher Schriftstellerinnen um 1800: eine Bibliographie mit Standortnachweisen.* Stuttgart: Metzler, 1993.

Garbe, Christine. "Sophie oder die heimliche Macht der Frauen: Zur Konzeption des Weiblichen bei Jean-Jacques Rousseau." In *"Wissen heißt leben. . ." Beiträge zur Bildungsgeschichte von Frauen im 18. und 19. Jahrhundert.* Ed. Ilse Brehmer. Frauen in der Geschichte, IV. Düsseldorf: Schwann, 1983. 67–87.

Genette, Gérard. *Narrative Discourse Revisited.* Trans. Jane E. Lewin. Ithaca, NY: Cornell UP, 1988.

———. *Palimpsestes: La Littérature au second degré.* Paris: Seuil, 1982.

Gnüg, Hiltrud, and Renate Möhrmann, ed. *Frauen, Literatur, Geschichte: Schreibende Frauen vom Mittelalter bis zur Gegenwart.* Stuttgart: Metzler, 1985.

Goetsch, Paul, ed. *Lesen und Schreiben im 17. und 18. Jahrhundert.* Studien zu ihrer Bewertung in Deutschland, England, Frankreich. ScriptOralia, 65. Tübingen: Narr, 1994.

———. "Leserfiguren in der Erzählkunst." Germanisch-Romanische Monatsschrift 64 (1983): 199–215.

Goodman, Katherine, and Edith Waldstein, ed. *In the Shadow of Olympus: German Women Writers around 1800.* Albany: State U of New York P, 1992.

Graevenitz, Gerhart von. "Innerlichkeit und Öffentlichkeit: Aspekte deutscher 'bürgerlicher' Literatur im frühen 18. Jahrhundert." *Deutsche Vierteljahrsschrift* 49, Sonderheft (1975): 1–82.

Greiner, Martin. *Die Entstehung der modernen Unterhaltungsliteratur: Studien zum Trivialroman des 18. Jahrhunderts.* Reinbek: Rowohlt, 1964.

Grenz, Dagmar. *Mädchenliteratur: Von den moralisch-belehrenden Schriften im 18. Jahrhundert bis zur Herausbildung der Backfischliteratur im 19. Jahrhundert.* Germanistische Abhandlungen 52. Stuttgart: Metzler, 1981.

Gross, Erich. *C. M. Wielands Geschichte des Agathon: Entstehungsgeschichte.* Germanische Studien, 86. 1930. Nendeln/Liechtenstein: Kraus Reprint Limited, 1967.

Gruenter, Rainer, ed. *Leser und Lesen im 18. Jahrhundert: Colloquium d. Arbeitsstelle 18. Jh, Gesamthochschule Wuppertal, Schloß Lüntenbeck, October 24–26, 1975.* Beiträge zur Geschichte der Literatur und Kunst des 18. Jahrhunderts, 1. Heidelberg: Winter, 1977.

Hadley, Michael. *Romanverzeichnis: Bibliographie der zwischen 1750–1800 erschienenen Erstausgaben.* Bern and Las Vegas: Lang, 1977.

Haenelt, Karin. "Die Verfasser der 'Frankfurter Gelehrten Anzeigen' von 1772: Ermittlung von Kriterien zu ihrer Unterscheidung durch maschinelle Stilanalyse." *Euphorion* 78 (1984): 368–82.

Häntzschel, Günter. "Nachwort." In *Geschichte des Fräuleins von Sternheim,* by Sophie von La Roche. Ed. Marlies Korfsmeyer. München: Winkler, 1976. 301–36.

Hahl, Werner. *Reflexion und Erzählung: Ein Problem der Romantheorie von der Spätaufklärung bis zum programmatischen Realismus.* Studien zur Poetik und Geschichte der Literatur, 18. Stuttgart: Kohlhammer, 1971.

Halperin, Natalie. "Die deutschen Schriftstellerinnen in der zweiten Hälfte des 18. Jahrhunderts." Ph.D. diss., Frankfurt/Main, 1935.

Hanebutt-Benz, Eva-Maria. *Die Kunst des Lesens: Lesemöbel und Leseverhalten vom Mittelalter bis zur Gegenwart.* Frankfurt/Main: Museum für Kunsthandwerk, 1985.

Hardin, James N., ed. *Reflection and Action: Essays on the Bildungsroman.* Columbia: U of South Carolina P, 1991.

Harrison, Mette. "Irony, Utopia, and Beyond: A Critique of Bourgeois Gender Polarity in Two Late Eighteenth-Century Bildungsromane." Ph.D. diss., Princeton University, 1995.

Hausen, Karin. "Die Polarisierung der 'Geschlechtscharaktere': Eine Spiegelung der Dissoziation von Erwerbs- und Familienleben." In *Sozialgeschichte der Familie in der Neuzeit Europas.* Ed. Werner Conze. Stuttgart: Klett, 1976. 363–93.

Heidenreich, Bernd. *Sophie von La Roche — eine Werkbiographie.* Frankfurt/Main; Bern and New York: Lang, 1986.

Heuser, Magdalene. "'Das beständige Angedencken vertritt die Stelle der Gegenwart': Frauen und Freundschaften in Briefen der Frühaufklärung und Empfindsamkeit." In *Frauenfreundschaft-Männerfreundschaft: literarische Diskurse im 18. Jahrhundert.* Ed. Wolfram Mauser and Barbara Becker-Cantarino. Tübingen: Niemeyer, 1991. 141–66.

———. "'Ich wollte dieß und das von meinem Buche sagen, und gerieth in ein Vernünfteln': Poetologische Reflexionen in den Romanvorreden." In *Untersuchungen zum Roman von Frauen um 1800.* Ed. Helga Gallas and Magdalene Heuser. Untersuchungen zur deutschen Literaturgeschichte, 55. Tübingen: Niemeyer, 1990. 52–65.

———. "'Spuren trauriger Selbstvergessenheit': Möglichkeiten eines weiblichen Bildungsromans um 1800: Friederike Helene Unger." In *Kontroversen, alte und neue: Akten des VII. internationalen Germanisten-Kongresses, Göttingen, 1985,* ed. Albrecht Schöne. Vol. 6, *Frauensprache-Frauenliteratur?* Ed. Inge Stephan and Carl Pietzcker. Tübingen: Niemeyer, 1986. 30–42.

Hillmann, Heinz. "Wunderbares in der Dichtung der Aufklärung: Untersuchungen zum französischen und deutschen Feenmärchen." *Deutsche Vierteljahrsschrift für Literaturwissenschaft und Geistesgeschichte* 43 (1969): 76–113.

Hohendahl, Peter Uwe. "Empfindsamkeit und gesellschaftliches Bewußtsein." *Jahrbuch der deutschen Schillergesellschaft* 16 (1972): 176–207.

Honegger, Claudia. *Die Ordnung der Geschlechter: Die Wissenschaften vom Menschen und das Weib 1750–1850.* Frankfurt/Main and New York: Campus, 1991.

———. "Weibliche Selbstreflexion um 1800." *Feministische Studien* 7, 2 (1989): 7–22.

Hull, Isabel V. *Sexuality, State, and Civil Society in Germany, 1700–1815.* Ithaca, NY and London: Cornell UP, 1996.

Ingold, Felix Philipp. *Das Buch im Buch.* Berlin: Merve, 1988.

Iser, Wolfgang. *Der Akt des Lesens: Theorie ästhetischer Wirkung.* München: Fink, 1976.

Jacobs, Jürgen. "Die Theorie und ihr Exempel: Zur Deutung von Wielands Agathon in Blanckenburgs Versuch über den Roman." *Germanisch-Romanische Monatsschrift* 31, 1 (1981): 32–42.

———. *Wielands Romane.* Bern and München: Franke, 1969.

Jahn, Wolfgang. "Zu Wielands Don Sylvio." In *Christoph Martin Wieland.* Ed. Hansjörg Schelle. Wege der Forschung, 421. Darmstadt: Wissenschaftliche Buchgesellschaft, 1981. 307–21.

Japp, Uwe. "Das Buch im Buch: Eine Figur des literarischen Hermetismus." *Neue Rundschau* 4 (1975): 651–70.

Jauss, Hans Robert. *Ästhetische Erfahrung und literarische Hermeneutik.* Frankfurt/Main: Suhrkamp, 1982.

———, ed. *Nachahmung und Illusion: Kolloquium Gießen Juni 1963. Vorlagen und Verhandlungen.* Poetik und Hermeneutik, 1. München: Eidos, 1964.

Joeres, Ruth-Ellen. "'That girl is an entirely different character!' Yes, But Is She a Feminist? Observations on Sophie von la Roche's 'Geschichte des Fräuleins von Sternheim.'" In *German Women in the Eighteenth and Nineteenth Centuries.* Ed. Ruth-Ellen Joeres and Mary Jo Maynes. Bloomington: Indiana UP, 1986. 137–56.

Jørgensen, Sven-Aage. "Der unverheiratete Held." *Orbis Litterarum* 42, 3–4 (1987): 338–52. [Festschrift für Bengt Algot Sørensen.]

———. "Warum und zu welchem Ende schreibt man eine Vorrede? Randbemerkungen zur Leserlenkung, besonders bei Wieland." *Text und Kontext* 4, 3 (1976): 3–20.

Kayser, Wolfgang. "Die Anfänge des modernen Romans im 18. Jahrhundert und seine heutige Krise." *Deutsche Vierteljahrsschrift* 28 (1954): 417–46.

Kermode, Frank. *The Genesis of Secrecy: On the Interpretation of Narrative.* Cambridge, MA: Harvard UP, 1979.

Kleinschmidt, Erich. "Fiktion und Identifikation: Zur Ästhetik der Leserrolle im deutschen Roman zwischen 1750 und 1780." *Deutsche Vierteljahrsschrift* 53, 1 (1979): 49–74.

Klüger, Ruth. "Zum Außenseitertum der deutschen Dichterinnen." In *Untersuchungen zum Roman von Frauen um 1800.* Ed. Helga Gallas and Magdalene Heuser. Untersuchungen zur deutschen Literaturgeschichte, 55. Tübingen: Niemeyer, 1990. 13–19.

Koebner, Thomas. "Lektüre in freier Landschaft: Zur Theorie des Lese-verhaltens im 18. Jahrhundert." In *Leser und Lesen im 18. Jahrhundert: Colloquium d. Arbeitsstelle 18. Jh, Gesamthochschule Wuppertal, Schloß Lüntenbeck, October 24–26, 1975*. Ed. Rainer Gruenter. Heidelberg: Winter, 1977. 40–58.

König, Dominik von. "Lesesucht und Lesewut." In *Buch und Leser*. Ed. Herbert G. Göpfert. Schriften des Wolfenbütteler Arbeitskreises für Geschichte des Buchwesens, 1. Hamburg: Hauswedell, 1977. 89–124.

Köpke, Wulf. "Die emanzipierte Frau in der Goethezeit und ihre Dar-stellung in der Literatur." In *Die Frau als Heldin und Autorin: Neue kritische Ansätze zur deutschen Literatur*. Ed. Wolfgang Paulsen. Amherster Kolloquium zur deutschen Literatur, 10. Bern and München: Franke, 1979. 96–110.

Kontje, Todd. "The German Bildungsroman as Metafiction: Artistic Autonomy in the Public Sphere." *Michigan German Studies* 13, 2 (Fall 1987): 140–55.

———. *The German Bildungsroman: History of a National Genre*. Co-lumbia, SC: Camden House, 1993.

———. *Private Lives in the Public Sphere: the German Bildungsroman as Metafiction*. University Park, PA: Pennsylvania State UP, 1992.

———. *Women, the Novel, and the German Nation*. Cambridge: Cam-bridge UP, 1998.

Kord, Susanne. *Sich einen Namen machen: Anonymität und weibliche Au-torschaft 1700–1900*. Stuttgart: Metzler, 1996.

Košenina, Alexander. "Wie die 'Kunst von der Natur überrumpelt' wer-den kann: Anthropologie und Verstellungskunst." In *Anthropologie und Literatur um 1800*. Ed. Jürgen Bankhoff and Eda Sagarra. Publications of the Institute of Germanic Studies, University of London, 54. München: iudicum verlag, 1992. 53–71.

Kreuzer, Helmut. "Gefährliche Lesesucht: Bemerkungen zu politischer Lektürekritik im ausgehenden 18. Jahrhundert." In *Leser und Lesen im 18. Jahrhundert: Colloquium d. Arbeitsstelle 18. Jh, Gesamthochschule Wuppertal, Schloß Lüntenbeck, October 24–26, 1975*. Ed. Rainer Gruen-ter. Heidelberg: Winter, 1977. 62–75.

Kurrelmeyer, Wilhelm. "Gil Blas and Don Sylvio." *Modern Language Notes* 34 (1919): 78–81.

———. "The Sources of Wieland's Don Sylvio." *Modern Philology* 16 (1918/19): 637–48.

Kurth, Lieselotte E. "Formen der Romankritik im 18. Jahrhundert." *Modern Language Notes* (October 1968): 655–93.

————. "Historiographie und historischer Roman: Kritik und Theorie im 18. Jahrhundert." *Modern Language Notes* 79, 3 (1964): 337–62.

————. *Die zweite Wirklichkeit: Studien zum Roman des achtzehnten Jahrhunderts.* Chapel Hill: U of North Carolina P, 1969.

Kurth-Voigt, Lieselotte E. *Perspectives and Points of View: The Early Works of Wieland and Their Background.* Baltimore and London: Johns Hopkins, 1974.

————. "Wielands 'Geschichte des Agathon': Zur journalistischen Rezeption des Romans." In *Wieland Studien 1.* Ed. Wieland Archiv Biberach and Hans Radspieler. Sigmaringen: Jan Thorbecke, 1991. 9–42.

————, ed. *Modern Language Notes* 99, 3 (April 1984). [Special issue on Wieland.]

Lachmanski, Hugo. "Die deutschen Frauenzeitschriften des achtzehnten Jahrhunderts." Ph.D. diss., Berlin, 1900.

Landes, Joan B. *Women and the Public Sphere in the Age of the French Revolution.* Ithaca, NY and London: Cornell UP, 1988.

Lange, Sigrid. "Über epische und dramatische Dichtung Weimarer Autorinnen: Überlegungen zur Geschlechterspezifika in der Poetologie." *Zeitschrift für Germanistik* NF 1, 2 (1991): 341–51.

Lange, Victor. "Erzählformen im Roman des achtzehnten Jahrhunderts." *Anglia* 76 (1958): 129–44.

————. "Zur Gestalt des Schwärmers im deutschen Roman des 18. Jahrhunderts." In *Festschrift für Richard Alewyn.* Ed. Herbert Singer and Benno von Wiese. Köln and Graz: Böhlau, 1967. 151–64.

Langen, August. *Der Wortschatz des deutschen Pietismus.* 1954. Tübingen: Niemeyer, 1968.

Langner, Margrit. *Sophie von La Roche — die empfindsame Realistin.* Heidelberg: Winter, 1995.

Laqueur, Thomas. *Making Sex: Body and Gender from the Greeks to Freud.* Cambridge, MA and London: Harvard UP, 1990.

Lehmann, Christine. *Das Modell Clarissa: Liebe, Verführung, Sexualität und Tod der Romanheldinnen des 18. und 19. Jahrhunderts.* Stuttgart: Metzler, 1991.

Leierseder, Brigitte. "Das Weib nach den Ansichten der Natur: Studien zur Herausbildung des bürgerlichen Frauenleitbildes an der Wende vom 18. zum 19. Jahrhundert." Ph.D. diss., München, 1981.

Leopold, Keith. "Wielands Don Sylvio: The First Modern German Novel?" In *Festschrift für Ralph Farrell.* Ed. A. Stephens, 9–16. Bern and Las Vegas: Lang, 1977.

Leventhal, Robert S. *The Disciplines of Interpretation: Lessing, Herder, Schlegel and Hermeneutics in Germany 1750–1800.* European Cultures, 5. Berlin and New York: de Gruyter, 1994.

———. "Semiotic Interpretation and Rhetoric in the German Enlightenment 1740–1760." *Deutsche Vierteljahrsschrift* 60, 2 (1986): 223–49.

Lipping, Margita. "Bürgerliche Konzepte zur weiblichen Sexualität in der zweiten Hälfte des 18. Jahrhunderts." In *Frauenkörper — Medizin — Sexualität.* Ed. Johanna Geyer-Kordesch and Annette Kuhn. Geschichtsdidaktik/Studien und Materialien, 64; 33. Düsseldorf: Schwann, 1986. 28–42.

Loster-Schneider, Gudrun. *Sophie La Roche: Paradoxien weiblichen Schreibens im 18. Jahrhundert.* Tübingen: Narr, 1995.

MacArthur, Elizabeth J. *Extravagant Narratives: Closure and Dynamics in the Epistolary Form.* Princeton: Princeton UP, 1990.

Manger, Klaus. "Kommentar." In *Geschichte des Agathon.* Ed. Klaus Manger. Bibliothek deutscher Klassiker, 11. Frankfurt/Main: Deutscher Klassiker Verlag, 1986.

Markley, Robert. "Sentimentality as Performance: Shaftesbury, Sterne, and the Theatrics of Virtue." In *The New Eighteenth-Century.* Ed. Felicity Nussbaum and Laura Brown. New York and London: Methuen, 1987. 210–30.

Marx, Friedhelm. *Erlesene Helden: Don Sylvio, Werther, Wilhelm Meister und die Literatur.* Heidelberg: Winter, 1995.

Martens, Wolfgang. *Die Botschaft der Tugend: Die Aufklärung im Spiegel der deutschen moralischen Wochenschriften.* Stuttgart: Metzler, 1968.

Martini, Fritz. "Nachwort." In Christoph Martin Wieland, *Werke.* Ed. Fritz Martini and Hans-Werner Seiffert. Vol. 1, ed. Fritz Martini and Reinhard Döhl. München: Hanser, 1964. 915–66.

Masten, Jeffrey. *Textual Intercourse: Collaboration, Authorship, and Sexualities in Renaissance Drama.* Cambridge Studies in Renaissance Literature and Culture, 14. Cambridge: Cambridge UP, 1997.

Maurer, Michael. *Aufklärung und Anglophilie in Deutschland.* Veröffentlichungen des Deutschen Historischen Instituts London, 19. Göttingen and Zürich: Vandenhoeck u. Ruprecht, 1987.

———. "Das Gute und das Schöne: Sophie von LaRoche (1730–1807)." *Euphorion* 79, 2 (1985): 111–38.

Mauser, Wolfram, and Barbara Becker-Cantarino, ed. *Frauenfreundschaft-Männerfreundschaft: literarische Diskurse im 18. Jahrhundert.* Tübingen: Niemeyer, 1991.

Mayer, Gerhart. *Der deutsche Bildungsroman: Von der Aufklärung bis zur Gegenwart.* Stuttgart: Metzler, 1992.

McCarthy, John A. "The Art of Reading and the Goals of the German Enlightenment." *Lessing Yearbook* 16 (1984): 79–94.

———. *Christoph Martin Wieland.* Boston: Twayne, 1979.

———. *Crossing Boundaries: A Theory and History of Essay Writing in German, 1680–1815.* Philadelphia: U of Pennsylvania P, 1989.

———. *Fantasy and Reality: An Epistemological Approach to Wieland.* Frankfurt/Main and Bern: Lang, 1974.

McKeon, Michael. *The Origins of the English Novel: 1600–1740.* Baltimore, London: Johns Hopkins, 1987.

Meise, Helga. "Der Frauenroman: Erprobungen der Weiblichkeit." In *Deutsche Literatur von Frauen.* Vol. 1. Ed. Gisela Brinker-Gabler. München: Beck, 1988. 434–52.

———. "'Papierne' Mädchen: Ansichten von der Unschuld im Frauenroman des 18. Jahrhunderts." In *Kontroversen, alte und neue: Akten des VII. internationalen Germanisten-Kongresses, Göttingen, 1985,* ed. Albrecht Schöne. Vol 6, *Frauensprache-Frauenliteratur?* Ed. Inge Stephan and Carl Pietzcker. Tübingen: Niemeyer, 1986. 18–23.

———. "Politisierung der Weiblichkeit oder Revolution des Frauenromans? Deutsche Romanautorinnen und die Französische Revolution." In *Die Marseillaise der Weiber.* Ed. Inge Stephan and Sigrid Weigel. 55–73. Das Argument: Argument Sonderband, AS 185; Literatur im historischen Prozeß, N. F. 26. Hamburg: Argument, 1989.

———. *Die Unschuld und die Schrift: Deutsche Frauenromane im 18. Jahrhundert.* Reihe Metro 14. Berlin/Marburg: Guttandin & Hoppe, 1983.

———. "'Wer ist sie?' Zum Verhältnis von weiblicher Identität und literarischem Diskurs in Frauenromanen des 18. Jahrhunderts." In *Das Subjekt des Diskurses.* Ed. Manfred Geier and Harold Woetzel. Berlin: Argument-Verlag, 1983. 108–21.

———. "Das Werk von Maria Anna Sagar: Konstitutionsbedingungen und Probleme des Romans von Frauen im 18. Jahrhundert." In *Untersuchungen zum Roman von Frauen um 1800.* Ed. Helga Gallas and Magdalene Heuser. Untersuchungen zur deutschen Literaturgeschichte, 55. Tübingen: Niemeyer, 1990. 79–91.

Meyer-Krentler, Eckhardt. "Die Leiden der jungen Wertherin: Weibliche Sozialisation durch die Literatur im späten 18. Jahrhundert." In *Zwischen Aufklärung und Restoration: Sozialer Wandel in der deutschen Literatur (1700–1848): Festschrift für Wolfgang Martens zum 65. Geburtstag.* Ed. Wolfgang Frühwald and Alberto Martino. Studien und Texte zur Sozialgeschichte der Literatur, 24. Tübingen: Niemeyer, 1989. 225–48.

Michelsen, Peter. *Laurence Sterne und der deutsche Roman des achtzehnten Jahrhunderts.* Göttingen: Vandenhoeck & Ruprecht, 1962.

Milch, Werner. *Sophie La Roche: Die Großmutter der Brentanos.* Frankfurt: Societätsverlag, 1935.

Miller, Nancy K. *The Heroine's Text: Readings in the French and English Novel 1722–1782.* New York: Columbia UP, 1980.

———. *Subject to Change: Reading Feminist Writing.* Gender and Culture. New York: Columbia UP, 1988.

Miller, Norbert. *Der empfindsame Erzähler: Untersuchungen an Romananfängen des 18. Jahrhunderts.* Literatur als Kunst. München: Hanser, 1968.

Miller, Steven R. *Die Figur des Erzählers in Wielands Romanen.* Göppinger Arbeiten zur Germanistik, 19. Göppingen: Alfred Kümmerle, 1970.

Minden, Michael. *The German Bildungsroman: Incest and Inheritance.* Cambridge: Cambridge UP, 1997.

Moser-Verrey, Monique. *Dualité et continuité du discours narratif dans Don Sylvio, Joseph Andrews et Jacques le Fataliste.* Bern and Frankfurt/Main: Lang, 1976.

Mücke, Dorothea E. von. *Virtue and the Veil of Illusion: Generic Innovation and the Pedagogical Project in Eighteenth-Century Literature.* Stanford: Stanford UP, 1991.

Myers, Sylvia H. "Learning, Virtue and the Term 'Bluestocking'": *Studies in Eighteenth-Century Culture* 15 (1986): 279–88.

Naumann, Ursula. "Das Fräulein und die Blicke: Eine Betrachtung über Sophie von La Roche." *Zeitschrift für deutsche Philologie* 107 (1988): 488–516.

Nenon, Monika. *Autorschaft und Frauenbildung: Das Beispiel Sophie von La Roche.* Epistemata: Reihe Literaturwissenschaft, 31. Würzburg: Königshausen & Neumann, 1988.

————. "Sophie von La Roche: Schreiben für 'Teutschlands Töchter': Überlegungen zur Funktion der Mutterrolle." In *Mütter und Mütterlichkeit: Wandel und Wirksamkeit einer Phantasie in der deutschen Literatur: Festschrift für Verena Ehrich-Haefeli*. Ed. Irmgard Roebling and Wolfram Mauser. Würzburg: Königshausen & Neumann, 1996. 65–76.

Nickisch, Reinhard M. G. "Briefkultur: Entwicklung und sozialgeschichtliche Bedeutung des Frauenbriefs im 18. Jahrhundert." In *Deutsche Literatur von Frauen*. Ed. Gisela Brinker-Gabler. München: Beck, 1988. 389–409.

————. "Die Frau als Briefschreiberin im Zeitalter der deutschen Aufklärung." *Wolfenbüttler Studien zur Aufklärung* 3 (1976): 29–65.

Nies, Fritz. *Bahn und Bett und Blütenduft: Eine Reise durch die Welt der Lesebilder*. Darmstadt: Wissenschaftliche Buchgesellschaft, 1991.

————. "Suchtmittel oder Befreiungsakt? Wertungen von Lektüre in der bildenden Kunst des 18. Jahrhunderts." In *Lesen und Schreiben im 17. und 18. Jahrhundert: Studien zu ihrer Bewertung in Deutschland, England, Frankreich*. Ed. Paul Goetsch. Tübingen: Narr, 1994. 151–68.

Noakes, Susan. "On the Superficiality of Women." In *The Comparative Perspective on Literature: Approaches to Theory and Practice*. Ed. Clayton Koelb and Susan Noakes. Ithaca, NY and London: Cornell UP, 1988. 339–55.

Nobis, Helmut. *Phantasie und Moralität: Das Wunderbare in Wielands Dschinnistan und der Geschichte des Prinzen Biribinker*. Kronberg/Ts.: Scriptor, 1976.

Nörtemann, Regina. "Die 'Begeisterung des Poeten' in den Briefen eines Frauenzimmers: Zur Korrespondenz der Caroline Christiane Lucius mit Christian Fürchtegott Gellert." In *Die Frau im Dialog: Studien zu Theorie und Geschichte des Briefes*. Ed. Anita Runge and Lieselotte Steinbrügge. Ergebnisse der Frauenforschung, 21. Stuttgart: Metzler, 1991. 13–32.

————. "Brieftheoretische Konzepte im 18. Jahrhundert und ihre Genese." In *Brieftheorie des achtzehnten Jahrhunderts: Texte, Kommentare, Essays*. Ed. Angelika Ebrecht. Stuttgart: Metzler, 1990. 211–24.

————. "Schwache Werkzeuge als Öffentliche Richterinnen." *Archiv für Kulturgeschichte* 72, 2 (1990): 381–403.

Norton, Robert E. *The Beautiful Soul: Aesthetic Morality in the Eighteenth Century*. Ithaca, NY and London: Cornell UP, 1995.

Nussbaum, Felicity A. "Eighteenth-Century Women's Autobiographical Commonplaces." In *The Private Self: Theory and Practice of Women's Autobiographical Writings.* Ed. Shari Benstock. Chapel Hill and London: U of North Carolina P, 1988. 147–71.

Oettinger, Klaus. *Phantasie und Erfahrung: Studien zur Erzählpoetik Christoph Martin Wielands.* München: Fink, 1970.

Petschauer, Peter. "Christina Dorothea Leporin (Erxleben), Sophia (Gutermann) von La Roche, and Angelika Kauffmann: Background and Dilemmas of Independence." *Studies in Eighteenth-Century Culture* 15 (1986): 127–43.

———. "Sophie von Laroche, Novelist between Reason and Emotion." *The Germanic Review* 57, 2 (Spring 1982): 70–77.

Plato, K. Th. *Sophie La Roche in Koblenz/Ehrenbreitstein.* Koblenz: Görres-Verlag, 1978.

Poitzsch, Manfred. *Zeitgenössische Persiflagen auf C. M. Wieland und seine Schriften.* Frankfurt/Main and Bern: Lang, 1972.

Preisendanz, Wolfgang. "Die Auseinandersetzung mit dem Nachahmungsprinzip in Deutschland und die besondere Rolle der Romane Wielands." In *Nachahmung und Illusion: Kolloquium Gießen Juni 1963: Vorlagen und Verhandlungen.* Ed. Hans Robert Jauss. Poetik und Hermeneutik, 1. München: Eidos, 1964. 72–95.

Prokop, Ulrike. "Die Einsamkeit der Imagination: Geschlechterkonflikt und literarische Produktion um 1770." In *Deutsche Literatur von Frauen.* Ed. Gisela Brinker-Gabler, vol 1:325–65. München: Beck, 1988.

———. "Die Melancholie der Cornelia Goethe." *Feministische Studien* 2 (1983): 46–78.

Redfield, Marc. *Phantom Formations: Aesthetic Ideology and the Bildungsroman.* Ithaca, NY: Cornell UP, 1996.

Ridderhoff, Kuno. "Introduction." *Geschichte des Fräuleins von Sternheim,* by Sophie von La Roche. Ed. Kuno Ridderhoff. Deutsche Literaturdenkmale des 18. und 19. Jahrhunderts. Dritte Folge 18. Berlin: Behr, 1907. 183.

———. "Sophie von La Roche, die Schülerin Richardsons und Rousseaus." Ph.D. diss., Göttingen, 1895.

Riley, Helene Kastinger. *Die weibliche Muse.* Columbia, SC: Camden House, 1986.

Robert, Marthe. *The Old and the New: From Don Quixote to Kafka.* Trans. Carol Cosman. Foreword by Robert Alter. Berkeley and Los Angeles: U of California P, 1977.

Rogan, Richard G. *The Reader in the Novels of C. M. Wieland.* European University Studies: Series 1, German language and literature. Las Vegas, Bern and Frankfurt/Main: Lang, 1981. 433.

——. "The Reader in Wieland's *Die Abenteuer des Don Sylvio von Rosalva.*" *German Studies Review* 4, 2 (1981): 177–93.

Runge, Anita, and Lieselotte Steinbrügge. *Die Frau im Dialog: Studien zu Theorie und Geschichte des Briefes.* Ergebnisse der Frauenforschung, 21. Stuttgart: Metzler, 1991.

Saariluoma, Liisa. *Die Erzählstruktur des frühen deutschen Bildungsromans.* Annales Academiae Scientiarum Fennicae. Dissertationes Humanarum Litterarum, 42. Helsinki: Suomalainen Tiedeakatemia, 1985.

Sagmo, Ivar. "Über die ästhetische Erziehung des Eros: Zu Wielands Roman *Don Sylvio von Rosalva.*" *Text und Kontext* 9, 2 (1981): 185–97.

Salvaggio, Ruth. *Enlightened Absence: Neoclassical Configurations of the Feminine.* Chicago: U of Illinois P, 1988.

Sammons, Jeffrey L. "The Bildungsroman for Nonspecialists: An Attempt at Clarification." In *Reflection and Action: Essays on the Bildungsroman.* Ed. James N. Hardin. Columbia: U of South Carolina P, 1991. 26–45.

Sauder, Gerhard. "Argumente der Fiktionskritik 1680–1730 und 1960–1970." *Germanisch-Romanische Monatsschrift* 26 (1976): 129–40.

——. *Empfindsamkeit.* Vol. 1. Stuttgart: Metzler, 1974; Vol. 3. Stuttgart: Metzler, 1980.

——. "Gefahren empfindsamer Vollkommenheit für Leserinnen und die Furcht von Romanen in einer Damenbibliothek." In *Leser und Lesen im 18. Jahrhundert: Colloquium d. Arbeitsstelle 18. Jh, Gesamthochschule Wuppertal, Schloß Lüntenbeck, October 24–26, 1975.* Ed. Rainer Gruenter. Heidelberg: Winter, 1977. 83–91.

——. "Lichtenbergs ungeschriebene Romane." *Zeitschrift für deutsche Philologie* 98, 4 (1979): 481–97.

Schaefer, Klaus. *Christoph Martin Wieland.* Stuttgart and Weimar: Metzler, 1996.

Schelle, Hansjörg, ed. *Christoph Martin Wieland.* Wege der Forschung, 421. Darmstadt: Wissenschaftliche Buchgesellschaft, 1981.

——. *Christoph Martin Wieland: North American Scholarly Contributions on the Occasion of the 250th Anniversary of His Birth. 1983.* Tübingen: Niemeyer, 1984.

Schenda, Rudolf. *Volk ohne Buch.* 1970. München: dtv, 1977.

Schiebinger, Londa. *The Mind Has No Sex? Women in the Origins of Modern Science.* Cambridge, MA and London: Harvard UP, 1989.

Schieth, Lydia. *Die Entwicklung des deutschen Frauenromans im ausgehenden 18. Jahrhundert: Ein Beitrag zur Gattungsgeschichte.* Helicon, 5. Frankfurt/Main, Bern, New York, and Paris: Lang, 1987.

Schings, Hans-Jürgen. "Agathon — Anton Reiser — Wilhelm Meister. Zur Pathogenese des modernen Subjekts im Bildungsroman." In *Goethe im Kontext: Kunst und Humanität, Naturwissenschaft und Politik von der Aufklärung bis zur Restauration.* Ed. Wolfgang Wittkowski. Tübingen: Niemeyer, 1984. 42–68.

———. "Der anthropologische Roman: Seine Entstehung und Krise im Zeitalter der Spätaufklärung." In *Die Neubestimmung des Menschen: Wandlungen des anthropologischen Konzepts im 18. Jahrhundert.* Ed. Bernhard Fabian, Wilhelm Schimdt-Biggemann and Rudolf Vierhaus. Studien zum Achtzehnten Jahrhundert, 3. München: Kraus, 1980. 247–75.

———. *Melancholie und Aufklärung: Melancholiker und ihre Kritiker in Erfahrungsseelenkunde und Literatur des 18. Jahrhunderts.* Stuttgart: Metzler, 1977.

Schmid, Pia. *Zeit des Lesens — Zeit des Fühlens: Anfänge des deutschen Bildungsbürgertums: Ein Lesebuch.* Berlin: Quadriga-Verlag Severin, 1985.

Schmidt, Erich. *Richardson, Rousseau und Goethe.* 1875. Jena: Frommannsche Buchhandlung Walter Biedermann, 1924.

Schön, Erich. *Der Verlust der Sinnlichkeit/oder Die Verwandlung des Lesers: Mentalitätswandel um 1800.* Stuttgart: Klett-Cotta, 1987.

———. "Weibliches Lesen: Romanleserinnen im späten 18. Jahrhundert." In *Untersuchungen zum Roman von Frauen um 1800.* Ed. Helga Gallas and Magdalene Heuser. Untersuchungen zur deutschen Literaturgeschichte, 55. Tübingen: Niemeyer, 1990. 20–40.

Schönert, Jörg. *Roman und Satire im 18. Jahrhundert: Ein Beitrag zur Poetik.* Stuttgart: Metzler, 1969.

Schor, Naomi. *Reading in Detail: Aesthetics and the Feminine.* New York and London: Methuen, 1987.

Schostack, Renate. "Wieland und Lavater: Beitrag zur Geistesgeschichte des ausgehenden 18. Jahrhunderts." Ph.D. diss., Freiburg, 1964.

Scott, Joan Wallach. *Gender and the Politics of History.* Gender and Culture. New York: Columbia UP, 1988.

Seiler, Christiane. "Alter(n): Eine 'zinsbare Kunst?' Betrachtungen zu Agathon mit einem Seitenblick auf Die Wahlverwandtschaften." In *Exile and Enlightenment: Studies in German and Comparative Literature*. Ed. Uwe Faulhaber and Jerry Glenn. Detroit: Wayne State UP, 1987. 105–14.

————. "Die Rolle des Lesers in Wielands Don Sylvio von Rosalva und Agathon." *Lessing Yearbook* 9 (1977): 152–65.

Selbmann, Rolf. *Der deutsche Bildungsroman*. Stuttgart: Metzler, 1994.

Sengle, Friedrich. *Wieland*. Stuttgart: Metzler, 1949.

Sharpe, Lesley. "Über den Zusammenhang der tierischen Natur der Frau mit ihrer geistigen: Zur Anthropologie der Frau um 1800." In *Anthropologie und Literatur um 1800*. Ed. Jürgen Bankhoff and Eda Sagarra. Publications of the Institute of Germanic Studies, University of London, 54. München: iudicum verlag, 1992. 213–25.

Shookman, Ellis. *Noble Lies, Slant Truths, Necessary Angels: Aspects of Fictionality in the Novels of Christoph Martin Wieland*. Chapel Hill and London: U of North Carolina P, 1997.

Smith, John H. "Sexual Difference, Bildung and the Bildungsroman." *Michigan German Studies* 13, 2 (Fall 1987): 206–25.

Spickernagel, Wilhelm. "Die Geschichte des Fräuleins von Sternheim von Sophie von La Roche und Goethes Werther." Ph.D. diss., Greifswald, 1911.

Spiegel, Marianne. *Der Roman und sein Publikum im frühen 18. Jahrhundert 1700–1767*. Bonn: Bouvier, 1967.

Spies, Bernhard. "Sophie von La Roches 'Geschichte des Fräuleins von Sternheim' und die moderne Trivialliteratur: Das moralische Vorbild als psychologische Kompensation." *Literatur für Leser*, 2 (1991): 80–89.

Starnes, Thomas C. *Christoph Martin Wieland: Leben und Werk aus zeitgenössischen Quellen dargestellt*. Sigmaringen: Thorbecke, 1987.

Steinbrügge, Lieselotte. "Die Aufteilung des Menschen: Zur anthropologischen Bestimmung der Frau in Diderots Encyclopedie." In *"Wissen heißt leben. . ." Beiträge zur Bildungsgeschichte von Frauen im 18. und 19. Jahrhundert*. Ed. Ilse Brehmer. Frauen in der Geschichte, 4. Düsseldorf: Schwann, 1983. 51–64.

————. *Das moralische Geschlecht: Theorien und literarische Entwürfe über die Natur der Frau in der französischen Aufklärung*. Weinheim/Basel: Freie Universität Berlin, 1987.

Stern, Guy. "Saint or Hypocrite? A Study of Wieland's 'Jacinte Episode.'" *Germanic Review* 29 (1954): 96–101.

———. "Wieland als Herausgeber der 'Sternheim.'" In *Christoph Martin Wieland: North American Scholarly Contributions on the Occasion of the 250th Anniversary of His Birth.* 1983. Ed. Hansjörg Schelle. Tübingen: Niemeyer, 1984. 195–208.

Stockhammer, Robert. *Leseerzählungen: Alternativen zum hermeneutischen Verfahren.* Stuttgart: M+P Verlag für Wissenschaft und Forschung, 1991.

Sudhof, Siegfried. "Sophie LaRoche." In *Deutsche Dichter des achtzehnten Jahrhunderts.* Ed. Benno von Wiese. Berlin: E. Schmidt, 1977. 300–319.

Suleiman, Susan R., and Inge Crosman, ed. *The Reader in the Text: Essays on Audience and Interpretation.* Princeton: Princeton UP, 1980.

Swales, Martin. *The German Bildungsroman from Wieland to Hesse.* Princeton: Princeton UP, 1978.

Thickstun, Margaret O. *Fictions of the Feminine: Puritan Doctrine and the Representation of Women.* Ithaca, NY and London: Cornell UP, 1989.

Thomé, Horst. "Menschliche Natur und Allegorie sozialer Verhältnisse: Zur politischen Funktion philosophischer Konzeptionen in Wielands 'Geschichte des Agathon.'" *Jahrbuch der deutschen Schillergesellschaft* 22 (1978): 205–34.

Touaillon, Christine. *Der deutsche Frauenroman des 18. Jahrhunderts.* 1919. Reprint Bern, Frankfurt/Main, and Las Vegas: Lang, 1979.

Tronskaja, Maria. *Die deutsche Prosasatire der Aufklärung.* Berlin: Rütten und Loening, 1969.

Tropsch, Stephan. "Wielands Don Sylvio und Cervantes' Don Quijote." *Euphorion* 4, Ergänzungsheft 4 (1899): 32–61.

Tschapke, Reinhard. *Anmutige Vernunft: Christoph Martin Wieland und die Rhetorik.* Stuttgarter Arbeiten zur Germanistik 228. Stuttgart: Heinz, 1990.

Vosskamp, Wilhelm. "Dialogische Vergegenwärtigung beim Schreiben und Lesen: Zur Poetik des Briefromans im 18. Jahrhundert." *Deutsche Vierteljahrsschrift* 45 (1971): 80–116.

———. *Romantheorie in Deutschland: Von Martin Opitz bis Friedrich von Blanckenburg.* Stuttgart: Metzler, 1973.

Wahrenburg, Fritz. *Funktionswandel des Romans und ästhetische Norm: Die Entwicklung seiner Theorie in Deutschland bis zur Mitte des 18. Jahrhunderts.* Stuttgart: Metzler, 1976.

Ward, Albert. *Book Production, Fiction, and the German Reading Public 1740–1800.* Oxford: Oxford UP, 1974.

Watt, Ian. *The Rise of the Novel: Studies in Defoe, Richardson and Fielding.* Berkeley and Los Angeles: U of California P, 1957.

Waugh, Patricia. *Metafiction: The Theory and Practice of Self-Conscious Fiction.* London and New York: Methuen, 1984.

Weber, Ernst. *Die poetologische Selbstreflexion im deutschen Roman des 18. Jahrhunderts: Zu Theorie und Praxis von "Roman," "Historie" und pragmatischem Roman.* Studien zur Poetik und Geschichte der Literatur, 34. Stuttgart, Berlin, Köln, and Mainz: Kohlhammer, 1974.

———, ed. *Der Buchmarkt der Goethezeit.* Hildesheim: Gerstenberg, 1986.

Weber, Ernst, and Christine Mithal, ed. *Deutsche Originalromane zwischen 1680 und 1780: eine Bibliographie mit Besitznachweisen (BRD + DDR).* Berlin: E. Schmidt, 1983.

Wellbery, Caroline Elisabeth. "Sensibility and Socialization: The German Sentimental Novel of the 1770s." Ph.D. diss., Stanford University, 1982.

Werner, Meike. "'Mein Herz ist unschuldig und rein': Die Geschichte des Fräuleins von Sternheim." In *Grenzen der Moral.* Ed. Ursula Konnertz. Tübingen: Ed. diskord, 1991. 125–45.

Wiede-Behrendt, Ingrid. *Lehrerin des Schönen, Wahren, Guten: Literatur und Frauenbildung im ausgehenden 18. Jahrhundert am Beispiel Sophie von LaRoche.* Frankfurt/Main, Bern, New York, and Paris: Lang, 1987.

Wiener Stadt- und Landesbibliothek. *Portheim Katalog: Personen.* Wien. [n. d.] Microfiche.

Wilson, W. Daniel. *The Narrative Strategy of Wieland's "Don Sylvio von Rosalva."* Canadian Studies in German Language and Literature, 24. Bern, Frankfurt/Main Las Vegas: Lang, 1981.

———. "'Prächt'ge Vase' or 'halber Topf'? A Horatian Verse in Wieland's *Agathon.*" *Modern Language Notes* 95, 3–4 (1980): 664–69.

Wölfel, Kurt. "Daphnes Verwandlung: Zu einem Kapitel in Wielands 'Agathon.'" In *Christoph Martin Wieland.* Ed. Hansjörg Schelle. Wege der Forschung, 421. Darmstadt: Wissenschaftliche Buchgesellschaft, 1981. 232–50.

———. "Friedrich von Blanckenburgs Versuch über den Roman." In *Deutsche Romantheorien: Beiträge zu einer historischen Poetik des Romans in Deutschland.* Ed. Reinhold Grimm. Frankfurt/Main: Athenäum, 1968. 29–60.

Wolpers, Theodor, ed. *Gelebte Literatur in der Literatur: Studien zu Erscheinungsformen eines literarischen Motivs: Bericht über Kolloquien der Kommission für literaturwissenschaftliche Motiv-u. Themenforschung 1983–1985.* Abhandlungen der Akademie der Wissenschaften in Göttingen. Philologisch-Historische Klasse Folge 3, 152. Göttingen: Vandenhoeck & Ruprecht, 1986.

Woodmansee, Martha. "Toward a Genealogy of the Aesthetic: The German Reading Debate of the 1790s." *Cultural Critique* 11 (Winter 1988–89): 203–21.

———. *The Author, Art, and the Market: Rereading the History of Aesthetics.* New York: Columbia UP, 1994.

Wunderlich, Heinke. "Buch und Leser in der Buchillustration des 18. Jahrhunderts." In *Die Buchillustration im 18. Jahrhundert: Colloquium der Arbeitsstelle 18. Jahrhundert, Gesamthochschule Wuppertal, Universität Münster,* 93–123. Heidelberg: Winter, 1980.

Würzner, M. H. "Die Figur des Lesers in Wielands 'Geschichte des Agathon.'" In *Christoph Martin Wieland.* Ed. Hansjörg Schelle. Wege der Forschung, 421. Darmstadt: Wissenschaftliche Buchgesellschaft, 1981. 399–406.

Wuthenow, Ralph-Rainer. *Im Buch die Bücher oder Der Held als Leser.* Frankfurt/Main: Europäische Verlagsanstalt, 1980.

———. "Lesende Figuren: Die Bücher im Buch." *Neue Rundschau* 100, 2 (1989): 152–62.

Zantop, Susanne. "Aus der Not eine Tugend . . . Tugendgebot und Öffentlichkeit bei Friederike Helene Unger." In *Untersuchungen zum Roman von Frauen um 1800.* Ed. Helga Gallas and Magdalene Heuser. Untersuchungen zur deutschen Literaturgeschichte, 55. Tübingen: Niemeyer, 1990. 132–47.

———. "Trivial Pursuits? An Introduction to German Women's Writing from the Middle Ages to 1830." In *Bitter Healing: German Woman Writers 1700–1830: An Anthology.* Ed. Jeannine Blackwell and Susanne Zantop. European women writers series. Lincoln: U of Nebraska P, 1990. 9–50.

Notes

Introduction

[1] Johann Georg Sulzer, *Allgemeine Theorie der schönen Künste in einzeln, nach alphabetischer Ordnung der Kunstwörter auf einander folgenden, Artikeln abgehandelt* (Neue vermehrte Ausgabe), 4 vols. (Leipzig: Weidmanns Erben und Reich, 1786), 4:101.

"One applies this term to whatever has in its content, tone, or expression the character that was dominant in the novels of old, such as adventurousness or extremity in actions, events, and sentiments. What is natural is just about the exact opposite of the novelistic." (All translations are mine unless otherwise noted.)

[2] "Since, in our times, the character of novels increasingly approaches the natural character of true history, and our authors increasingly make it a rule to school their taste by following the ancients . . . it is to be expected that it [the novelistic] will slowly disappear."

[3] Ernst Weber's important study, *Die poetologische Selbstreflexion im deutschen Roman des 18. Jahrhunderts* (Stuttgart, Berlin, Köln, Mainz: Kohlhammer, 1974), focuses on aesthetic reflection in prefaces of novels (5–85 on the period 1700–1760; 86–122 on the period 1760–1790). Magdalene Heuser concentrates on the theoretical stances taken in prefaces to texts by female authors in her article, "'Ich wollte dieß und das von meinem Buche sagen, und gerieth in ein Vernünfteln': Poetologische Reflexionen in den Romanvorreden," in *Untersuchungen zum Roman von Frauen um 1800,* ed. Helga Gallas and Magdalene Heuser (Tübingen: Niemeyer, 1990), 52–65. See also Sven-Aage Jørgensen, "Warum und zu welchem Ende schreibt man eine Vorrede? Randbemerkungen zur Leserlenkung, besonders bei Wieland," *Text und Kontext* 4, 3 (1976): 3–20.

[4] The following bibliographies of eighteenth-century novels provide a sense of the variety and numbers of novels published: Marianne Spiegel, *Der Roman und sein Publikum im frühen 18. Jahrhundert 1700–1767* (Bonn: Bouvier, 1967); Michael Hadley, *Romanverzeichnis: Bibliographie der zwischen 1750–1800 erschienenen Erstausgaben* (Bern and Las Vegas: Lang, 1977); Ernst Weber and Christine Mithal, ed., *Deutsche Originalromane zwischen 1680 und 1780: eine Bibliographie mit Besitznachweisen (BRD + DDR)* (Berlin: E. Schmidt, 1983); Helga Gallas and Anita Runge, *Romane und Erzählungen deutscher Schriftstellerinnen um 1800: eine Bibliographie mit Standortnachweisen* (Stuttgart: Metzler, 1993).

[5] For an account of some of the difficulties with the definition and usage of the term "Bildungsroman" see Todd Kontje, *The German Bildungsroman: History of a National Genre* (Columbia, SC: Camden House, 1993); Jeffrey L. Sammons, "The Bildungsroman for Nonspecialists: An Attempt at Clarification," in *Reflection and Action: Essays on the Bildungsroman,* ed. James N. Hardin (Columbia: U of South Carolina P, 1991), 26–45; Rolf Selbmann, *Der deutsche Bildungsroman* (Stuttgart: Metzler, 1994); Marc Redfield, *Phantom Formations: Aesthetic Ideology and the Bildungsroman* (Ithaca: Cornell UP, 1996). The term "Frauenroman," promoted by Christine Touaillon's influential study *Der deutsche Frauenroman des 18. Jahrhunderts* of 1919 (reprint, Bern, Frankfurt Main, and Las Vegas: Lang, 1979), is still used in newer criticism. Lydia Schieth's book *Die Entwicklung des deutschen Frauenromans im ausgehenden 18. Jahrhundert. Ein Beitrag zur Gattungsgeschichte* (Frankfurt/Main, Bern, New York, and Paris: Lang, 1987), 1–22, addresses the history and some of the difficulties with the designation (although she does retain it).

[6] See, for example, the varied ways in which Wieland's *Agathon* is considered as precursor or originator of the Bildungsroman by Martin Swales, *The German Bildungsroman from Wieland to Hesse* (Princeton: Princeton UP, 1978); Gerhart Mayer, *Der deutsche Bildungsroman: Von der Aufklärung bis zur Gegenwart* (Stuttgart: Metzler, 1992); Robert E. Norton, *The Beautiful Soul: Aesthetic Morality in the Eighteenth Century* (Ithaca and London: Cornell UP, 1995); Klaus Schaefer, *Christoph Martin Wieland* (Stuttgart and Weimar: Metzler, 1996); and Michael Minden, *The German Bildungsroman: Incest and Inheritance* (Cambridge: Cambridge UP, 1997).

[7] For example Chris Cullens, "Female Difficulties, Comparativist Challenge: Novels by English and German Women, 1752–1814," in *Borderwork: Feminist Engagements with Comparative Literature,* ed. Margaret R. Higonnet (Ithaca, NY and London: Cornell UP, 1994), 100–19; also Schieth, 28–49 and passim. In his book *Women, the Novel, and the German Nation 1771–1871* (Cambridge: Cambridge UP, 1998), Todd Kontje adopts the term "domestic fiction," coined by Nancy Armstrong in *Desire and Domestic Fiction: A Political History of the Novel* (New York and Oxford: Oxford UP, 1987), to designate the novel tradition initiated by La Roche.

[8] A notable exception is Jeannine Blackwell, "Bildungsroman mit Dame: The Heroine in the German Bildungsroman from 1770–1900" (Ph.D. diss., Indiana University, 1982), who analyzes the portrayal of the heroine in novels by Gutzkow and Fontane as well as in novels by women authors. Mette Harrison is, to my knowledge, unique in considering novels by La Roche and Goethe together as examples of the Bildungsroman in "Irony, Utopia, and Beyond: A Critique of Bourgeois Gender Polarity in Two Late Eighteenth-Century Bildungsromane" (Ph.D. diss., Princeton University, 1995). Harrison aims to redefine the genre of Bildungsroman as a critique of the limitations that polar gender construction places on the novel's plot. John H. Smith, "Sexual Dif-

ference, Bildung and the Bildungsroman," *Michigan German Studies* 13, 2 (Fall 1987): 206–25, and Dorothea E. von Mücke, *Virtue and the Veil of Illusion: Generic Innovation and the Pedagogical Project in Eighteenth-Century Literature* (Stanford: Stanford UP, 1991) also consider the importance of gender for an understanding of the German Bildungsroman and its relation to a new model of male subjectivity. *The Voyage In: Fictions of Female Development*, ed. Elizabeth Abel, Marianne Hirsch, and Elizabeth Langland (Hanover and London: UP of New England, 1983) addresses the limitations of the Bildungsroman paradigm for stories of female subjectivity.

[9] For example, the essays collected in *Untersuchungen zum Roman von Frauen um 1800*, ed. Gallas and Heuser; *Bitter Healing: German Woman Writers 1700–1830: An Anthology*, ed. Jeannine Blackwell and Susanne Zantop (Lincoln: U of Nebraska P, 1990); Barbara Becker-Cantarino, *Der lange Weg zur Mündigkeit: Frau und Literatur (1500–1800)* (Stuttgart: Metzler, 1987); Magdalene Heuser, "'Spuren trauriger Selbstvergessenheit': Möglichkeiten eines weiblichen Bildungsromans um 1800: Friederike Helene Unger," in *Kontroversen, alte und neue: Akten des VII. internationalen Germanisten-Kongresses, Göttingen, 1985*, ed. Albrecht Schöne, vol. 6, *Frauensprache-Frauenliteratur?* ed. Inge Stephan and Carl Pietzcker (Tübingen: Niemeyer, 1986), 30–42; Helga Meise, *Die Unschuld und die Schrift: Deutsche Frauenromane im 18. Jahrhundert* (Berlin/Marburg: Guttandin & Hoppe, 1983).

[10] Blackwell and Harrison bridge this divide. La Roche and some of her male contemporaries, particularly Goethe, are treated together in studies of the sentimental or epistolary novel, for example by Peter Uwe Hohendahl, "Empfindsamkeit und gesellschaftliches Bewußtsein," *Jahrbuch der deutschen Schillergesellschaft* 16 (1972): 176–207; Wilhelm Vosskamp, "Dialogische Vergegenwärtigung beim Schreiben und Lesen: Zur Poetik des Briefromans im 18. Jahrhundert," *Deutsche Vierteljahrsschrift* 45 (1971): 80–116; and Caroline Wellbery, "Sensibility and Socialization: The German Sentimental Novel of the 1770s" (Ph.D. diss., Stanford University, 1982), but the aspect of gendered writing is largely ignored. Heuser's article "Poetologische Reflexionen" is one of the few that looks at theoretical positions taken by women writers. Gudrun Loster-Schneider, *Sophie La Roche: Paradoxien weiblichen Schreibens im 18. Jahrhundert* (Tübingen: Narr, 1995), approaches the poetological aspects of La Roche's texts through Wieland's theoretical formulations.

[11] Patricia Waugh, *Metafiction: The Theory and Practice of Self-Conscious Fiction* (London and New York: Methuen, 1984), 2.

[12] Isabel V. Hull, in *Sexuality, State, and Civil Society in Germany, 1700–1815* (Ithaca and London: Cornell UP, 1996), presents the self-understanding of these "practitioners of civil society," 214–15.

[13] Albert Ward, *Book Production, Fiction, and the German Reading Public 1740–1800* (Oxford: Oxford UP, 1974), and Ernst Weber, *Der Buchmarkt der Goethezeit* (Hildesheim: Gerstenberg, 1986), provide information on the

book market; see also the bibliographies of eighteenth-century novels listed above, note 4.

[14] The following studies share my interests in how novels present reading and readers: Lieselotte Kurth, *Die zweite Wirklichkeit: Studien zum Roman des achtzehnten Jahrhunderts* (Chapel Hill: U of North Carolina P, 1969), examines novels whose reading characters create "second realities" in the context of novel theories, yet her discussions do not successfully integrate the theoretical concerns into the presentation of the individual novels. Uwe Japp's article "Das Buch im Buch. Eine Figur des literarischen Hermetismus," *Neue Rundschau* 4 (1975): 651–70, considers literary hermeticism; "the book in the book" is a figure of augmentation rather than reduction, he argues, grounded in language and history. Hans Blumenberg's work on the book as metaphor, *Die Lesbarkeit der Welt* (Frankfurt/Main: Suhrkamp, 1981), is likewise relevant here. Ralph-Rainer Wuthenow, *Im Buch die Bücher oder Der Held als Leser* (Frankfurt/Main: Europäische Verlagsanstalt, 1980), proceeds primarily descriptively in his consideration of the figure of the book in the book from Dante to Borges. Edgar Bracht, *Der Leser im Roman des 18. Jahrhunderts* (Frankfurt/Main and Bern: Lang, 1987), has attempted a comprehensive work on the reader in the eighteenth-century novel; his interest in developing a methodology of "Motivgeschichte," however, excludes substantial considerations of theoretical issues. Robert Stockhammer's readings of eighteenth-century texts in *Leseerzählungen: Alternativen zum hermeneutischen Verfahren* (Stuttgart: M+P Verlag für Wissenschaft und Forschung, 1991) and Friedhelm Marx's *Erlesene Helden: Don Sylvio, Werther, Wilhelm Meister und die Literatur* (Heidelberg: Winter, 1995) are closest to my interest.

Chapter 1

[1] Fritz Wahrenburg discusses the developing theory of the novel through 1740 in *Funktionswandel des Romans und ästhetische Norm: Die Entwicklung seiner Theorie in Deutschland bis zur Mitte des 18. Jahrhunderts* (Stuttgart: Metzler, 1976). Wilhelm Vosskamp's investigation *Romantheorie in Deutschland: Von Martin Opitz bis Friedrich von Blanckenburg* (Stuttgart: Metzler, 1973) includes novel theory of the second half of the century up to 1774. I follow the work of both authors here. The following anthologies contain many of the theoretical texts I discuss here in easily accessible form: Ernst Weber, ed., *Texte zur Romantheorie,* 2 vols. (München: Fink, 1981), henceforth cited in the text as *T;* Dieter Kimpel and Conrad Wiedemann, ed., *Theorie und Technik des Romans im 17. und 18. Jahrhundert,* 2 vols. (Tübingen: Niemeyer, 1970), henceforth cited in the text as *TT;* Eberhard Lämmert, ed., *Romantheorie: Dokumentation ihrer Geschichte in Deutschland 1620–1880* (Frankfurt/Main: Athenäum, 1988), henceforth cited in the text as *R.*

[2] Vosskamp distinguishes among three directions of novel criticism on moralistic grounds: Calvinists, Pietists, and aesthetic-cultural critics attacked the

genre for slightly different theological and ethical reasons (*Romantheorie,* 121–41). See also Wahrenburg's chapter on religious opponents of the novel, 167–82.

[3] On the topos of the poetry as lies see Hans Blumenberg, "Wirklichkeitsbegriff und Möglichkeit des Romans," in *Nachahmung und Illusion: Kolloquium Gießen Juni 1963. Vorlagen und Verhandlungen,* ed. Hans Robert Jauss, Poetik und Hermeneutik, 1 (München: Eidos, 1964), 9–27, and Gerhard Sauder, "Argumente der Fiktionskritik 1680–1730 und 1960–1970," in *Germanisch-Romanische Monatsschrift* 26 (1976): 129–40.

[4] Novels "fully arrest the head, as it were, set the person into a sweat of *passions,* consequently ruin one's health and make one *melancholy* and cowardly."

[5] Hieronymous Freyer, "Teutsche Programma vom Roman lesen" (1730), *T* 1:545.

[6] Review of G. Heidegger's *Mythoscopia Romantica* (1700), *R* 57; correspondence with Duke Anton Ulrich von Braunschweig (1712–1714), *TT* 1:67–69.

[7] "Schertz- und Ernsthaffter, Vernünfftiger und Einfältiger Gedancken über allerhand Lustige und nützliche Bücher und Fragen" (1688); reviews of E. G. Happel (1689) and of D. C. Lohenstein (1689): See *R* 38–50 and *T* 1:262–82.

[8] "Indeed, I am amazed that our *author* did not say that Eve, just before eating from the forbidden tree, had read a *novel* or a *histoire galante, presented* by the despicable snake."

[9] For a detailed discussion of the treatment of the novel in moral weeklies see Wolfgang Martens, *Die Botschaft der Tugend: Die Aufklärung im Spiegel der deutschen moralischen Wochenschriften* (Stuttgart: Metzler, 1968), 492–520.

[10] These arguments were voiced as early as the turn of the century with respect to a male readership by Weise and others; see Vosskamp (*Romantheorie,* 96–120) and Wahrenburg on the development of the novel as a bourgeois genre from the beginning of the century to 1740 (132–261).

[11] Georg Friedrich Meier, "Ob es erlaubt sey, die so genanten Romainen oder erdichteten Geschichte zu lesen?" *Der Gesellige* (1750), *R* 88.

[12] "The desire that captivates the reader diminishes the effort and he reveals his entire heart, without knowing or suspecting it in the least."

[13] Johann Christoph Gottsched, *Versuch einer critischen Dichtkunst,* 4th ed. (1751; reprint, Darmstadt: Wissenschaftliche Buchgesellschaft, 1977), 505–28. On Gottsched cf. Vosskamp, *Romantheorie,* 145–51 and Wahrenburg, 159–67.

[14] Johann Jakob Bodmer, "Von dem Charakter des Don Quixote und des Sancho Pansa" (1741), in Johann Jakob Bodmer and Johann Jakob Breitinger, *Schriften zur Literatur,* ed. Volker Meid (Stuttgart: Reclam, 1980), 261–82. One interesting product of the Quixote fashion prior to Wieland's

Don Sylvio is Wilhelm Ehrenfried Neugebauer's novel *Der teutsche Don Quichotte* (1753), which vigorously engages questions of poetics.

[15] Johann Adolf Schlegel, "Von der Eintheilung der Künste" in Schlegel's translation of Charles Batteux, "Einschränkung der schönen Künste auf Einen einzigen Grundsatz" (Leipzig, 1751), *R* 97.

[16] Christian Fürchtegott Gellert, "Praktische Abhandlung von dem guten Geschmacke in Briefen" (1751), in Gellert, *Werke,* ed. Gottfried Honnefelder, 2 vols. (Frankfurt/Main: Insel, 1979), 2:137–88.

[17] Karl Friedrich Troeltsch, "Vorrede von dem Nuzen der Schauspiels-Regeln bei den Romanen," preface to *Geschichte einiger Veränderungen des menschlichen Lebens* (1753), *T* 2:154–74.

[18] "The more the poet places hindrances along the way that heighten the uncertainty of the reader and increase his desire, the better and more touchingly he will know how to win over the reader."

[19] See, for example, Gotthold Ephraim Lessing, review of Toussaint, *Histoire des passions* (1751), *R* 91–92; Johann Carl Dähnert, review of *Amusemens d'un Prisonnier* (1751), *R* 89–91.

[20] These arguments are made, for example, in "Schreiben über einige englische Romane" in the journal *Neue Erweiterung der Erkenntnis und des Vergnügens* (1755), *T* 2:191–95.

[21] "If the aesthetic magician wants to show me his miracles, then his first miracle must be to capture my faith. . . . He must enchant my sentiments or I will not believe him."

[22] Johann Heinrich Merck, *Werke,* ed. Arthur Henkel (Frankfurt/Main: Insel, 1968), 535–39, 566–71.

[23] Merck, "Über den Mangel des epischen Geistes in unserm lieben Vaterland," in Merck, *Werke,* 385–91.

[24] Georg Christoph Lichtenberg, *Sudelbücher* D 367, in Lichtenberg, *Schriften und Briefe,* ed. Wolfgang Promies (München: Hanser, 1968), 1:286–87.

[25] Lichtenberg's "Vorschlag zu einem Orbis Pictus für deutsche dramatische Schriftsteller, Romanen-Dichter und Schauspieler," in *Schriften und Briefe* 3:376–92, for example, proposed compiling a collection of expressions, oaths, and physical characteristics from all walks of life; his *Sudelbücher* also contain entries of this type. On Lichtenberg's positions on the novel, see Gerhard Sauder, "Lichtenbergs ungeschriebene Romane," *Zeitschrift für deutsche Philologie* 98, 4 (1979): 481–97, here especially 487.

[26] Johann Georg Sulzer, *Die schönen Künste, in ihrem Ursprung, ihrer wahren Natur und besten Anwendung betrachtet* (Leipzig: bey Weidmanns Erben und Reich, 1772), 17–18.

[27] "They are the sirens, whose song no one is able to resist."

[28] "Without this guidance toward a higher purpose, the muses would be seductive harlots."

[29] Christian Heinrich Schmid's *Theorie der Poesie nach den neuesten Grundsätzen* (1767; reprint, Frankfurt/Main: Athenäum, 1972) offered an earlier systematic approach to the novel as an epic art form; his ideal of the successful novel was the work of Richardson.

[30] On Blanckenburg's indebtedness to Lessing, Mendelssohn, and Garve, see Kurt Wölfel, "Friedrich von Blanckenburgs Versuch über den Roman," in *Deutsche Romantheorien: Beiträge zu einer historischen Poetik des Romans in Deutschland*, ed. Reinhold Grimm (Frankfurt/Main: Athenäum, 1968), 29–60.

[31] Johann Jakob Engel, *Ueber Handlung, Gespräch und Erzählung* (1774; reprint, ed. Ernst Theodor Voss, Stuttgart: Metzler, 1964).

[32] On the limitations of Blanckenburg's reading of *Agathon* see Jürgen Jacobs, "Die Theorie und ihr Exempel: Zur Deutung von Wielands Agathon in Blanckenburgs Versuch über den Roman," *Germanisch-Romanische Monatsschrift* 31, 1 (1981): 32–42; Eberhard Lämmert's afterword to his edition of Blanckenburg (Stuttgart: Metzler, 1965); Vosskamp, *Romantheorie*, 177–205; Wölfel, "Blanckenburgs Versuch."

[33] Robert S. Leventhal's study, *The Disciplines of Interpretation: Lessing, Herder, Schlegel and Hermeneutics in Germany 1750–1800* (Berlin and New York: de Gruyter, 1994), and his "Semiotic Interpretation and Rhetoric in the German Enlightenment 1740–1760," *Deutsche Vierteljahrsschrift* 60, 2 (1986): 223–49, which I follow here, detail the emergence of critical hermeneutics. Dorothea von Mücke interprets the move from the paradigms of *Anschaulichkeit* to *Bildung* in *Virtue and the Veil of Illusion*. See also Robert Stockhammer's eclectic "Excurs" on reception theories in *Leseerzählungen*, 123–51.

[34] Leventhal, "Semiotic Interpretation," 238. Leventhal translates "hermeneutische Billigkeit" as "hermeneutic economy" (236).

[35] On this shift see Erich Kleinschmidt, "Fiktion und Identifikation: Zur Ästhetik der Leserrolle im deutschen Roman zwischen 1750 und 1780," *Deutsche Vierteljahrsschrift* 53, 1 (1979): 49–74. See also John A. McCarthy, "The Art of Reading and the Goals of the German Enlightenment," *Lessing Yearbook* 16 (1984): 79–94, on the Enlightenment concept of the ideal reader after 1750.

[36] In his studies, Fritz Nies offers an interesting history of Western iconography of readers, which I draw on here: *Bahn und Bett und Blütenduft: Eine Reise durch die Welt der Lesebilder* (Darmstadt: Wissenschaftliche Buchgesellschaft, 1991) and "Suchtmittel oder Befreiungsakt? Wertungen von Lektüre in der bildenden Kunst des 18. Jahrhunderts," in *Lesen und Schreiben im 17. und 18. Jahrhundert: Studien zu ihrer Bewertung in Deutschland, England, Frankreich*, ed. Paul Goetsch (Tübingen: Narr, 1994), 151–68. See also Heinke Wunderlich, "Buch und Leser in der Buchillustration des 18. Jahrhunderts," in *Die Buchillustration im 18. Jahrhundert. Colloquium der Ar-*

beitsstelle 18. Jahrhundert, Gesamthochschule Wuppertal, Universität Münster (Heidelberg: Winter, 1980), 93–123 and Eva-Maria Hanebutt-Benz, *Die Kunst des Lesens: Lesemöbel und Leseverhalten vom Mittelalter bis zur Gegenwart* (Frankfurt/Main: Museum für Kunsthandwerk, 1985).

[37] Erich Schön, *Der Verlust der Sinnlichkeit oder Die Verwandlung des Lesers: Mentalitätswandel um 1800* (Stuttgart: Klett-Cotta, 1987), 163–97. Schön traces not only an accommodation to the body but also the tendency toward restricting the body while reading.

[38] Nies, *Bahn und Bett*, 56.

[39] Nies outlines the development of images presenting the eroticized woman reader, *Bahn und Bett*, 37, 55–56.

[40] See Dominik von König, "Lesesucht und Lesewut," in *Buch und Leser*, ed. Herbert G. Göpfert (Hamburg: Hauswedell, 1977), 89–124, on this terminology's appearance in the early 1770s, its relation to the earlier "Büchersucht," and the victims of "Lesesucht" as women and youths.

[41] See Pia Schmid, *Zeit des Lesens — Zeit des Fühlens. Anfänge des deutschen Bildungsbürgertums: Ein Lesebuch* (Berlin: Quadriga-Verlag Severin, 1985), 119.

[42] Martha Woodmansee traces the contours of this debate at the end of the century, with a view to aesthetic theories, in "Toward a Genealogy of the Aesthetic: The German Reading Debate of the 1790s," *Cultural Critique* 11 (Winter 1988–89): 203–21. See also Bracht's chapter on "Die Lesesuchtdebatte" in *Der Leser im Roman*, 390–448; Rudolf Schenda, *Volk ohne Buch* (München: dtv, 1977), 53–66; Pia Schmid, *Zeit des Lesens*, 100–131; Schön, *Verlust*, 46–49 and 238–86, and Schön, "Weibliches Lesen: Romanleserinnen im späten 18. Jahrhundert," in *Untersuchungen zum Roman von Frauen um 1800*, ed. Gallas and Heuser, 20–40. Helmut Kreuzer addresses the politics of the debate in "Gefährliche Lesesucht: Bemerkungen zu politischer Lektürekritik im ausgehenden 18. Jahrhundert," in *Leser und Lesen im 18. Jahrhundert: Colloquium d. Arbeitsstelle 18. Jh, Gesamthochschule Wuppertal, Schloß Lüntenbeck, October 24–26, 1975*, ed. Rainer Gruenter (Heidelberg: Winter, 1977), 62–75.

[43] See, for example, the images of "Büchernarren" in Hanebutt-Benz, 176–86.

[44] Nies, *Bahn und Bett*, 42.

[45] Thomas Koebner discusses (male) desire for reading and the "Lektüretraum" as a sign and critique of the social conditions rather than of reader incompetence: "Lektüre in freier Landschaft: Zur Theorie des Leseverhaltens im 18. Jahrhundert," in *Leser und Lesen im 18. Jahrhundert*, ed. Gruenter, 40–58.

[46] Stockhammer discusses how Klopstock, for example, equates the most competent with the most masculine reader, in *Leseerzählungen*, 30–32.

[47] Susan Noakes illuminates this tradition with examples from Plato to Flaubert in her article "On the Superficiality of Women," in *The Comparative Perspective on Literature: Approaches to Theory and Practice*, ed. Clayton Koelb and Susan Noakes (Ithaca and London: Cornell UP, 1988), 339–55.

[48] "As an aesthetic judge I have a right to play (the role of) the strong intellect and to mistrust his mysterious arts."

[49] Carl Friedrich Pockels, *Versuch einer Charakteristick des weiblichen Geschlechts*, vol. 1–4, 1797–1801, 410, cited from Schön, "Weibliches Lesen," 28.

"It is quite natural. Women almost always find in novels . . . what they assiduously seek. The woman who is inclined towards love sees her own heart."

[50] The following studies offer historical analyses of these processes: Ursula Becher, "Weibliches Selbstverständnis in Selbstzeugnissen des 18. Jahrhunderts," in *Weiblichkeit in geschichtlicher Perspektive: Fallstudien und Reflexionen zu Grundproblemen der historischen Frauenforschung*, ed. Ursula A. J. Becher and Jörn Rüsen (Frankfurt/Main: Suhrkamp, 1988), 217–33; Ute Frevert, *Frauen-Geschichte Zwischen Bürgerlicher Verbesserung und Neuer Weiblichkeit* (Frankfurt/Main: Suhrkamp, 1986); and Karin Hausen, "Die Polarisierung der 'Geschlechtscharaktere.' Eine Spiegelung der Dissoziation von Erwerbs- und Familienleben," in *Sozialgeschichte der Familie in der Neuzeit Europas*, ed. Werner Conze (Stuttgart: Klett, 1976) 363–93. Silvia Bovenschen, *Die imaginierte Weiblichkeit: Exemplarische Untersuchungen zu kulturgeschichtlichen und literarischen Präsentationsformen des Weiblichen* (Frankfurt/Main: Suhrkamp, 1979), provides critical insights on the eighteenth-century cultural imagination of gender, as does Brigitte Leierseder, "Das Weib nach den Ansichten der Natur: Studien zur Herausbildung des bürgerlichen Frauenleitbildes an der Wende vom 18. zum 19. Jahrhundert" (Ph.D. diss., München, 1981). Claudia Honegger's study, *Die Ordnung der Geschlechter: Die Wissenschaften vom Menschen und das Weib 1750–1850* (Frankfurt/Main and New York: Campus, 1991) likewise focuses on the transformations in the notions of gender in the second half of the century in Germany.

[51] See particularly Thomas Laqueur, *Making Sex: Body and Gender from the Greeks to Freud* (Cambridge, MA, and London: Harvard UP, 1990), chapters 5 and 6, and Londa Schiebinger, *The Mind Has No Sex? Women in the Origins of Modern Science* (Cambridge, MA, and London: Harvard UP, 1989), chapters 6–10.

[52] Lesley Sharpe, "Über den Zusammenhang der tierischen Natur der Frau mit ihrer geistigen: Zur Anthropologie der Frau um 1800," in *Anthropologie und Literatur um 1800*, ed. Jürgen Bankhoff and Eda Sagarra (München: iudicum verlag, 1992), 213–25, here 215. Barbara Duden investigates the medical discourse on women in the early eighteenth century in *Geschichte unter der Haut* (Stuttgart: Klett-Cotta, 1987).

[53] Johann Georg Jacobi, ed., *Iris* 1, 3 (Dec. 1774): 121–28, here 121–22. Further references to *Iris* will be cited in the text. "Strength and weakness. With weakness, beauty, charm and acquiescence, in order to please the strong one, to win him over, not to be oppressed by him. Courage and timidity; with timidity, the cunning to escape violence. Power and obedience, severity and patience, protection and loyalty, profundity and lightheartedness, work and aid and refreshment, suffering and comfort. Desire and responding desire, with modesty, which controls itself so that the master will honor the subjugated beauty and will disarm himself at her feet. Love between both and a new lineage for whom they care in common. That is *man* and *woman*."

[54] On Rousseau and his enormous influence in shaping cultural understandings of gender see Lieselotte Steinbrügge, *Das moralische Geschlecht: Theorien und literarische Entwürfe über die Natur der Frau in der französischen Aufklärung* (Weinheim/Basel: Freie Universität Berlin, 1987), 67–96; Bovenschen, *Die imaginierte Weiblichkeit*, 164–81; Meise, *Die Unschuld und die Schrift*, 36–45. See also Schiebinger's chapter on "Complementarity" in *The Mind Has No Sex?* 213–44, and Leierseder's outline of anthropological conceptions of Woman as "civilizing" supplement to Man, "Das Weib nach den Ansichten der Natur," 63–69.

[55] "The mind of the man awakens to a brighter morning, to a new creation. He investigates, discovers, investigates again, compares, invents. Knowledge and desire for knowledge increase; his heart expands, he must express thoughts, share emotions. . . . In this society, in the face of these changes, the purpose of the woman remains constant. She must please the stronger one, be the helpmate of her husband and the caregiver of her children."

[56] "The male mind also wants to find pleasure through the female mind; therefore the particular capacities and charms of the latter gradually develop, sharpen and increase."

[57] Martens, *Die Botschaft der Tugend*, 538, remarks the critique of female "Schöngeisterei" found in journals especially in the 1770s.

[58] Wunderlich, "Buch und Leser," 112, notes a polarity in eighteenth-century iconography of reading women: either they preside over a happy family (for example, they read aloud to children), or they are so absorbed in their books that the children are totally neglected.

[59] See Sharpe, "Über den Zusammenhang," 220–22.

[60] Margita Lipping, "Bürgerliche Konzepte zur weiblichen Sexualität in der zweiten Hälfte des 18. Jahrhunderts," in *Frauenkörper — Medizin — Sexualität*, ed. Johanna Geyer-Kordesch and Annette Kuhn (Düsseldorf: Schwann, 1986), 28–42, here 31–32.

[61] . . . "or too obscure for the lighthearted and frivolous, or too strong and violent, or some other 'too' for the tender heart and the flowery fantasy of the young beauties."

[62] "Therefore we consider it useful, and hope to gain the gratitude of our beautiful public, if we offer to it from these forbidden gardens that are secured and full of traps at least some of the most beautiful flowers and the best fruits, which anyone who knows what is good will recognize as salutary — if we copy for our female readers some of the most excellent passages from the newly published books that are considered dangerous, difficult to understand, and so on."

[63] Barbara Becker-Cantarino, *Der lange Weg zur Mündigkeit,* provides a social history of German women's writing. See especially chapters 3 and 4, 149–302, on education and on female authors.

[64] Margaret W. Ferguson treats this association for the period 1400–1700 in "A Room Not Their Own: Renaissance Women as Readers and Writers," in *The Comparative Perspective on Literature: Approaches to Theory and Practice,* ed. Clayton Koelb and Susan Noakes (Ithaca and London: Cornell UP, 1988), 93–116. For the eighteenth century, see Sylvia H. Myers, "Learning, Virtue and the Term 'Bluestocking,'" *Studies in Eighteenth-Century Culture* 15 (1986): 279–88.

[65] Ruth P. Dawson shows how female authors were judged according to their feminine virtues in "Im Reifrock den Parnaß besteigen: Die Rezeption von Dichterinnen im 18. Jahrhundert (am Beispiel von Philippine Gatterer-Engelhard)," in *Frauensprache-Frauenliteratur?* ed. Stephan and Pietzcker, 24–29. Susanne Zantop analyzes the female-authored novel as a "Trojan horse," duplicitous writing that has emancipatory potential by the very act of engaging in public discourse, in "Aus der Not eine Tugend. . .Tugendgebot und Öffentlichkeit bei Friederike Helene Unger," in *Untersuchungen zum Roman von Frauen um 1800,* ed. Gallas and Heuser, 132–47, here 142.

[66] On epistolary theory and gender see particularly: Angelika Ebrecht, ed., *Brieftheorie des achtzehnten Jahrhunderts: Texte, Kommentare, Essays* (Stuttgart: Metzler, 1990) and Anita Runge and Lieselotte Steinbrügge, ed., *Die Frau im Dialog: Studien zu Theorie und Geschichte des Briefes* (Stuttgart: Metzler, 1991).

[67] In *Reading in Detail: Aesthetics and the Feminine* (New York and London: Methuen, 1987), Naomi Schor shows the connotation of the detail with femininity in the aesthetics of the eighteenth-century (see especially her chapters on Reynolds and Hegel, 11–41); Sigrid Lange's article on gender and aesthetics in eighteenth-century Germany illuminates some of the pitfalls of an essentialist attribution of narrative style: "Über epische und dramatische Dichtung Weimarer Autorinnen: Überlegungen zur Geschlechterspezifika in der Poetologie," *Zeitschrift für Germanistik* NF 1, 2 (1991): 341–51.

[68] Wilhelm von Humboldt, "Plan einer vergleichenden Anthropologie," in *Werke in fünf Bänden,* ed. Andreas Flitner and Klaus Giel, vol. 3 (Darmstadt: Wissenschaftliche Buchgesellschaft, 1980), 370.

"Experience teaches that women do not take on those genres whose success depends primarily on their artistic shape, only possible through genius, such as epic and dramatic poetry and the plastic arts. Instead they try their hand almost exclusively at those which provide more surface, as it were, that allow the simple attraction and richness of the material more space: music, painting, the novel."

[69] Cf. Wölfel, "Blanckenburg's Versuch," 41.

[70] See Hans-Jürgen Schings, "Der anthropologische Roman: Seine Entstehung und Krise im Zeitalter der Spätaufklärung," in *Die Neubestimmung des Menschen: Wandlungen des anthropologischen Konzepts im 18. Jahrhundert,* ed. Bernhard Fabian, Wilhelm Schimdt-Biggemann and Rudolf Vierhaus (München: Kraus, 1980), 247–75, here 256.

[71] See Kleinschmidt, "Fiktion und Identifikation," 57, and Koebner, "Lektüre in freier Landschaft," 42.

[72] Rolf Engelsing, *Der Bürger als Leser: Lesergeschichte in Deutschland 1500–1800* (Stuttgart: Metzler, 1974), 310. Male novel-readers of the eighteenth-century were either young, or professional literati. The professionalization of bourgeois society and the attendant lack of free time cost men the chance to read, while the same gender polarization and relegation of women to the private sphere made reading a substitute for inaccessible experience of the world. Schieth's chapter on pressures of publication at the end of the eighteenth century also documents the importance of gender considerations for the book market (*Frauenroman,* 70–113).

[73] Hull, *Sexuality, State, and Civil Society,* 241–42.

[74] Dorothea von Mücke interprets the literary mechanisms that contribute to shaping the "male individual as masculine citizen" in *Virtue and the Veil of Illusion,* 58–60 and passim.

[75] Jeffrey Masten, *Textual Intercourse: Collaboration, Authorship, and Sexualities in Renaissance Drama* (Cambridge: Cambridge UP, 1997), 5.

[76] Nancy Armstrong has argued that "no history, literary or otherwise, can claim to be historical if it accedes to a notion of history that does not acknowledge the role of gender," in "Literature as Women's History," *Genre* 19, 4 (Winter 1986): 347–69, here 351. Gender is, speaking with Joan Wallach Scott, the historically specific social organization of perceived sexual difference; to analyze gender is to examine a constitutive element of social relationships based on cultural understandings of the differences between the sexes: *Gender and the Politics of History* (New York: Columbia UP, 1988), 42–45.

Chapter 2

[1] Christoph Martin Wieland, "Wie man liest," *Der teutsche Merkur* (January 1781): 70–74, in Wieland, *Werke,* ed. Fritz Martini and Hans-Werner Seiffert (München: Hanser, 1964–1968), 3:429–31.

[2] *Wielands Briefwechsel,* ed. Deutsche Akademie der Wissenschaften zu Berlin and Hans-Werner Seiffert, 5 vols. (Berlin: Akademie Verlag, 1963–1983), 3: Nr. 170, 169–70.

"It is a kind of satirical novel that is philosophical enough, under its appearance of frivolity and which I imagine will not bore any sort of reader, except the austere ones."

[3] "To my surprise, this entertainment became so interesting that I made a project out of it and decided to make something as sensible as I possibly could from my material that is foolish enough in itself."

[4] This has been shown by Peter Michelsen, *Laurence Sterne und der deutsche Roman des achtzehnten Jahrhunderts* (Göttingen: Vandenhoeck & Ruprecht, 1962), 181–99.

[5] Kurth, *Die zweite Wirklichkeit.*

[6] Monique Moser-Verrey, *Dualité et continuité du discours narratif dans Don Sylvio, Joseph Andrews et Jacques le Fataliste* (Bern and Frankfurt/Main: Lang, 1976), 11–71, traces the reading styles of the novel's characters and also addresses the relationship they have to narrative in the novel, yet her findings are so schematized as to hinder her investigation. Elizabeth Frenzel's article is primarily an influence study, and considers only Don Sylvio as a reader: "Mißverstandene Literatur. Musäus' Grandison der Zweite und Wielands Die Abenteuer des Don Sylvio von Rosalva — zwei deutsche Donquichottiaden des 18. Jahrhunderts," in *Gelebte Literatur in der Literatur,* ed. Theodor Wolpers (Göttingen: Vandenhoeck & Ruprecht, 1986), 110–33. Likewise, Bracht, *Der Leser im Roman,* 46–88, presents Sylvio's reading style and merely mentions other figures as readers. Stockhammer, *Leseerzählungen,* 89–110, focuses on the hero's reading attitude to consider how *Don Sylvio* presents the power of fiction as a cure against limiting misreading.

[7] W. Daniel Wilson, in *The Narrative Strategy of Wieland's "Don Sylvio von Rosalva"* (Bern, Frankfurt/Main and Las Vegas: Lang, 1981), describes the narrative tactic of *Don Sylvio* as one which distinguishes between implied readers with various degrees of interpretive competence. The less critical reader, he argues, is gradually drawn into the novel as a fairy tale while presuming to read a satire. The more critical reader will recognize the devices which facilitate this transition from ostensible satire against the genre to delightful participation within it, and will enjoy the sophistication of the literary design. Studies of the fictive or implied reader include Steven R. Miller, *Die Figur des Erzählers in Wielands Romanen* (Göppingen: Alfred Kümmerle, 1970); Richard G. Rogan, "The Reader in Wieland's *Die Abenteuer des Don Sylvio von Rosalva,*" *German Studies Review* 4, 2 (1981): 177–93; Christiane Seiler, "Die Rolle des Lesers in Wielands 'Don Sylvio von Rosalva' und 'Agathon,'" *Lessing Yearbook* 9 (1977): 152–65.

[8] For example Michelsen, *Laurence Sterne,* and particularly Ellis Shookman, *Noble Lies, Slant Truths, Necessary Angels: Aspects of Fictionality in the Novels*

of Christoph Martin Wieland (Chapel Hill and London: U of North Carolina P, 1997), 27–45.

[9] Wolfgang Preisendanz analyzes the novel's emancipatory strategy in the context of contemporary theoretical positions, and remarks on its innovative turn toward psychologizing poetic criteria in his article "Die Auseinandersetzung mit dem Nachahmungsprinzip in Deutschland und die besondere Rolle der Romane Wielands," in *Nachahmung und Illusion*, ed. Jauss, 72–95. Klaus Oettinger, *Phantasie und Erfahrung. Studien zur Erzählpoetik Christoph Martin Wielands* (München: Fink, 1970), 103–19, has also addressed the narrative strategy and poetics of the novel, yet his analysis is unable to account adequately for Wieland's irony.

[10] Wolfgang Kayser, "Die Anfänge des modernen Romans im 18. Jahrhundert und seine heutige Krise," *Deutsche Vierteljahrsschrift* 28 (1954): 417–46, here 425–35.

[11] Marx, *Erlesene Helden*, 53–110.

[12] "The Victory of Nature over Enthusiasm or The Adventures of Don Sylvio of Rosalva: A Story in Which Everything Miraculous Occurs Naturally." The preface title is: "Afterword by the Editor, Which Was Made into a Foreword Through the Mistake of the Scribe." The novel will be cited from the text of the first edition of 1764 in Christoph Martin Wieland, *Werke,* ed. Fritz Martini and Hans-Werner Seiffert, vol. 1 (München: Hanser, 1964), here 9. Further page references will be given in the text. All translations are mine.

[13] On Sterne and the eighteenth-century German novel, see Michelsen, *Laurence Sterne,* particularly 177–224 on Wieland.

[14] For example, Lieselotte E. Kurth-Voigt reads the editor as the model of the "rational man" and conflates him with the narrator of the novel, in *Perspectives and Points of View: The Early Works of Wieland and Their Background* (Baltimore and London: Johns Hopkins, 1974), 121.

[15] "She actually feared that I had become insane, a concern which, I admit, did no honor to my reason."

[16] "In short, I could easily have pulled all of my neighbors into the game and who knows if the laughter would not have rolled along from alley to alley and have in the end shaken up the entire city including the suburbs, if I had not had the good sense to put away my manuscript."

[17] Bracht's interpretation of the preface as "deutlich genug ein Nachklang des barocken 'gros rire,' das von der Schwermut reinigt und hier als sozialer Funke überspringt" (72–73) neglects these aspects of the preface.

[18] "Krampfhaft, zu Muskelverzerrungen führend" according to the edition cited, 876.

[19] Hans-Jürgen Schings, *Melancholie und Aufklärung: Melancholiker und ihre Kritiker in Erfahrungsseelenkunde und Literatur des 18. Jahrhunderts* (Stuttgart: Metzler, 1977), 197–98 and, for background information, 171–84, discusses how the theological discourse on these topics is embedded in the

preface of *Don Sylvio*. See also Victor Lange, "Zur Gestalt des Schwärmers im deutschen Roman des 18. Jahrhunderts," in *Festschrift für Richard Alewyn*, ed. Herbert Singer and Benno von Wiese (Köln and Graz: Böhlau, 1967), 151–64.

[20] Miguel de Cervantes, *The Adventures of Don Quixote de la Mancha* (1605; 1615), translated by Tobias Smollett, 1755 (New York: Farrar-Straus-Giroux, 1986), I, 1, chap. 6, 52–57.

[21] See Jørgensen, "Warum und zu welchem Ende," 7.

[22] In *Roman und Satire im 18. Jahrhundert: Ein Beitrag zur Poetik* (Stuttgart: Metzler, 1969), Jörg Schönert writes: "[D]er Untertitel 'Satire' wird zu einem Markenetikett, das den Verkaufserfolg zu garantieren verspricht" (5).

[23] "The character of a kind of aunt." See, for example, Kayser, "Die Anfänge des modernen Romans"; Norbert Miller, *Der empfindsame Erzähler: Untersuchungen an Romananfängen des 18. Jahrhunderts* (München: Hanser, 1968), 89–94; John A. McCarthy, *Christoph Martin Wieland* (Boston: Twayne, 1979), 67.

[24] . . . "by perpetuating a feud with the entire realm of love that was just as evident and irreconcilable as that of the Maltese knights with the Muslims."

[25] *Amadis de Gaula* by Garci Roderiguez de Montalvo was written before 1492, first published in 1508 and translated into German in 1569–98.

[26] "The sillier the ideas that the foolish fellow, the author, lets loose, the more I laugh, and that is everything that I seek thereby."

[27] "For as much as she valued the books about knights, which she categorized together with chronicles, histories and travel literature, she disdained all these little games of wit, which are simply written to entertain children or to pass the time for adults, and which can only recommend themselves to people of taste through their pleasant narrative style."

[28] "The abhorrence that she demonstrated for the tales of a Boccaccio and even for the most innocent jokes of a Lope de Vega did not hinder her from always keeping the book of conversations that some modern Sotades ascribed to the famous Aloysia Sigea under her pillow; a habit which she perhaps thought to justify with the example of Saint Chrysostom, who paid the same honor to the equally sotadic comedies of Aristophanes."

[29] See Schön, *Verlust*, on women and *Lesesucht*, especially 90–92 and 238–39 on reading in bed. See also Pia Schmid, *Zeit des Lesens*, 119–31.

[30] "An exemplum, that aloofness provokes the wrath of Venus."

[31] Felicia has been read by Wolfgang Jahn as the embodiment of both primary feminine roles in the eighteenth century: to him, Felicia represents the victory of both nature and society over Don Sylvio's faulty reading: "Zu Wielands Don Sylvio," in *Christoph Martin Wieland*, ed. Hansjörg Schelle (Darmstadt: Wissenschaftliche Buchgesellschaft, 1981), 307–21, here 310.

[32] Wilhelm Kurrelmeyer, "Gil Blas and Don Sylvio," *Modern Language Notes* 34 (1919): 78–81, has traced these connections.

[33] Peter J. Brenner is concerned with its position in the "epic whole" in "Kritische Form: Zur Dialektik der Aufklärung in Wielands Roman 'Don Sylvio von Rosalva,'" *Jahrbuch der deutschen Schillergesellschaft* 20 (1976): 162–83, here 165; Jahn, in "Zu Wielands," 311, reads it as a reference to generic convention of Spanish novellas, adding that it is "kompositorisch sonst kaum zu rechtfertigen"; Kurth, in *Die zweite Wirklichkeit*, 151, simply notes that Hyacinthe's narrative is "romanhaft." In her later work, Kurth-Voigt rightly observes that both Hyacinthe's story and the tale "Biribinker" exemplify the subjectivity of personal points of view (*Perspectives*, 135), but she does not correlate this to the figures' reading practices.

[34] Hyacinthe "narrates her theatrical story in such a miserable tone, that the biographies are certainly told better on the island Felsenburg." *Allgemeine deutsche Bibliothek* (1765) I, 2:97–107, here 105.

[35] Guy Stern, "Saint or Hypocrite? A Study of Wieland's 'Jacinte Episode,'" *Germanic Review* 29 (1954): 96–101, here 102. Stern's thesis is echoed uncritically by other scholars.

[36] See Nancy K. Miller's study of eighteenth-century French and English novels, *The Heroine's Text: Readings in the French and English Novel 1722–1782* (New York: Columbia UP, 1980), esp. 4–20.

[37] "If it is correct, as I am inclined to believe, the beautiful Hyacinthe began her story, that a woman is all the more worthy, the less reason she gives people to talk about her, then I am unhappy enough, that, at an age where most have barely begun to creep out timidly from under the wings of a tender mother, I must tell a tale of my adventures; and I would indeed be inconsolable, if I had to attribute the blame (for this circumstance) to myself."

[38] "I imagined how I would act towards the Marquis, my fantasy painted for me a number of adventures that I had read in old novels, and my small vanity found itself flattered by the thought that I myself could probably become the heroine of a novel."

[39] Stern's failure to recognize this difficulty as a generic one leads him to misread the figure of Hyacinthe as a female hypocrite who "artfully plays the prude with a wedding ring as her incentive" ("Saint or Hypocrite?" 100), although he admits that this interpretation clashes with how Hyacinthe is figured in the rest of *Don Sylvio*. See Robert Markley on the "theatrics of virtue" in "Sentimentality as Performance: Shaftesbury, Sterne, and the Theatrics of Virtue," in *The New Eighteenth-Century*, ed. Felicity Nussbaum and Laura Brown (New York and London: Methuen, 1987), 210–30.

[40] "As interesting as the love story of Don Eugenio and the beautiful Hyacinthe probably is for them themselves and perhaps also for their immediate audience, we cannot hold it against our readers, if they wish to see the end of

it. Indeed, there is no more boring creature in the world, for people who are sober, than a lover who tells the story of his heart."

[41] "If you had wished, said Hyacinthe, for me to turn my story into a fairy tale, why did you hide that from me? If I had believed that I could make it more pleasing for you thereby, it would have been easy for me to turn the old gypsy into a Carabosse, the good Lady of Calatrava into a Lumineuse, and Don Fernand of Zamora, if not into a rascally dwarf, at least into a sylph or a salamander."

[42] Wilson, *Narrative Strategy*, 52–55.

[43] "He read nothing else, he marveled at and composed nothing else, he occupied himself the entire day with nothing else, and he dreamed all night of nothing else."

[44] Wilson, *Narrative Strategy*, 96–97 and passim shows how such techniques are a fundamental aspect of Wieland's narrative design.

[45] "Now I certainly must believe that everything that you have told me is the truth. Truly, if I didn't see it with my own eyes, I would not have believed it. That is miraculous! But from whom else could you possibly have it except for a fairy?"

[46] "She is only painted so small here, because the smallness of the space allows nothing else, but that doesn't prevent her from being at least as tall as Diana . . . and even if she were somewhat shorter, she would thereby be all the more similar to the graces, who are represented by poets and painters as smaller than other goddesses in order to express their grace and loveliness."

[47] "That is a terrible story, Pedrillo said, by my soul, it began so nicely! it is a terrible shame that it did not end on a better note. But — if a simple fellow is allowed one question — do you really believe, good master, that you truly experienced all those things?"

[48] Wilson, *Narrative Strategy*, 91.

[49] *Wielands Briefwechsel* 3: Nr. 205, 206–7.

[50] "Figments of the imagination, which the old whore, your grandmother, inherited from her old mother."

[51] . . . "a very convoluted narrative of all the little stories of this kind, which since unimaginable times have crossed the paths of the aunts and grandmothers in his circle, thanks to an uninterrupted tradition from grandmother to grandmother."

[52] "You know the story, don't you, master? It is from an old book that I had to accept for thirteen Maravedis from the inheritance of my grandmother, even though it no longer had a cover or a title page; there were a number of painted figures in it which amused me when I was still a young boy, and then my grandmother read me the stories that were next to the pictures, I feel as though I could still see her sitting in front of me, the good old woman, may God comfort her!"

[53] "Suddenly he remembered all the ghost-stories that he had heard from childhood on, every minute he thought he saw something suspicious and he shook at the slightest sound that he heard, as loudly or even louder than a Klopstockian devil!"

[54] "I thought, one courtesy was worth another, and if I accept your salamander as valid, then you could also let my giants stand. Who knows, anyway, if they aren't more closely related than one imagines?"

[55] Cervantes, *Don Quixote*, II, 1, chap. 4, 448.

[56] Cervantes, for instance, *Don Quixote*, II, 1, chap. 4, 460.

[57] "The confusion that this apparition left in his head and in his heart was so great, that the mere effort to describe it throws us into nearly the same state of confusion."

[58] "An example that an eye-witness is not always as reliable as one tends to believe."

[59] "Do you therefore have to include all these insignificant circumstances, whereby your narrative becomes as sluggish and soporific as an old fairy tale?"

[60] "Gracious master . . . I would have thought that I had earned more trust from you, than that you would think I was trying to trick you. If the salamanders that I saw with the donkeys were not salamanders, then that is their problem and not mine; what is it to me, or why should I need to know, if they are this thing or that?"

[61] See Kurth-Voigt's interpretation of Pedrillo's lack of concern with "narrative detail," *Perspectives*, 133. Certainly, Pedrillo's comic confusion of literary references is one of the narrative tactics stressing the novel's fictionality. Yet the character Pedrillo still believes in the authority of literature as the precedent of possibility rather than simply dismissing its importance because it is invented. See also Moser-Verrey on Pedrillo as reader, *Dualité et continuité*, 16–20.

[62] "The gracious reader will be so courteous as to accept the mention of this circumstance as yet another proof of the precision with which we aim to fulfill the duties of historical truth, since it would have been easy for us, if we were only concerned about the honor of our wit, to awaken our hero through some other more noble or more marvelous means."

[63] "That is the pure truth, and if you find otherwise, you may kill me or throw me to the fleas, which are as hungry in this house as the wolves in the Pyrenees."

[64] "Upon my soul! I thought, when I saw the legions of fleas descending on me, that it would mean nothing good! I assure Your Grace, I am nothing but a wound on my entire body, and I would swear by a book that those were no natural fleas, but rather all sorts of enchanted hedgehogs and porcupines, with which these nasty sorcerers hoped to plague us to death. Pedrillo chattered in this tone until he was done packing up his bag, for he was still con-

cerned that his master might discover the truth, if he gave him time to consider."

[65] "Yet Pedrillo has, as one should have noticed long ago, a far more important role to play; and even if our intention in introducing him into this story was in part to amuse the readers, it is still certain that this (to express ourselves in a learned way) was only a finis secundarius."

[66] S. Miller, *Die Figur des Erzählers*, 86.

[67] Helmut Nobis, *Phantasie und Moralität: Das Wunderbare in Wielands Dschinnistan und der Geschichte des Prinzen Biribinker* (Kronberg/Ts.: Scriptor, 1976), 107–8.

[68] For major treatments of the Biribinker story see Heinz Hillmann, "Wunderbares in der Dichtung der Aufklärung: Untersuchungen zum französischen und deutschen Feenmärchen," *DVLG* 43 (1969): 76–113; Nobis, *Phantasie;* Friedmar Apel, *Die Zaubergärten der Phantasie* (Heidelberg: Winter, 1978). Ivar Sagmo offers a convincing reading of the inserted fairy tale as part of the "aesthetic education of eros" found in the novel in "Über die Ästhetische Erziehung des Eros: Zu Wielands Roman *Don Sylvio von Rosalva*," *Text und Kontext* 9, 2 (1981): 185–97.

[69] "How could we know if an author who lived three thousand years ago and whose history and character are totally unknown to us only wanted to tell us the truth? And if we assume he did have this in mind, could he not be credulous? Could he not have drawn from impure sources? Could he not have been deceived himself by his prejudices or by false reports? Or even if that was all not the case, can the story not have been changed, falsified and augmented by inserted additions at the hands of the copyists over the time of two or three thousand years?"

Chapter 3

[1] Jacobs, "Die Theorie und ihr Exempel," exposes Blanckenburg's misreadings of *Agathon*.

[2] Letter to Salomon Gessner, April 28, 1763. *Wielands Briefwechsel* 3: Nr. 161, 162.

"I regard *Agathon* as a book that can hardly be anything but successful in the world; it is for every type of person, and what is solid is combined with what is pleasing and interesting throughout."

[3] On the reception of the first edition, see Erich Gross, *C. M. Wielands Geschichte des Agathon: Entstehungsgeschichte* (1930; Nendeln/Liechtenstein: Kraus Reprint Limited, 1967), 159–79; Klaus Manger, "Kommentar," *Geschichte des Agathon*, ed. Klaus Manger (Frankfurt/Main: Deutscher Klassiker Verlag, 1986), 858–71; and Lieselotte E. Kurth-Voigt, "Wielands 'Geschichte des Agathon': Zur journalistischen Rezeption des Romans," *Wieland Studien 1*, ed. Wieland Archiv Biberach and Hans Radspieler (Sigmaringen: Jan Thorbecke, 1991), 9–24.

[4] Albrecht von Haller, review of *Agathon, Göttingsche Anzeigen* 141, 23 (1767) 1127–28, cited here from Kurth-Voigt, "Wielands 'Geschichte des Agathon,'" 12.

". . . in general *Agathon* is the wittiest novel that the Germans have to show."

[5] Gotthold Ephraim Lessing, *Hamburgische Dramaturgie* 69 (December 29, 1767), in *Werke,* ed. Herbert G. Göpfert (München: Hanser, 1970–79), 4:555.

"It is the first and only novel for the thinking mind, in classical taste. Novel? We will go ahead and give it this title, perhaps it will receive a few more readers thereby."

[6] Johann Georg Meusel, review of *Agathon, Deutsche Bibliothek der schönen Wissenschaften,* cited from Kurth-Voigt, "Wielands 'Geschichte des Agathon,'" 15.

[7] The charges that Wieland lacked originality, which were to damage his reputation most severely, came from the Romantics at the turn of the century: their polemics against the authoritative Enlightenment author in Weimar colored Wieland reception even past the renewed critical interest in Wieland of the 1950s, which was instigated by Friedrich Sengle's important biography, *Wieland* (Stuttgart: Metzler, 1949). In the past fifty years, critics have ensconced *Agathon* as first important developmental novel or Bildungsroman. See, for example, Michael Beddow, *The Fiction of Humanity: Studies in the Bildungsroman from Wieland to Thomas Mann* (Cambridge: Cambridge UP, 1982); Jürgen Jacobs, *Wielands Romane* (Bern and München: Franke, 1969); Liisa Saariluoma, *Die Erzählstruktur des frühen deutschen Bildungsromans* (Helsinki: Suomalainen Tiedeakatemia, 1985); Swales, *The German Bildungsroman.*

[8] Heinrich Wilhelm von Gerstenberg, *H. W. Gerstenbergs Rezensionen in der Hamburgischen Neuen Zeitung, 1767–1771,* ed. O. Fischer, Deutsche Literatur-Denkmale des 18. und 19. Jahrhunderts, 128, 3. Folge, Nr. 8. (Berlin: 1904), 47–48.

[9] Christian Friedrich Daniel Schubart, letter to Christian Gottfried Böckh, June 6, 1766, cited from Manger, "Kommentar," 861.

[10] Probably Issak Iselin. See Manger, "Kommentar," 863–64.

[11] As Friedrich Heinrich Jacobi writes to Wieland, October 27, 1772, *Wielands Briefwechsel* 5: Nr. 19, 15.

[12] Letter to Gessner, May 7, 1768, *Wielands Briefwechsel* 3: Nr. 522, 512.

"In particular, poor Agathon is so terribly praised and so stupidly criticized that one doesn't know if one should laugh, cry, or reach for the Spanish cane. . . . The funny thing is, that nobody, not a single person, has figured out the intention and the unity of the whole."

[13] Letter to Johann Georg Zimmermann, August 24, 1768, *Wielands Briefwechsel* 3: Nr. 555, 542.

"The kind of reception Agathon has received has radically cured me from the idea of wanting to be of service to the heads and hearts of my contemporaries."

[14] W. Daniel Wilson discusses the differences between the first and third version of *Agathon* with respect to its motto and Horatian poetics in "'Prächt'ge Vase' or 'halber Topf'? A Horatian Verse in Wieland's Agathon," *Modern Language Notes* 95, 3–4 (1980): 664–69. The first version rejects an artificial reconciliation between the two terms as inappropriate for its status as the story of a soul, while the last version attempts to achieve a classical poetic harmony between them.

[15] Wieland, *Theorie und Geschichte der Red-Kunst und Dichtkunst* (1757), in *Wielands Gesammelte Schriften,* ed. Deutsche Kommission der Königlich Preußischen Akademie der Wissenschaften (Berlin: 1909ff), I, 4, 330.

[16] *Agathon,* cited from the text of the first edition of 1766–67, *Geschichte des Agathon,* ed. Klaus Manger (Frankfurt/Main: Deutscher Klassiker Verlag, 1986), 48. Further page references to this edition will be included in the text.

"He had everything that could make the type of wisdom he practiced seductive."

[17] The widespread interest in physiognomy, most prominently represented by Johann Caspar Lavater's controversial *Physiognomische Fragmente* (1775–78), was one expression of eighteenth-century efforts to approach the realm of psychology with scientific claims and to channel and control knowledge of sentiment, "Empfindung," through rational categories. In *Agathon,* ten years older than Lavater's publications, Agathon's "natural ability to read in souls" provides him with a source of knowledge which compensates for his lack of worldly experience (II, 8, 69). On the personal relationship of Wieland and Lavater, as well as on their aesthetic controversies, see Renate Schostack, "Wieland und Lavater: Beitrag zur Geistesgeschichte des ausgehenden 18. Jahrhunderts" (Ph.D. diss., Freiburg, 1964), especially 4–52.

[18] Horst Thomé traces the elements of "radical Enlightenment" in the discourse of Hippias in his article "Menschliche Natur und Allegorie sozialer Verhältnisse: Zur politischen Funktion philosophischer Konzeptionen in Wielands 'Geschichte des Agathon,'" *Jahrbuch der deutschen Schillergesellschaft* 22 (1978): 205–34, here 209. John A. McCarthy states that Agathon counters the intellectual arguments of Hippias by simply trusting his heart and his passions: *Fantasy and Reality: An Epistemological Approach to Wieland* (Frankfurt/Main and Bern: Lang, 1974), 80.

[19] The relation between seduction and knowledge, and the potential seducer lurking in the educator, is certainly familiar from such texts as Plato's *Symposion* or Rousseau's modern version of Abelard and Héloïse, "the most dangerous and most edifying novel in the world" (*Agathon,* 348).

[20] . . . "because he imagined that Hippias's eloquence would provide the kind of enjoyment offered to us by a skilled magician, who makes us see for one moment something that we do not see, without taking it so far, for the clever

person, that one would even doubt, in this very same moment, that one was being deceived."

[21] The effect of rhetorical brilliance on listeners was described by the Sophists in analogy to magic and to narcotics; the issue of responsibility in the employment of this power over others surfaces in their earliest texts on rhetoric. See Renato Barilli, *Rhetoric,* trans. Giuliana Menozzi (Minneapolis: U of Minnesota P), 1989, 3–5.

[22] Wieland mitigates the degree of outrage his positive seductress Danae might elicit with recourse to the customs and morals of his Greek setting, as Wulf Köpke notes in "Die emanzipierte Frau in der Goethezeit und ihre Darstellung in der Literatur," in *Die Frau als Heldin und Autorin: Neue kritische Ansätze zur deutschen Literatur.* ed. Wolfgang Paulsen (Bern and München: Franke, 1979), 96–110. Furthermore, the gender division of their roles account for the possibility of a positive seduction. It is not necessarily tragic for a young man to be seduced by an experienced woman, as would be the opposite case — see Ursula Fries, *Buhlerin und Zauberin: Eine Untersuchung zur deutschen Literatur des 18. Jahrhunderts* (München: Fink, 1970), 121–33. Dietlinde S. Bailet, *Die Frau als Verführte und als Verführerin in der deutschen und französischen Literatur des 18. Jahrhunderts* (Bern: Lang, 1981), argues that Danae's seduction of Agathon is, for him, "eine positive Etappe der Menschwerdung" (201). Yet, as discussed in Sven-Aage Jørgensen's article "Der unverheiratete Held," *Orbis Litterarum* 42, 3–4 (1987): 338–52, Wieland's novel is unable to overcome the crisis in the "codification of intimacy" (Luhmann) to arrive at a reconciliation of terms, for example in the form of marriage between Agathon and Danae. For a general discussion of Wieland's often liberal views on gender relations, see Elizabeth Boa, "Sex and Sensibility: Wieland's Portrayal of Relationships between the Sexes in the Comische Erzählungen, Agathon, and Musarion," *Lessing Yearbook* 12 (1980): 189–218.

[23] "The great art was to arouse his desires under the mask of friendship, while simultaneously appearing to rebuff them through an unaffected reserve."

[24] See Kurt Wölfel, "Daphnes Verwandlung: Zu einem Kapitel in Wielands 'Agathon,'" in *Christoph Martin Wieland,* ed. Hansjörg Schelle, 232–50.

[25] "One must undoubtedly admit that the painting which presented itself to our hero in this moment was not well suited to leave either his heart or his senses tranquil; but Danae's intention was only to prepare him, through the eyes, for the pleasures of another sense, and her pride demanded no smaller triumph than to obliterate such an attractive image in his soul through the magical power of her voice and her strings."

[26] Homer, *The Iliad,* translated and with an introduction by Richmond Lattimore, 1951 (Chicago: U of Chicago P, 1961), 14, v. 185 and 214–17, 299–300.

[27] "'If the sirens, whom the clever Ulysses had to pass, sung this way,' (thought Agathon), 'then he truly had cause to have himself bound by his hands and feet to the mast.'"

[28] . . . "how much he was beside himself and how much effort it cost him to hold himself back, not to throw himself out of his seat into the water and to swim over to her, and to expire, dissolved in delight and love, at her feet."

[29] . . . "a tender softness had to first gain mastery over his entire soul and his senses, swimming in pleasure, had to be captured by a sweet uneasiness and a lustful longing."

[30] . . . "siren-songs . . . which sank the soul into an enchanted forgetting of itself and, after it disarmed all its more noble powers, delivered the aroused and willing sensuality up to the entire force of lust which was entering from all sides."

[31] In Dorothea von Mücke's trenchant study of the final version of *Agathon* (*Virtue and the Veil of Illusion*, 229–73), she reads this challenge to Agathon's identity as a temporary loss of the "narcissistic integrity" on which the new paradigms of organizing male subjectivity in the late eighteenth-century are founded.

[32] "His entire being was in his sense of hearing and his entire soul dissolved into the sentiments that dominated her song."

[33] "An Ionic ear not only wants to be pleased, it wants to be enchanted . . . in short, the style of reading ought to put the ear in the place of all the other senses."

[34] "There is a certain art of removing from sight whatever could make a negative impression; so much depends on the turn of phrase; a single small circumstance gives an event such a different appearance from the one it would have had without this small circumstance."

[35] "But as regards those places where she considered as inadequate all the art that one could apply towards making them more beautiful . . . these she cleverly decided to conceal with complete silence."

[36] Lieselotte E. Kurth, "Historiographie und historischer Roman: Kritik und Theorie im 18. Jahrhundert," *Modern Language Notes* 79, 3 (1964): 337–62.

[37] "Truth . . . resides therein, that everything be commensurate with the way of the world, that characters are not arbitrary and simply generated from the fantasy or the intentions of the author, but are instead drawn from the inexhaustible sources of Nature herself; . . . and thus that everything is invented in such a way, that no sufficient reason can be given, why it could not have happened, or might not once happen, exactly as it was told. This truth alone can make works of this sort useful."

[38] Wieland defends the label "history" for his work and positions himself in relation to Xenophon and Fielding in "Über das Historische in Agathon," 573. See Shookman's reading of the ambivalences in the concept of history for *Agathon* in *Noble Lies*, 52–58.

[39] In "Unterredungen mit dem Pfarrer von ***" (1775), Wieland defends his artistic works and his person against charges of ethical transgressions. Danae's guidelines are expressly recalled as poetic ones: "Ich bin als Dichter bekannt. . . . Man würde sagen, daß ich (wie Danae) mehr die Gesetze des Schönen und Anständigen als der historischen Treue zum Augenmerke genommen" (*Wielands Gesammelte Schriften*, I, 14, 30).

[40] "Danae narrated her story with the innocent aim of pleasing. She naturally regarded her performance, her weaknesses, even her missteps in a milder and (let us tell the truth) in a truer light than did the world."

[41] "He compared her own narrative with that of Hippias and now, once mistrust had taken over his mind, he thought to perceive a hundred traces in the first which supported the truth of the second."

[42] "It is undoubtedly good, when an author who has aimed to reach a more important goal than merely pleasing his readers, given certain situations, does not imitate the unbridled wantonness of many of the newer Frenchmen, but rather imitates the modest reservation of the innocent Virgil, who . . . finds it sufficient to tell us: 'that Dido and the hero came to a cave.' However if this reservation were carried so far that the obscurity with which one covers a delicate circumstance could give rise to misunderstanding and error: then, we think, it would be misplaced modesty and in such instances we think it advisable to lift the curtain a little bit, rather than to risk exposing innocence itself to unfounded suspicions because of exaggerated caution."

[43] "And here, without unnecessarily detaining the reader with what she said further and what he answered, we will leave the brush to a Correggio and slip away."

[44] "And how do we even know that Agathon himself, for all his candor, did not hold back any circumstance which he foresaw, like a good painter or poet, could hinder the beautiful effect of the whole. Who will vouch for the fact that the seductive priestess did not achieve more influence over him than he admitted?"

[45] "'How praiseworthy, excellent, divine!' shout the enthusiastic admirers of heroic virtue — we would gladly shout out with them, if one could first show us what benefit this elevated virtue has ever been to the human race."

[46] "Such a character does indeed make a good impression . . . and awakens the wish that he might be more than a beautiful chimera. But we admit that, for weighty reasons, with increasing experience, we are becoming ever more mistrustful of the human — and so why not of the superhuman virtues?"

[47] "One imagined one was hearing Mercury or Apollo speak, the connoisseurs . . . admired most, that he rejected the tools of artifice through which the Sophists were accustomed to give a bad thing the shape of a good one — no colors whose shine had to conceal the deceptiveness of false or uselessly posited sentences; no artificial distribution of light and shadow. His expression

resembled the sunshine, whose lively and almost spiritual radiance shone on the objects without taking away anything from their own shape and color."

[48] "What more can we demand, in all strictness, than that his intentions are noble and virtuous?"

[49] "In moral novels we admittedly find heroes who remain constant in all respects — and therefore are to be praised — . . . But in life we find it is different. So much the worse for those who, in life, always remain constant."

[50] Many critics have studied the relationships constructed between narrator and fictive reader. See, for example: Jacobs, *Wielands Romane;* Jørgensen, "Warum und zu welchem Ende schreibt man eine Vorrede?"; Rogan, "The Reader in Wieland's *Die Abenteuer des Don Sylvio von Rosalva,*"; Seiler, "Die Rolle des Lesers"; M. H. Würzner, "Die Figur des Lesers in Wielands 'Geschichte des Agathon,'" in Schelle, ed., *Christoph Martin Wieland,* 399–406.

[51] "Dion proved . . . that philosophy usually only causes us to avoid those mistakes for which we have no affinity and only supports us in those virtues toward which we are inclined anyway."

[52] Plato, "Gorgias," 463b, in *The Collected Dialogues of Plato,* ed. Edith Hamilton and Huntington Cairns (New York: Pantheon, 1961).

[53] *The Odyssey,* 12, v. 184–194, translated by Johann Heinrich Voss: *Homers Odüßee übersezt von Johann Heinrich Voß.* 2 vols. (Vienna: 1789), I, 219.

"'Come hither on your way, renowned Odysseus, great glory of the Achaeans; stop your ship that you may listen to the voice of us two. For never yet has any man rowed past the island in his black ship until he has heard the sweet voice from our lips; instead, he has joy of it, and goes his way a wiser man. For we know all the toils that in wide Troy the Argives and Trojans endured through the will of the gods, and we know all things that come to pass upon the fruitful earth.' So they spoke, sending forth their beautiful voice, and my heart desired to listen, and I commanded my comrades to free me, nodding to them with my brows; but they fell to their oars and rowed on." *The Odyssey,* with an English translation by A. T. Murray, revised by George E. Dimock, 2 vols. (Cambridge, MA and London: Harvard UP, 1995), v. 184–194, I, 461–63.

Chapter 4

[1] See Wilhelm Spickernagel, "Die Geschichte des Fräuleins von Sternheim von Sophie von La Roche und Goethes Werther" (Ph.D. diss., Greifswald, 1911). Touaillon, *Der deutsche Frauenroman,* 107–8, 174–79, also notes La Roche's probable literary influence on these younger male authors, as does Susanne Zantop, "Trivial Pursuits? An Introduction to German Women's Writing from the Middle Ages to 1830," in *Bitter Healing,* ed. Blackwell and Zantop, 9–50, here 34. Helene Kastinger Riley, *Die weibliche Muse* (Columbia, SC: Camden House, 1986), 27–52, reads *Sternheim* as precursor to Goethe's *Die Leiden des jungen Werther.*

[2] On the reception history of *Sternheim* see Kuno Ridderhoff's detailed presentation in his edition of the novel, "Introduction," *Geschichte des Fräuleins von Sternheim*, ed. Kuno Ridderhoff (Berlin: Behr, 1907), xxi–xxxiii; Touaillon, *Der deutsche Frauenroman*, 121–23; Günter Häntzschel, "Nachwort," *Geschichte des Fräuleins von Sternheim*, ed. Marlies Korfsmeyer (München: Winkler, 1976), 301–36, here 319–24; Bernd Heidenreich, *Sophie von La Roche — eine Werkbiographie* (Frankfurt/Main, Bern, and New York: Lang, 1986), 64–66. Barbara Becker-Cantarino's edition of the novel, *Geschichte des Fräuleins von Sternheim*, ed. Barbara Becker-Cantarino (Stuttgart: Reclam, 1983), includes documents of its contemporary reception, 363–76.

[3] Charlotte Craig, "Sophie LaRoche — a 'praecepta filiarum Germaniae'?" *Studies on Voltaire and the 18th Century* 193 (1980): 1996–2002.

[4] For example Siegfried Sudhof, "Sophie LaRoche," in *Deutsche Dichter des achtzehnten Jahrhunderts*, ed. Benno von Wiese (Berlin: E. Schmidt, 1977), 300–319; Peter Petschauer, "Sophie von Laroche, Novelist between Reason and Emotion," *The Germanic Review* 57, 2 (Spring 1982): 70–77; K. Plato, *Sophie La Roche in Koblenz/Ehrenbreitstein* (Koblenz: Görres-Verlag, 1978); Michael Maurer, "Das Gute und das Schöne: Sophie von LaRoche (1730–1807)," *Euphorion* 79, 2 (1985): 111–38. Biographical studies that consider La Roche's socio-historical position as female author have been indispensable to an adequate understanding of her work: see especially Becker-Cantarino's studies, "Freundschaftsutopie: Die Fiktionen der Sophie La Roche," in *Untersuchungen zum Roman von Frauen um 1800*, ed. Gallas and Heuser, 92–113, and "'Muse' und 'Kunstrichter': Sophie LaRoche und Wieland," *MLN* 99, 3 (April 1984): 571–88; Maurer's edition of La Roche's letters, *"Ich bin mehr Herz als Kopf" Sophie von La Roche: Ein Lebensbild in Briefen*, ed. Michael Maurer (München: Beck, 1983); Touaillon, *Der deutsche Frauenroman*, 69–206. Monika Nenon's book on La Roche, *Autorschaft und Frauenbildung: Das Beispiel Sophie von La Roche* (Würzburg: Königshausen & Neumann, 1988), has a strong biographical orientation; Verena Ehrich-Haefeli offers a "psychobiographical" reading of La Roche and her first novel in "Gestehungskosten tugendempfindsamer Freundschaft: Probleme der weiblichen Rolle im Briefwechsel Wieland-Sophie La Roche bis zum Erscheinen der Sternheim (1750–1771)," in *Frauenfreundschaft-Männerfreundschaft: literarische Diskurse im 18. Jahrhundert*, ed. Wolfram Mauser and Barbara Becker-Cantarino (Tübingen: Niemeyer, 1991), 75–136. Heidenreich's *Werkbiographie* disappointingly falls back on a reductive reading of *Sternheim* as virtue rewarded through marriage, 43–45.

[5] Touaillon underscores La Roche's unique achievements in this genre (*Der deutsche Frauenroman*, 26, 72, 115–19). Ridderhoff's study "Sophie von La Roche, die Schülerin Richardsons und Rousseaus" (Ph.D. diss., Göttingen, 1895), places La Roche in the European context with an emphasis on her novelty in Germany. Hohendahl, "Empfindsamkeit und gesellschaftliches Bewußtsein," also reads La Roche in the European context.

[6] La Roche's achievements as a female author writing feminocentric texts in a literary world dominated by men have been celebrated, from many ideological standpoints, since her first novel was published. Touaillon's work of 1919 (*Der deutsche Frauenroman*, 69–206 on La Roche) firmly established the image of La Roche as the first female novelist writing in German, contested only recently by the interest in Maria Anna Sagar stimulated by Helga Meise's studies, including *Die Unschuld und die Schrift* and "Das Werk von Maria Anna Sagar — Konstitutionsbedingungen und Probleme des Romans von Frauen im 18. Jahrhundert," in *Untersuchungen zum Roman von Frauen um 1800,* ed. Gallas and Heuser, 79–91.

[7] Kurt Ingo Flessau, *Der moralische Roman* (Köln: Böhlau, 1968), 52–68.

[8] Flessau, *Der moralische Roman;* Touaillon, *Der deutsche Frauenroman;* Riley, *Die weibliche Muse.*

[9] Martin Greiner, *Die Entstehung der modernen Unterhaltungsliteratur: Studien zum Trivialroman des 18. Jahrhunderts* (Reinbek: Rowohlt, 1964); Marion Beaujean, *Der Trivialroman in der zweiten Hälfte des 18. Jahrhunderts* (Bonn: Bouvier, 1964); Bernhard Spies, "Sophie von La Roches 'Geschichte des Fräuleins von Sternheim' und die moderne Trivialliteratur: Das moralische Vorbild als psychologische Kompensation," *Literatur für Leser,* 2 (1991): 80–89.

[10] Bovenschen's cultural-historical study of representations of femininity and her chapter on La Roche (*Die imaginierte Weiblichkeit,* 190–200) mark a turn in the scholarly investigations; Meise's study of texts by German women writers in the eighteenth century, *Die Unschuld und die Schrift,* provides a multifaceted literary and social topography in which La Roche features strongly, for example 111–13, 143–64; Schieth's *Die Entwicklung des deutschen Frauenromans* devotes considerable attention to *Sternheim* as paradigmatic for the genre, 28–49, 173–78. Ingrid Wiede-Behrendt, *Lehrerin des Schönen, Wahren, Guten: Literatur und Frauenbildung im ausgehenden 18. Jahrhundert am Beispiel Sophie von LaRoche,* (Frankfurt/Main, Bern, New York, and Paris: Lang, 1987), reads La Roche in the context of eighteenth-century discussions on female education. Margrit Langner, *Sophie von La Roche — die empfindsame Realistin* (Heidelberg: Winter, 1995), traces La Roche's interest in pedagogical theories (54–78 and passim) and points to aspects of the author's particular social and political engagement hitherto neglected (especially in section VI, 160–262).

[11] Meise's interest in writing and reading in the "Frauenroman" is a notable exception (*Die Unschuld und die Schrift,* 66–82, 165–200). Touaillon constructs a typology of the "sentimental" and the "rational" *Frauenroman;* her comments on style and form take recourse to an essentialist understanding of the difference between female and male writing (*Der deutsche Frauenroman,* 73, 112, 115–17); Schieth, *Die Entwicklung,* is concerned primarily with plot designs and thematic focus of the genre. Recent criticism on eighteenth-century novels written by women increasingly engages questions of poetics,

e.g., Heuser, "Poetologische Reflexionen." Loster-Schneider's investigation of La Roche in *Sophie La Roche* correctly insists on the theoretical aspects and self-consciousness of her writing (see especially chapter 4, 233–92).

[12] On the history of this term and the difficulties of its application see Schieth, *Die Entwicklung des deutschen Frauenromans*, 1–22; Wiede-Behrendt, *Lehrerin des Schönen, Wahren, Guten*, 14–18; *Untersuchung zum Roman von Frauen um 1800*, ed. Gallas and Heuser, especially the articles in that volume by Brandes (41–51); Heuser (52–65); Schieth (114–131). See also Elizabeth Abel, Marianne Hirsch and Elizabeth Langland, ed. *The Voyage In: Fictions of Female Development* (Hanover and London: UP of New England, 1983).

[13] For example in Joan DeJean, *Tender Geographies: Women and the Origins of the Novel in France* (New York and Oxford: Columbia UP, 1991) and in Nancy K. Miller, *The Heroine's Text*.

[14] Loster-Schneider's *Sophie La Roche*, especially chapters 2 and 3, devotes careful attention to Wieland's proscription of public theoretical discourse for La Roche and to the paradoxes inherent in his delineation of her writing, as well as to the function that Wieland's fashioning of La Roche as author holds for his own public profile as author.

[15] Janet Gurkin Altman, *Epistolarity: Approaches to a Form* (Columbus: Ohio State UP, 1982), 88, 111–12.

[16] On considerations of epistolarity and femininity in Germany see the collections *Brieftheorie des achtzehnten Jahrhunderts*, ed. Ebrecht, especially Regina Nörtemann's article "Brieftheoretische Konzepte im 18. Jahrhundert und ihre Genese," 211–24, and the extensive bibliography; also *Die Frau im Dialog*, ed. Runge and Steinbrügge. See also Becker-Cantarino, "Leben als Text: Briefe als Ausdrucks- und Verständigungsmittel in der Briefkultur und Literatur des 18. Jahrhunderts," in *Frauen, Literatur, Geschichte: Schreibende Frauen vom Mittelalter bis zur Gegenwart*, ed. Hiltrud Gnüg and Renate Möhrmann (Stuttgart: Metzler, 1985), 83–103. On the epistolary novel in the context of eighteenth-century narrative theory see Vosskamp, "Dialogische Vergegenwärtigung."

[17] Elizabeth J. MacArthur, *Extravagant Narratives: Closure and Dynamics in the Epistolary Form* (Princeton: Princeton UP, 1990). MacArthur adopts Roman Jakobson's terms to describe the two tendencies toward stability and meaning (the axis of selection, of metaphor) and toward self-perpetuating mobility and desire (the axis of combination, of metonymy) in epistolary narrative, 25–31 and passim.

[18] Loster-Schneider, *Sophie La Roche*, 81–85, recognizes a theoretical dimension to Wieland's comments, but few critics do. Häntzschel, "Nachwort," offers an early positive reading of Wieland's editorial pose, a "diplomatic and clever recommendation" of the novel, 316. Becker-Cantarino, "'Muse' und 'Kunstrichter,'" outlines Wieland's split stance of support and critical control of La Roche's production to ultimately credit him with the "baptism" of the *Frauenroman*, 572. Stern describes Wieland as *Sternheim's* "ideal utopian

reader," yet writes that Wieland never meant to encourage his friend to publish, in "Wieland als Herausgeber der 'Sternheim,'" in *Christoph Martin
Wieland: North American Scholarly Contributions on the Occasion of the 250th
anniversary of His Birth 1983*, ed. Hansjörg Schelle (Tübingen: Niemeyer,
1984), 195–208, here 201.

[19] *Geschichte des Fräuleins von Sternheim*, ed. Becker-Cantarino, 15. Further
citations following this edition will be referenced in the text.

[20] . . . "to make a present to all virtuous mothers, all lovable young daughters
of our nation, of this work, which seemed to me well suited to foster wisdom
and virtue — the sole great advantages of humanity, the sole sources of true
happiness — among your sex and even among mine."

[21] "It is equally certain that our nation is still far from having an excess of
original works of this sort, which are at once entertaining and suited to encourage the love of virtue."

[22] "I have no need to speak to you of the widespread usefulness that writing in
the genre to which your Sternheim belongs can bring, if it is good. All reasonable people are of one opinion on this point and it would be greatly superfluous, after all that Richardson, Fielding and so many others have said
about this topic, to add even one word to confirm a truth which nobody
doubts."

[23] Dagmar Grenz, *Mädchenliteratur: Von den moralisch-belehrenden Schriften
im 18. Jahrhundert bis zur Herausbildung der Backfischliteratur im 19. Jahrhundert* (Stuttgart: Metzler, 1981), describes the shift during the eighteenth
century from a positive to a negative view on learned women. See Myers,
"Learning, Virtue and the Term 'Bluestocking,'" and Nörtemann, "Die 'Begeisterung des Poeten' in den Briefen eines Frauenzimmers: Zur Korrespondenz der Caroline Christiane Lucius mit Christian Fürchtegott Gellert," in
Die Frau im Dialog, ed. Runge and Steinbrügge, 13–32, on the interlocking
notions of women's virtue and learnedness. The image Wieland constructs of
La Roche in his early letters to her reflects the female ideal of the first half of
the century (cf. Nenon, *Autorschaft und Frauenbildung*, 38, Ehrich-Haefeli,
"Gestehungskosten . . .," and Loster-Schneider, *Sophie La Roche*, 48–66).

[24] "You, my friend, never thought to write for the world or to produce a work
of art. Even with all your familiarity with the best authors of various lan-
guages, whom one can read without being learned, it was always your habit
to be attentive to the value of the content, but less so to the beauty of the
form."

[25] Ehrich-Haefeli, "Gestehungskosten . . .," considers the image of the female
author as mother in the correspondence between Wieland and La Roche
during the composition of *Sternheim*, 120–26.

[26] The famous gloss in a review of *Sternheim* long attributed to Goethe, now
to Merck, that *Sternheim* is a "human soul" rather than a book reflects this
interpretation (*Frankfurter Gelehrte Anzeigen* [1772], 101). See Karin Haenelt

on this attribution, "Die Verfasser der "Frankfurter Gelehrten Anzeigen" von 1772: Ermittlung von Kriterien zu ihrer Unterscheidung durch maschinelle Stilanalyse," *Euphorion* 78 (1984): 368–82.

[27] "if only my daughters would learn to think and act like Sophie Sternheim!"

[28] . . . "the singularity of our heroine, her enthusiasm for the ethically beautiful, her particular ideas and moods, her somewhat obstinate predilection for the Mylords."

[29] . . . "for precisely the reason that she is a phenomenon, she ought, as adorable eccentric, to be able to make considerable conquests."

[30] Riley, *Die weibliche Muse*, 27–52, offers a reinterpretation of Sophie Sternheim as such a negative example, whose orientation towards an outdated model of virtue is regressive. This reversal of Sternheim from positive to negative example is too facile and the attribution of dominant irony to La Roche remains unconvincing. Yet Riley's careful analysis of the difficulties *Sternheim's* heroine faces in various social milieus arising from the contradictions in the concept of virtue she espouses is perceptive and revealing.

[31] Thus Ruth-Ellen Joeres, in "'That girl is an entirely different character!' Yes, But Is She a Feminist? Observations on Sophie von la Roche's 'Geschichte des Fräuleins von Sternheim,'" in *German Women in the Eighteenth and Nineteenth Centuries*, ed. Ruth-Ellen Joeres and Mary Jo Maynes (Bloomington: Indiana UP, 1986), 137–56, here 153.

[32] "She *wants* to do good and she *will* do good and will thereby justify the step that I have dared to take."

[33] See particularly Bovenschen, *Die imaginierte Weiblichkeit*, 193–98, on this conflation.

[34] Becker-Cantarino, "Freundschaftsutopie," discusses friendship among women as constitutive of the text and central to shaping female identity, in contrast to the hierarchical model of friendship portrayed in Wieland's preface, 98.

[35] Emilia's primary function in the narrative, however, is that of passive "archivist" of Sophie's letters. See Altman, *Epistolarity*, 53, on this role of the "epistolary confidant."

[36] "Drawn by a Female Friend of the Same from Original Papers and Other Reliable Sources."

[37] . . . "this most lovable young lady entangled in difficulties and circumstances . . . which suddenly destroyed the lovely plan of a happy life which she had made for herself, but which, through the test of her inner worth, make her story edifying for the best of our sex."

[38] Ridderhoff, *Sophie von La Roche*, 13–14, highlights La Roche's innovations over Richardson and Rousseau in this regard. Cf. also Wiede-Behrendt, *Lehrerin des Schönen, Wahren, Guten*, 144–50, 173–74.

[39] "All aspects of the young lady's character give me hope for a triumph of virtue. But it must be achieved before the eyes of the world."

[40] "My uncle aroused in me the desire to see the prince humbled, and I imagined virtue's resistance as a delightful dramatic performance."

[41] "Today, my friend, today at the court theater she will be subjected to the gaze of the prince for the first time; I am not well, but I must go there, even were it to cost me my life."

[42] "My joy was indescribable; . . . the joy of the lady supported my idea that she would be, through her virtue, a new fleeing Daphne."

[43] "But how painfully, how despicably her false virtue betrayed me, as she soon thereafter threw herself into Apollo's arms!"

Theories of acting which focused on this dilemma of necessary duplicity and the difficulties of correct interpretation were of central interest in the eighteenth century. Markley's "Sentimentality as Performance" illuminates the "affective semiotics" of sentimentality.

[44] "The most intense, extreme disdain animated his comments about her feigned virtue and the miserable sacrifice of the same; about the impudence of making a spectacle of herself in front of all the nobility and wearing the most pleased expression all the while."

[45] "How cruel my own amour propre was towards that adorable girl! At first I didn't want to speak of my love until, fully in accordance with my conception, she had shown herself in the complete splendor of triumphant virtue. She followed her own pretty path and because she didn't follow my idealistic plan, I presumed the power of punishing her for that most severely."

[46] "Soon I will put an end to your silly tales, which I have only tolerated this long in order to see how far you would push your boasting in the face of your master. And you would feel the scourge of my satire today, if I didn't wish to show you the sketch of a German courtly tale which I am preparing to perform. . . . So do not continue to boast to me, my good B*, for one cannot sing a song of triumph over victories like yours."

[47] "She shall have bloomed for me, that much is certain."

[48] "Certainly she shall make new discoveries in the land of pleasure, if her enlightened and fine spirit will apply all its talents to that end."

[49] "You would have been the most suitable lover for her and I would have liked to be her confidant and her biographer."

[50] "The comedy of the prince and my Sternheim, which I wrote to you about recently, has been taken to such tragic heights through the romantic foibles of Seymour that nothing but death or the flight of the heroine can serve to develop the story; the first, I hope, the goddess of youth will prevent and Venus may take care of the second through my intervention."

[51] "But wait: how have I arrived at this nonsense? This is how poor Seymour's letters sounded when he was in love with the beautiful Y**: is this country lass to make an enthusiast of me?"

[52] "Just as enthusiasts who wish to gain personal access to spirits spend time fasting and praying, so I must give up all pleasures I have indulged until now in order to please this enthusiastic soul."

[53] "And yet her ruin is not determined. If she loves me, if the possession of her provides me all the alternate, lively pleasures which I imagine it will; then she shall become Lady Derby and make me the patriarch of a new motley lineage . . . The devil only knows how I arrived at this piece of domestic physics! My friend, things will look bad if this continues, but I will endure the test to the last extreme."

[54] "She wrote a grand letter in the extravagant tone of high virtue."

[55] "This foolish novel was a bit costly; yet she deserved it all. If only she had loved me and foresworn her enthusiasm!"

[56] La Roche corresponded with Wieland on *Sternheim* as early as 1766; it is not unlikely that correspondences between the novels might be traced.

[57] Nancy K. Miller, *The Heroine's Text;* part I takes up the "euphoric" plot; part II discusses the "dysphoric" plot.

[58] "The girl presents an entirely new genre of character!"

"Character" is a prime catchword for *Sternheim*. Touaillon remarks Sophie's "exoticism" ascribed to her English heritage (*Der deutsche Frauenroman,* 108). As pertinent question on the new type of character, Joeres asks "Yes, but is she a feminist?" ("'That girl is an entirely different character!'" 150–53). Nenon, *Autorschaft und Frauenbildung,* emphasizes the "reason and autonomy" of La Roche's sentimental heroine, which distinguishes her from Rousseau's ideal of femininity, 84. Christine Lehmann, *Das Modell Clarissa: Liebe, Verführung, Sexualität und Tod der Romanheldinnen des 18. und 19. Jahrhunderts.* (Stuttgart: Metzler, 1991), 40, discusses the novelty of Sternheim's active character compared to Richardson's model in Clarissa.

[59] Marion Beaujean, "Das Bild des Frauenzimmers im Roman des 18. Jahrhunderts," *Wolffenbüttler Studien zur Aufklärung* 3 (1976): 9–28, concludes that, despite the impetus toward individuation of the late eighteenth century, the image of women in novels remains role-bound. Heuser, "Spuren trauriger Selbstvergessenheit," discusses the dilemma for the feminocentric novel between generic "woman" and individual heroines, with a focus on F. H. Unger. See also Caroline Wellbery, "Sensibility and Socialization," on the concept of individuality in *Sternheim,* 55–66. Ursula Becher, "Weibliches Selbstverständnis," traces the conflict between the general focus on the self and the actual fetters placed on women's self-realization in the late eighteenth century, as does Ulrike Prokop, "Die Einsamkeit der Imagination: Geschlechterkonflikt und literarische Produktion um 1770," in *Deutsche Literatur von Frauen,* ed. Gisela Brinker-Gabler (München: Beck, 1988), 1:325–65.

[60] "Lord Sternheim led the twelve-year-old girl by the hand to the portrait of her mother, and spoke of her virtue and her goodness of heart with such emotion that the young lady kneeling next to him sobbed and often wished to die in order to be with her Lady Mother."

[61] "That a specific type of conjuring must be chosen for each ghost and the horror which I caused the Count by my appearance makes me think that I am under the protection of a more powerful spirit than the one that helps him learn to conjure."

[62] "But the word 'virtue' which I uttered numerous times was the incantation with which I appeased her anger."

[63] Meike Werner's article, "'Mein Herz ist unschuldig und rein': Die Geschichte des Fräuleins von Sternheim," in *Grenzen der Moral,* ed. Ursula Konnertz (Tübingen: ed. diskord, 1991), 125–45, elaborates on the scene and its importance. Lehmann, *Das Modell Clarissa,* takes the position that Sophie has been sexually violated through the gaze, that she is a "Betrogene ohne eine Berührte zu sein" (46), and concludes that the sexual act has no central importance in the novel. Meise, *Die Unschuld und die Schrift,* reads Sophie's transformation of what Derby sees from "Schönheit" to "Scham" as a move which robs the seduction of its force, "'Wer ist sie?' Zum Verhältnis von weiblicher Identität und literarischem Diskurs in Frauenromanen des 18. Jahrhunderts," in *Das Subjekt des Diskurses,* ed. Manfred Geier and Harold Woetzel (Berlin: Argument-Verlag, 1983), 108–21, here 115.

[64] "Dringen in" can carry both the meanings "to press" and "to penetrate."

[65] "I saw that they believed that I was innocent and pitied my heart; I could regard them as witnesses to my innocence and virtue."

[66] "You are rending my heart and my love for you; I will never forgive you this lack of noble sentiment!"

[67] "I knew the value of all that I had lost; but my illness and my observations showed me that I still truly possess the genuine property of our life. My heart is innocent and pure; my mind's knowledge is undiminished; the powers of my soul and my good inclinations have retained their full measure; and I still have the ability to do good."

[68] "I won't choose; I want to enjoy my freedom which I had to purchase with so much bitterness."

[69] "I have so strongly experienced that one can make others happy without becoming happy oneself, that I do not have the heart to venture one more time onto this uncertain ground."

[70] "The perspective from which you see my suggestions does in truth have much that is deterrent."

[71] Wiede-Behrendt emphasizes the radical nature of *Sternheim's* educational program, as it champions a measure of female independence (*Lehrerin des Schönen, Wahren, Guten,* 187). Ruth P. Dawson cites marriage and education as the two key debates, not surprisingly, in the proto-feminist texts at the end

of the century, "'And this Shield is called Self-Reliance': Emerging Feminist Consciousness in the late Eighteenth Century," in *German Women in the Eighteenth and Nineteenth Centuries,* ed. Ruth-Ellen Joeres and Mary Jo Maynes, 157–74.

[72] Pfeffel's review can be found in Robert Hassencamp, "Aus dem Nachlaß der Sophie von La Roche," *Euphorion* 5 (1898): 475–502, here 494–95. See Michael Maurer, *Aufklärung und Anglophilie in Deutschland* (Göttingen and Zürich: Vandenhoeck & Ruprecht, 1987), for a study of eighteenth-century German anglophilia and a discussion of La Roche in this context (142–81).

[73] Hohendahl, "Empfindsamkeit und gesellschaftliches Bewußtsein," 195, criticizes the "Grundfarbe der Erfolgsmoral" under the "Lack der Philanthropie." See also Burghard Dedner, *Topos, Ideal und Realitätspostulat: Studien zur Darstellung des Landlebens im Roman des 18. Jahrhunderts* (Tübingen: Niemeyer, 1969), 64; Häntzschel, "Nachwort," 330–33, and Riley, *Die weibliche Muse,* 29–52. It should not be overlooked, however, that the literary depiction and discussion of social ills in any form was still a novelty in Germany and that outspoken criticism of the social order by a woman or her female figure was a daring act. As Hohendahl notes, the resistance to the social criticisms in *Werther* was symptomatic of the pressures of the time, which were more stringently applied to women. Markley's article on (English) "Sentimentality as Performance" is pertinent to *Sternheim's* ideologies of class and sentimental charity; it reveals how the "strategy of defusing class conflict by sentimentalizing its victims" and the "myths of 'natural' benevolence and class-specific virtue" are constitutive of sentimentality itself, thereby rendering impossible a true interrogation of socio-economic injustices from the ideological position of sentimentality (212 and passim).

[74] The "German" traits of *Sternheim* have been noted in scholarship, from various ideological perspectives. Ridderhoff, *Sophie von La Roche,* for example, celebrates the La Roche's "patriotism" and the "character of a German work" that she maintains in her novel (iv; "Introduction" to *Sternheim*), whereas Erich Schmidt (as others after him) laments "der leidige Hang zum Moralischen," *Richardson, Rousseau und Goethe,* 1875 (Jena: Frommannsche Buchhandlung Walter Biedermann, 1924), 62.

[75] See Maurer, *Aufklärung und Anglophilie,* 16–30, on the relationships between class and nation in the three-way configuration of France-England-Germany in eighteenth-century Germany.

[76] "Why have most of our cavaliers not brought back from their trips to Paris, among the myriad, corrupting reports on fashion, also these reports that would have improved everything else, for their sisters and female relatives? But since they only collect ridiculous and damaging things *for themselves,* why should they seek what is proper and useful *for us?*"

[77] "Our fathers, husbands, brothers would not be able to speak so much about their gallant adventures and observations on their travels, etc.; otherwise the prohibition and this practice would present a harmful contrast."

For this citation, I differ from Becker-Cantarino's edition. There the first line reads: "Väter, *Mütter* und Brüder," apparently an editorial oversight. The difference in gender drawn in the text is crucial to the argument Sternheim makes. In the following editions of the novel the line reads "Männer" rather than "Mütter": Brüggemann (219, l. 35) and Häntzschel, "Nachwort," 233, both following the first edition of 1771, and Ridderhoff (259, l. 22–23), who follows the edition he labels "C," the third edition of 1771, as does Becker-Cantarino. The original edition "C" [A.III] I consulted also reads "Väter, Männer und Brüder" (vol. 2, 144) [Staatsbibliothek Preußischer Kulturbesitz Sig. 325 735].

[78] "I would wish to have collected moral paintings of the virtues of all classes, especially of our sex; and in this respect the French women are more fortunate than we are. Among the French, female merit is honored in a more public and a more lasting manner."

La Roche's letters, and later articles in her journal *Pomona,* attest to her admiration for French female novelists (i.e., Lambert; Graffingy) and the recognition they received (cf. Schieth, *Die Entwicklung des deutschen Frauenromans,* 126–29; Nenon, *Autorschaft und Frauenbildung,* 48–49; Ehrich-Haefeli, "Gestehungskosten . . .," 85). She looks to a novel tradition in France that is a feminine, epistolary tradition as a source for her own inspiration; not as clearly articulated as the association with Richardson and Rousseau, the male masters, it is nonetheless crucial background for the first German feminocentric novel.

[79] Cf. Altman, *Epistolarity,* 109, on the circulation of the letter between private and public domains and the concern to account for the publication of private documents as a typical characteristic of the eighteenth-century epistolary novel.

[80] "What horror overtook me, my Emilia, when I saw the handwriting of Lord Derby."

[81] "Moral wisdom, knowledge and experience should thus be lost on me and a pernicious enemy should have the two-fold power, not only to tear my outer appearance of fortune from me like a robber tears a dress, but also to destroy even in my soul my convictions, the practice of my duties and the love of virtue?"

[82] "Say: that, loyal to virtue, but unfortunate and in the arms of the most bitter sorrow, I gave my soul back to its maker."

[83] . . . "on which the description of her virtues and her misfortune shall be inscribed next to the signs of his eternal remorse."

[84] See Werner's cogent analysis of this symbolic death and the dual plots Sophie enacts as a sign of the "ambivalent image of femininity" in "Mein Herz ist unschuldig und rein"; also traced by Bovenschen, *Die imaginierte Weiblichkeit,* 131.

[85] "If it is appropriate that the stronger one not only carry his own full burden but also the burden of the weaker one, then I am fulfilling my duty, since I am not only sighing under the heavy measure of my sentiments but also must render my brother's overflowing emotion. My letters to you are the support which relieves my soul."

[86] "O God! I must have her or die — who will speak for me? I cannot say anything."

[87] Altman identifies the Super Reader as a crucial figure for the construction of meanings in epistolary novels (*Epistolarity*, 94, 111f).

[88] The name "Leidens" also functions as a sign of religious penitence that reflects the Pietist sense of "üben" as "to test" or "to try," in addition to its meaning as the active "practice" of virtue; see August Langen, *Der Wortschatz des deutschen Pietismus*, 1954 (Tübingen: Niemeyer, 1968), 75. See also Wiede-Behrendt, *Lehrerin des Schönen, Wahren, Guten*, 183–88, on "Tätige Tugend," and Touaillon, *Der deutsche Frauenroman*, 104–5, on Pietist influence in the novel.

[89] "The excerpts from my papers written with graphite will show you how hard and thorny was the path which I had to follow the last years. But how pleasant the exit from it has become for me, since I was led by the hand of the most affable virtue."

[90] "At the same time his glances surveyed my entire person with an expression, as if he wanted to judge which I deserved more, the pursuit of a lover or the compassion of a virtuous lady."

[91] "I demanded writing utensils and paper. The next day I wrote to clarify for the lady her doubts about little Lidy and I demonstrated the reasons why I had assumed the care of the child."

[92] "What does Providence still have planned for me?"

[93] "Here, read his letters with those of Lord Derby and send them back to me with all of my letters to you."

[94] "Reading Derby's letters you will shudder at his abuse of wit, virtue and love. Would I not have had to be evil myself to suspect his intrigues? What is Seymour's heart in comparison? I wish we had a spirit in common so that I could have access to your advice."

[95] MacArthur, *Extravagant Narratives*, 25–31.

[96] "With a moving, significant expression he approached me, kissed the pages of my journal, pressed them to his chest and begged my forgiveness that he had made a copy of them, over which and the original, however, he gave me full jurisdiction. 'But allow me' he continued 'to request from you this original image of your sentiments; allow me, my angelic friend, to possess these features of your soul and grant my brother Seymour his desire.'"

[97] "Then I cried and resolved to become Lady Seymour."

[98] Becker-Cantarino's view that there is no conflict between friendship and sexuality in the novel ("Freundschaftsutopie," 101) is unconvincing. Rich's renunciation of love which guarantees familial harmony and unity reveals similarities between *Sternheim* and, for example, Rousseau's *Nouvelle Héloïse* or Gellert's *Schwedische Gräfin* that are overlooked when the conflict is seen simply as one between Sternheim and Derby.

[99] "Her beautiful letters are not herself."

[100] "My brother has become the best husband and most worthy lord of several hundred subjects; bliss is in his face when he sees his son suckle virtue at the breast of the best wife and every passing day removes some of the blazing fire which had penetrated into all of his sentiments."

[101] "On our trip back she became a mother — and what a mother! O doctor! I would have had to be more, much more than human, not to have wished in my heart a thousand times that she were my wife, the mother of my children!"

[102] "This child is the support of my reason and my tranquillity."

[103] Becker-Cantarino, in "Nachwort" and "Freundschaftsutopie," 102–3.

[104] . . . "our little Sophie (since you are so gracious as to call her yours as well)." See Ehrich-Haefeli, "Gestehungskosten . . .," 125.

[105] The structure of enclosure of women's stories in male-authored texts described by Jeannine Blackwell seems to apply, then, to *Sternheim* as well: "Herzensgespräche mit Gott. Bekenntnisse deutscher Pietistinnen im 17. und 18. Jahrhundert," in *Deutsche Literatur von Frauen*, ed. Gisela Brinker-Gabler, 1: 265–89, here 289.

[106] With this terminology, MacArthur, *Extravagant Narratives,* argues convincingly against the interpretive limitations of traditional discussions on narrative closure for the particular dynamics of the epistolary novel form. See also Altman, *Epistolarity,* 160–62.

Chapter 5

[1] "O what kind of dull story will this be about the two of us? Look, one can fit all the events of our lives into two lines. They will read: Nanette and Karoline, two sisters born of honest parents, the one born 1761, the other 1763, ate and drank, grew up and were both married on the same day in the year 1771 and died in the year — I don't know that yet."

Maria Anna Sagar, *Karolinens Tagebuch* (Prag: bey Wolfgang Gerle, 1774), 302–3. Further references to the novel will be given in the text. Since the novel is not well known, I will at times quote at length. Translations unless otherwise noted are mine.

[2] Elisabeth Friedrichs, *Die deutschsprachigen Schriftstellerinnen des 18. und 19. Jahrhunderts* (Stuttgart: Metzler, 1981), 261, and the *Deutsches Biographisches Archiv,* ed. Bernhard Fabian, reference the extant biographical articles,

which are sparse and contradictory as to date of death and Sagar's maiden name: Radoschny; Rodoschny; Roskoschny. The latter name appears most plausible, as a German transcription of the common Czech name Rozkosny. (I thank Peter Demetz for this information.) The *Portheimkatalog* of the Vienna libraries gives the death date cited above. Apparently Sagar had to earn her living in Vienna after the death of her father, and met her future husband during this time. De Luca writes that Sagar knew J. Sonnenfels; under his guidance "ward sie mit dem, einem Frauenzimmer nöthigen Bücherkenntnisse bekannt, er brachte ihr etwas von den schönen Wissenschaften bey, und so wurde sie Schriftstellerinn" (Ignaz De Luca, *Das gelehrte Österreich*, I, 2, 1778; cited from *Deutsches Biographisches Archiv*, 284).

[3] Touaillon discusses *Karolinens Tagebuch* as unique for eighteenth-century women's writing, yet she concludes that Sagar's "typically feminine" work is lacking in depth (*Der deutsche Frauenroman*, 242). In Touaillon's typology, Sagar is a representative of the "rationalistische Gegenwartsroman" more closely linked with the male novel tradition than the sentimental novel (233–42). Meise brought Sagar's work to contemporary critical attention in *Die Unschuld und die Schrift*, on Sagar particularly 189–200, and in her subsequent studies; Meise emphasizes Sagar's concern with women's writing and her theoretical positions. See also Heuser, "Poetologische Reflexionen," 65.

[4] Meise's article "Das Werk von Maria Anna Sagar" provides an analysis of *Die verwechselten Töchter* focused on questions of female identity and the poetics of the novel.

[5] Touaillon sees in Sagar's open presentation of the creative writing process a pre-figuration of romantic irony indicative of Sagar's "surprising intellectual and artistic independence" (*Der deutsche Frauenroman*, 238).

[6] See Meise, "Wer ist sie," 119–20.

[7] "What, my dear female readers, you have read the title page and yet still want to leaf further in the book; didn't it warn you to put this little work aside right away? do you want to splinter your time with nothing — and what else is a journal without extraordinary events? I'll tell you once more, it is nothing. What can you expect from a Bohemian woman, how can she even light on the idea of writing a book? What else can it be but . . ."

[8] Heuser notes that the image of feminine writing as deficiency is typical of eighteenth-century women's poetic self-understanding, and wonders why the authors favored this figure over one of difference ("Poetologische Reflexionen," 59). Sagar is an exception: she confidently plays with the figure of "deficiency" and boldly turns it into a sign of positive difference.

[9] "Yet perhaps my candor pleases you? Well, it may be that many a woman from somewhere else would not warn the readers about her little work, be it ever so unimportant, quite as sincerely as I do; but perhaps I also know my sex better and understand how to pique its curiosity, I draw these conclusions based on how I am myself. For the more somebody wants to keep me from

something, the more I desire it. But quiet now! Let that remain just between us women."

[10] Heuser remarks Sagar's unusual directness in incorporating the aim to entertain openly into her prefaces ("Poetologische Reflexionen," 57). See also Meise on Sagar's use of "nothing" in the preface, *Die Unschuld und die Schrift*, 172–74.

[11] "Now don't reproach me for ruining so much paper and time: for I think I do better to do so than to spend the empty hours in front of the mirror in order to research which glance and position present me in the best light. Besides, you know that most of my work consists of making meaningless little knots, whereby I ruin string or silk instead of paper, without using the time any more usefully."

[12] Ute Frevert, *Frauen-Geschichte Zwischen Bürgerlicher Verbesserung und Neuer Weiblichkeit* (Frankfurt/Main: Suhrkamp, 1986), describes the "emptiness" of a girl's life in the eighteenth century before marriage (39).

[13] The communicative function of the letters is superfluous, as emphasized in the comments of the figure Leopold, Karoline's brother (38).

[14] The name Cyrilli carries the ring of authority and wisdom, as it recalls Saint Cyril, the Christian missionary and theologian (827–869); the reference holds literary overtones as well, for the old Slavic — Cyrillic — alphabet is ascribed to this saint.

[15] "My judge a loving sister, my supreme judge our gentle writing master!"

[16] Heuser, "Poetologische Reflexionen," 58.

[17] Touaillon overemphasizes the importance of the male teacher and fully neglects the fictive female reader Nanette (*Der deutsche Frauenroman*, 241).

[18] "What will these two people not be able to forgive their favorite?"

[19] "I even charge you in the name of our entire sex to push certain little things that are common to us all behind a fold so that one may not discover in your totally open heart the important Nothing of the whole woman, otherwise you will find in me a judge who is just as unrelenting as I am now your well-meaning sister."

[20] Ruth Salvaggio, *Enlightened Absence: Neoclassical Configurations of the Feminine* (Chicago: U of Illinois P, 1988), discusses this figure for Woman in the (English) Enlightenment: "the very idea of woman became a metaphor and figure of the essence of exclusion — of not being, of absence" (5) and "the very notion of 'lack' took on the attributes of the feminine gender" (6).

[21] See Steinbrügge's study of the definition of "woman" in French Enlightenment discourse generally, *Das moralische Geschlecht*.

[22] Frank Kermode, *The Genesis of Secrecy: On the Interpretation of Narrative* (Cambridge, MA: Harvard UP, 1979), contemplates secrecy as the essence of narrative interpretation and the mark of a text's authority; the divining reader's search for a spiritual (hidden) meaning in opposition to the superfi-

cial carnal view. But the biblical distinction between the carnal and the spiritual, so often also employed as metaphor of the distinction between women and men in the Pauline tradition, becomes complicated when the diviners of a text's secrets are communities of women. Then the carnal reading of Sagar's narrative secret is (a male) one that "solves" the riddle and reduces women to the gendered body, to the supposed nothing that defines them, while the spiritual reading of the (female) initiates perceives the multiplicity and freedom from that limitation. On the "Pauline metaphysics of gender" see Margaret O. Thickstun, *Fictions of the Feminine: Puritan Doctrine and the Representation of Women* (Ithaca, NY and London: Cornell UP, 1989). Heuser discusses German eighteenth-century male fear of female solidarity which would exclude men, a long-standing cultural topos, "'Das beständige Angedencken vertritt die Stelle der Gegenwart': Frauen und Freundschaften in Briefen der Frühaufklärung und Empfindsamkeit," in *Frauenfreundschaft-Männerfreundschaft: literarische Diskurse im 18. Jahrhundert,* ed. Wolfram Mauser and Barbara Becker-Cantarino, 141–66, esp. 142–43.

[23] "How incongruous, you may think, and perhaps even doubt that it is possible for a girl of such youth and such a decent way of thought, under the care and protection of a reasonable and virtuous mother, to end up having adventures. . . . I even ask myself often if it is really true that I, in my barely developed age, am that novel heroine whose experiences I describe here. Now listen to me."

[24] "I want to know why I must be here and who presumes to subject me, a freeborn person, to violence. And why I was torn away from my mother, who alone, after God, has the right to exert force over me. I don't want to assume that the laws are unknown here."

[25] "I finally submitted somewhat more quietly to my fate, for she had something so captivating about her, in which education, broad reading and charming virtues shimmered forth in unison, that one could not contradict her."

[26] "But my God, Lady Fani, what will I do here alone and speechless?"

[27] "Now, Miss Eleonora, just try to make a mockery of the prejudice that all women without exception are chatterboxes and cannot live if they lack opportunity to talk."

[28] See Ferguson's discussion of the common equation of women's speech with lust, chatter with wantonness; thus silence was considered a mandatory element of control ("A Room Not Their Own," 100). See Felicity Nussbaum on eighteenth-century definitions that woman's identity consisted of "an interior core that cannot be overcome and cannot meet the male measure," "Eighteenth-Century Women's Autobiographical Commonplaces," in *The Private Self: Theory and Practice of Women's Autobiographical Writings,* ed. Shari Benstock (Chapel Hill and London: U of North Carolina P, 1988) 147–71, here 154–55.

[29] "I freely admitted to her that I would rather chatter in the arms of my Mama and sister than earn this fame."

[30] Ruth Bottingheimer, *Grimm's Bad Girls and Bold Boys* (New Haven: Yale UP, 1987), examines the presentation of silence and silencing in Grimm's fairy tales in the historical and national-cultural context and analyzes them in terms of gendered power relationships; she considers "historical, narrative, textual, lexical, and editorial" levels (52; see 51–80).

[31] "O how happy I was to find myself surrounded again by people, and especially those of my own sex: we looked at each other like four silent statues."

[32] "You kept your word and patiently submitted to the test; for this constraint you deserve a compensation which I promise to provide for you soon . . . prepare yourself for one of the most curious tales, one that will touch your heart that is already so sensitive."

[33] "You were an innocent sacrificial victim of a friendship that was made too readily."

[34] Cf. Natalie Halperin, "Die deutschen Schriftstellerinnen in der zweiten Hälfte des 18. Jahrhunderts" (Ph.D. diss., Frankfurt/Main, 1935), 31, on the attributes of the sentimental heroine including obedience to the husband, even if he is in the wrong. Rousseau's *Émile* (1762) had enormous influence on the theorization of gender attributes: see Meise, *Die Unschuld und die Schrift*, 35–50, and especially Steinbrügge, *Das moralische Geschlecht*, 67–96.

[35] "A hitherto unknown pride asserted itself in me, . . . a natural light showed me my dignity, which I might not have recognized so soon given a more uniform treatment from my spouse. I reflected, my consciousness awakened, and I discovered that I was being insulted."

[36] "What does she want there, who is she, I almost asked, so busy was I for the first time with my self. Until then I only sought to use the mirror to fix my clothes and didn't notice my self that had only now become important to me. O how many considerations I now launched about the dear 'me,' perhaps not without the direction of my self-love, to which my reading of some books — not exactly select ones — may have contributed quite a bit. I had chosen them from the library myself, and what kinds of wares will an inexperienced young thing not choose for herself, if left on her own?"

[37] "I spent the most time on the sad passages that I read, and I found a certain attractiveness in them, interspersed with the tears, because they illuminated what was strange about my own adventures as a trial which promised to make me more perfect."

[38] Meise stresses discrepancies between Henriette's story and the sentimental "heroine's text" claiming she does not withstand her trials, that external circumstances are more central than inner tests, and that she oversteps boundaries with her "bürgerliche Auftritt" late in Karoline's novel (*Die Unschuld und die Schrift*, 190). Yet even as Karoline's tale becomes increasingly extravagant

and pushes the boundaries of the genre she employs and satirizes, she does cites these sentimental paradigms.

[39] "So, those are our enemies? from now on no mirror shall occupy me, O out of my room with all of them . . . the cursed glass!"

[40] "It is not the fault of the mirror if our obstinacy uses it to arouse corrupting passions. Rather, the mirror is our friend, she continued, if we know how to use it well. It shows us our imperfections which even our best friends keep silent about, out of fear of disturbing us. With these and other such edifying comments, with which I will not annoy you, for I am familiar with your liveliness and impatience, we went to bed."

[41] "It was no small surprise to me when I noticed in myself, with the help of the mirror, all the features I had given my heroine on paper."

[42] "How many hours I spent in front of my portrait lost in quite foolish observations, and thus I pined away with complaints about the miserable life of the original so much that I finally became ill."

[43] As analyzed by Meise, *Die Unschuld und die Schrift*, 106–38 and "'Papierne' Mädchen": the illness figures the relationship of the woman to herself more than her relationship to men.

[44] "But my dear sister! My intent, in addition to benefitting myself, is also to entertain you. Yet the preceding tale, as I now recognize myself, is much too frosty, not to say tasteless, for you. But wait . . ."

[45] "One can always rather endure objections or even very bitter comments."

[46] "Comments — o they don't deter me, I can compensate for them myself; can I not also allow myself the same thing about others? And I want to try it out right away: look, in the second-to-last line of the letter from Lusani, the expression she does not want to disobey her mother *intentionally*. What does she mean? is that not a mischievous reservation in case of a surprise of the heart? or am I perhaps mischievous to interpret the word 'intentionally' in that way?"

[47] Meise, "Der Frauenroman: Erprobungen der Weiblichkeit," in *Deutsche Literatur von Frauen,* ed. Gisela Brinker-Gabler, 1:434–52, here 447.

[48] Like the corresponding term *Lesesucht,* the emphasis on the activity of writing also carries a reprimand against it. Cf. Nörtemann on the correspondence between Caroline Christiane Lucius and Gellert: Lucias also used the term "Schreibsucht" to describe her passion to write, and describes her writing, which tells of the limitations on female literary production, as "ohne Inhalt" ("Die 'Begeisterung des Poeten'").

[49] "Today I think I have rather satisfied my addiction to writing, or should I not rather say, I am tired of bringing foreign wares to market, since I am in love with my own chatting. But I admit it to you, my dear sister, I cannot hide the fact that I am simply trying to buy your attention by copying other people's adventures, since the index of what I do and don't do, or my

thoughts, must probably make you yawn often, even if they may seem very important at times in my imagination. . . ."

[50] "No, it is more difficult than I had believed to give you an account of my thoughts. Inside my head it often looked like a destroyed ball of string that seems to have no beginning and no end, there were simply many disconnected fragments of thoughts, just half-beginnings or quarter-beginnings of a thought, each of which pushed out the other, in a word, my head grasped nothing but fleeting ideas. Why? — I didn't have to think about anything definite."

[51] "Mr Cyrilli always says that one must learn to think. All right, I can already do that, but he should teach me to control the thoughts, so that they don't appear in such confusion but rather in an orderly fashion."

[52] "I want to imitate the clever politician, who himself knows how to make a clever mistake at the right time in order to figure out what one thinks of him — O don't make a satirical face about that, sister dear! What do you know about statesmanship? Only we authors know about that."

[53] "But today . . . my imagination is so full of indefinite and fleeting images that I don't know how or where I should begin. . . . Ruling would please me, I feel, if my own freedom would not be the price of my desire to rule! I always argue and do nothing; a thousand resolutions follow one on another, and each one makes me less resolved than before."

[54] "Today for example I sat as usual at my writing desk — don't laugh at me for calling my little table that, I never call it anything else in front of those in our house, it gives me an important image, for the servants talk about it when they are out of the house and spread my reputation as a learned woman. Hm! yet another satire about myself? O well it is already written now, but — don't think, sister, that I am doing it in order to take the pleasure away from others. O no, they can make fun of me as much as they wish, I grant them that. I am a pious child, I go get the switch myself; but who can be so rude as to wish to beat me with it after I have shown myself to be so obedient? You see? yet another new strategy? . . . but I have completely lost the thread of my story."

[55] Cf. Meise, "Das Werk von Maria Anna Sagar," 90–91.

[56] "I need have no reservations or disguise towards you, you are my dearest and most trusted sister, you may as well know openly that I envy my friend [Eleonora] her sleep. No longer can I too — you already know what I mean."

[57] Touaillon, *Der deutsche Frauenroman*, overlooks the conflicting feelings about marriage, but they are part of the "Seelenzwiespalt" she notes of Sagar's heroine (241), which motivates much of the figure Karoline's writing (239–40).

[58] "Well I can't help myself, I would like to melt myself down or, if it wouldn't hurt, to be ground up in a mortar like a harlequin in order to produce a new creature. But that is no good either, for it would always only produce another harlequin. So just leave me the way I am."

[59] "I have asked my mirror to forgive my all my virgin sins and to teach me expressions that will attract respect, or contrite expressions of grown women. It has already shared with me a few such expressions: but before the ceremonial breaking-of-the-neck I will not make use of them. So allow me dear sister to remain without constraint until then, for I still have many stories to tell you in my natural way."

[60] Reminiscent of Karoline's heroine Henriette's fate as "unschuldiges Schlachtopfer" (cited above, note 351).

[61] "Listen, Karl, come on in, do whatever you wish, my sister won't perceive a thing, she is completely buried in important things."

[62] "My poor brain"; "in my head the cursed word *bride* buzzes and roars so awfully that it truly disgusts me."

[63] "Is that the fate of all brides? O then I rather wish never in my life to be a bride!"

[64] "But all men on the other hand . . . well . . . what is it . . . o nothing . . . No, I don't want to have anything to do with these impetuous creatures — away with them, I rather wish to continue to describe my friend's adventures to you."

[65] "But now I must renounce this pleasure for some time. Serious considerations are occupying me. Household and cares are appearing to me in a terrible form."

[66] "I presume the freedom of warning you to be a little more cautious . . . You have entangled yourself considerably, how are you going to help yourself out of this mess, and where did you get all that stuff?"

[67] "Where are you headed, with the jumble of errant knights and their strange heroines? It is perhaps supposed to be a satire on the review of the *Verwechselte Töchter* (The Switched Daughters) because of the reproach that the little work had too little action? As for myself, I smiled when you recently became irritated with the scholars because they still wished to read about extraordinary events in novels: but you can't judge everyone based on me."

[68] "I advise you again, my Sirs the readers! don't reproach anything about my little work, don't even shake your head over it or else I will take revenge through a sequel." Sagar, *Die verwechselten Töchter* [iv].

[69] "Dear Sir and Master!"; "I hope that this title meets with your approval, for it pleases me — but why are you rushing me? I would have thought you would have more patience, forgive me, my best and dearest teacher. I had planned an unexpected development for my story, you are depriving yourself of the surprise. Or if your outline pleases you more, so be it, I don't want to pretend to be more clever than you are."

[70] "O I am sorry for the honest tutor, but I can't help myself in any other way. He too must die, or else I won't be able to cover everything with my resources, because I used them too generously at the beginning."

[71] "Who knows how far my wit would have taken me."

[72] "Yet fare well and believe me when I say I remain your obedient female apprentice Karoline. P.S. note the term 'female apprentice,' I invented it myself."

[73] "I am done with my fits and my enthusiasms — and I need to be before I begin to play the solid matron. . . . I am to marry, and the new thought of being called a respectable woman destroys all silliness in my head."

[74] "I had seriously intended to have streams of tears fall and would have perhaps, to please myself, even cried too."

[75] "Karl R. is to melt me down, he is to give me his name, he already has permission to do so from our good father. You see I know all that: but in what kind of council was this decided? I would have thought that I ought to have had a voice in this council as well, but I am only a child, I won't be allowed to take issue with the word of my father."

[76] "I was not prepared for today's comedy, thus the men should not reproach me if I don't answer well according to the design of the play, for it is well known that extemporized performances are rarely successful."

[77] "Did I play my role well?"; "Here is the comedy I promised."

[78] Meise notes that Karoline's written consideration of the need to sacrifice her writing to marriage is remarkably similar to Cornelia Goethe's articulation of this impasse, and a general dilemma of the 1770s in Germany ("Der Frauenroman," 447). Cf. Prokop, "Die Einsamkeit der Imagination," 325–65.

[79] "Should I already stop writing, is our wedding to occur in such a straightforward manner? no unusual events? No duel, no test of resilient virtue? . . . O what kind of dull story will this be about the two of us?"

[80] "O sister don't abandon me then either! I beseech you. Poor Karoline, how will things turn out for you if Karl is not the best of all men? . . ."

[81] "Will I always be an internal contradiction? Don't make fun of me, sister, but if you won't grant me that, then cry now and then over me. I deserve both. Farewell!"

Index